Black in Place

COMRADE
ZACCAi,
Hope All is well.

A luta Continua,

Will

Aug. 2020

Comrade
Hope All is well.

Black in Place

The Spatial Aesthetics of Race
in a Post-Chocolate City

. . . .

BRANDI THOMPSON SUMMERS

The University of North Carolina Press Chapel Hill

© 2019 The University of North Carolina Press
All rights reserved
Set in Charis and Lato by Westchester Publishing Services

The University of North Carolina Press has been a member of the
Green Press Initiative since 2003.

Library of Congress Cataloging-in-Publication Data
Names: Summers, Brandi Thompson, author.
Title: Black in place : the spatial aesthetics of race in a post–Chocolate
    City / Brandi Thompson Summers.
Description: Chapel Hill : University of North Carolina Press, [2019] |
    Includes bibliographical references and index.
Identifiers: LCCN 2019010826 | ISBN 9781469654003 (cloth : alk. paper) |
    ISBN 9781469654010 (pbk : alk. paper) | ISBN 9781469654027 (ebook)
Subjects: LCSH: Gentrification—Washington (D.C.). | Washington
    (D.C.)—Race Relations—Economic aspects. | Washington (D.C.)—
    Social conditions—21st century. | H Street (Washington, D.C.)—
    Economic aspects. | Aesthetics, Black—Economic aspects—
    Washington (D.C.)
Classification: LCC HT177.W3 S84 2019 | DDC 305.8009753—dc23
    LC record available at https://lccn.loc.gov/2019010826

Cover illustration: Shawn Theodore, *Mimema* (2014). Used with
permission of the artist.

Portions of chapters 2 and 5 include material from "H Street, Main Street,
and the Neoliberal Aesthetics of Cool," in *Capital Dilemma: Growth and
Inequality in Washington, D.C.*, ed. Derek Hyra and Sabiyha Prince
(New York: Routledge, 2015), 299–314. Used by permission.

For my daughter, Cameron January,
who reminds me to breathe and dream

Contents

Figures and Table

Figures

Table

Preface

Living in and Researching "Chocolate City"

. . . .

It was my relocation to Washington, D.C., in 2011 to research political organizing that enabled me to explore the rich, exciting, cosmopolitan environment of the city firsthand and discover the monumental changes taking place—including the transformation and rapid gentrification of the H Street, Northeast (NE) corridor. Prior to my decision to study the neighborhood, I spent several days and nights observing the goings-on of the rebranded "Atlas District." One of the first things I noticed after moving to Washington, D.C., and spending time on H Street was how much gentrification in D.C. differs from the way it is described in other contexts. I became particularly interested in the postracial discourse and neoliberal urban development strategies that often accompany gentrification in this city that has been long defined by its blackness, and a city where America's first Black president resided. Through these early informal observations, I started to discover how blackness was deployed in the physical transformation of H Street—particularly how blackness was valued and used to invite spectators to the region.

As an African American woman living in a city with a large Black population, I was able to blend into daily life along the corridor. Until 2017, I continued to visit H Street regularly, as I traveled to my home in D.C. each weekend from Richmond, Virginia. I attended community meetings and street festivals, visited pop-up art galleries, and dined at restaurants and bars along the corridor. It was important to me that I maintained relationships with the business owners, political actors, and activists I had met over the years. Their wisdom and candid insights enabled me to maintain a clear picture of the changes taking place on H Street and in D.C. generally. *Black in Place* is theoretically motivated by my interest in the continuing significance of blackness in a place like Washington, D.C., how it contributes to our understanding of race and the city, and how it laid an important foundation for how Black people were thought to exist in cities.

Known as one of three neighborhoods devastated by uprisings following the 1968 assassination of Dr. Martin Luther King Jr. in 2011, H Street, NE was named *USA Today*'s top "up and coming" neighborhood. In recent years, community organizations and government agencies have placed significant efforts into the rebuilding and rebranding of the H Street corridor, privileging "diversity" and the possibility of a global community. Given the history of the neighborhood, I was curious about the remaking and literal embodiment of H Street as a space of diversity. This remaking requires changing the prevailing narrative that defines the neighborhood as a "Black ghetto," or an area of urban blight, to a more desirable narrative of diversity and multiculturalism. Therefore, I wondered, how has diversity been discursively sutured to this neighborhood to produce a brand-new spatial identity? As Stuart Hall writes, identities operate "as points of identification and attachment only *because* of their capacity to exclude, leave out, to render 'outside,' abjected. Every identity has at its 'margin,' an excess, something more."[1] So, what happens to the marginal excesses of blackness in the nation's first "Chocolate City" that do not fit into the revised story of H Street's multicultural past?

The name "Chocolate City" is a culturally resonant designation that reaches beyond simple characterizations of majority-Black urban centers. While the Chocolate City label originally referred to Washington, D.C., Parliament's 1975 song of the same name opened up the designation to include cities like Newark, Gary, and Los Angeles where Blacks became the clear majority once white residents fled to the suburbs. The concept of a majority Black Chocolate City is linked to the political and cultural imaginations of the civil rights and Black Power periods. Chocolate City instilled and reflected a sense of pride and hope for the future of a Black city but also recognized its limits, like unfulfilled promises from the federal government for Black people to achieve true equality. The Chocolate City of the funk era referenced an aesthetic of Black empowerment and nationalism in music, fashion, politics, and the visual arts. Chocolate City emphasized Black distinction, separate from a white world. In contrast, a current post–Chocolate City aesthetic markets a depoliticized Black cool in the multicultural, neoliberal city.

Today, the "chocolate" in Chocolate City arguably no longer connotes blackness as in the moment of integration, civil rights, Black nationalism, and political organization; instead, we might say it signals diversity of an American sort, across a broader spectrum, not a sense of diversity with any special resonance for African Americans. The form and function of blackness over time in D.C. are an expressly spatial matter in that they have referenced a particular, recognizable location. The title Chocolate City has made us think about not only Washington, D.C., but a particularly *Black* Washington, D.C. Yet, what is so interesting about a place like D.C. is that it is recognized as "chocolate" not only because of the people who inhabit it but because of its juxtaposition with a power structure steeped in white privilege (white politicians, white residents). In other words, "D.C." is Black and "Washington" is white. Chocolate City as a metaphor for the circulation of Black culture was at one point fully saturated. Now we are experiencing a shift in the geographic distribution of Black people and an increasing commitment to diversity that is in many ways independent of Black people, yet inclusive of projections of blackness.

Washington, D.C.

Before the nation found its first dynamic and prolific "postracial" leader in Barack Obama, Washington, D.C., had Adrian Fenty, who served as mayor from 2007 until 2011, and was similarly thought to transcend race and class. The Fenty administration, and that of his predecessor Anthony Williams, fostered pro-development agendas that ushered in a new wave of gentrification, disproportionately impacting lower-income Black residents. At this point, the divisions between race and class in D.C. became starker, as wealthy Black and white residents were benefiting from their connections with the government. Race did not become irrelevant, but its significance changed. For the first Chocolate City, which has only had Black mayors in its brief independent political history, to elect its youngest, "postracial," biracial, Black mayor who preached colorblindness (and established a mostly white cabinet) signaled the end of a particular era of service-oriented Black leadership that was steeped in identity politics.[2] D.C. was already experiencing a dramatic demographic shift with the concurrent influx of white residents, and a precipitous decline in Black residents. With this shift came changes to the social and political terrain around matters of race.

Washington, D.C., has had a long and unique Black cultural and political history. Throughout the nineteenth and twentieth centuries, the District was the center for antilynching, antisegregation, and voting rights campaigns. In the early nineteenth century, Washington welcomed runaway slaves and freedmen and freedwomen seeking refuge. Because federal legislators preferred to stay in Washington only a few months out of the year, Blacks had more freedom and economic opportunities. Nevertheless, Black Washingtonians have experienced years of social and economic policies that disproportionately affected them—race has been a key factor in many of these decisions often determined by politicians and leaders in the federal government.

Washington became the first major city with a majority-Black population in 1957. However, the 1960 census failed to account for thousands of Black residents in the highly impoverished slums, thus significantly understating the city's Black and overall population. In 1968, the city's population total was informally revised upward to 854,000 with Black residents representing 67 percent of the city.[3] Plagued by a sordid history between the federal government and Black constituents, D.C. only received limited home rule after the enfranchisement of Blacks in other locations in the United States. The D.C. Home Rule Act was not passed until 1973. This act allowed the city to elect a mayor and city council members and designated an annual payment for the District, but final say over the District's budget and legislative power over city matters remained with the House Committee on D.C., which also has veto power over any city legislation. The federal government continues to have distinct political power over and within the District. Residents have no voting congressional representation, despite the fact that they pay federal taxes, and have only been able to vote in presidential elections since 1964. As a result, D.C. residents live under some of the least democratic conditions in the country. Nevertheless, despite the challenges D.C. residents have faced, the tone and tenor of Washington, D.C., and its cultural relevance to Black life are almost unparalleled. In D.C., Black folks built vibrant neighborhoods complemented by thriving commercial districts. As D.C. poet Kenneth Carroll wrote in 1998 about his hometown, "Even before [George] Clinton put a beat to it, Chocolate City was a metaphorical utopia where Black folks' majority status was translated into an assertion of self-consciousness, self-determination and self-confidence."[4]

In the period after the 1968 uprisings following the assassination of Dr. Martin Luther King Jr., identity politics became popular as well as the gradual move to welfare programs that perpetually had a Black face representing them, most notably, "welfare queens." With the onset of the crack epidemic, cultural narratives about deviant and criminal Black users and dealers and about absentee parents with their "crack babies" impacted how the divested urban core was designated, disciplined, and developed using white notions of blackness as a way to organize the space. At the same time, middle- and upper-middle-class white families were continuing to build exclusive communities at the outer edges of the city and into the thriving suburbs.

Multiple political and economic systems were at work to make blackness legible from the mid-twentieth century and beyond. The politics and cultural narratives developed in conjunction with President Johnson's Great Society and later Reaganomics contributed to the ways that blackness was represented in media but also how these ideologies were used to map the spaces in which Black people lived. In D.C., blackness and Black people have been seen as disruptive (as in Blacks' relationship with police), criminal (as in the crack epidemic), corrupt (as in Mayor Marion Barry and his political machine), undeserving (as in disinvested neighborhoods), and more recently, marketable (as in branding spaces as "Black" to draw in tourists). Most often cities wanted to hide the ugly realities of Black life in urban spaces and instead privilege positive elements (Black labor, culture, and entertainment largely supported tourism in these cities).

Blackness—specifically, Black Americanness—means and meant something very distinct in D.C. The uprisings of 1968 signaled an important shift in D.C. history. In its aftermath emerged a new relationship between the federal government and the District. Home rule meant that D.C. could, for the first time, operate like an independent municipality, with several stringent rules attached. New provisions afforded many Blacks unprecedented opportunity. Nevertheless, D.C. remained a contentious environment for its high concentration of poverty, unemployment, and class and racial stratification.

Today, with its dense population of over 700,000 residents, D.C. remains largely segregated, as the population on the eastern side of the city remains almost exclusively Black, and on the western end mostly white. Nevertheless, with its Black population dipping below 50 percent in 2010, D.C. joins a collection of U.S. cities like Oakland, Chicago, and St. Louis where the population of Black residents has been in decline, largely due to economic factors (primarily income inequality and a dearth of economic opportunities) that have led to higher unemployment rates, declining wealth accumulation, and lower educational attainment in comparison with their white counterparts.

Washington, D.C., is undergoing an economic renaissance, as the city has experienced a tremendous growth in population, private-sector jobs, and housing stock. In fact, considering the District's low unemployment rate, job growth, per-capita GDP, average weekly wages, and wage growth, D.C. has consistently ranked as one of the top areas in the country with the strongest economy. Despite these advances, Black Washingtonians—specifically, long-term Black residents—have been largely left behind. According to a 2017 Georgetown University report on Black employment, population, and housing trends, the median annual income for white D.C. families is $120,000, while it is $41,000 for Black households. The report, which explicitly attributes the decline of Black residents to gentrification, also notes that between 2007 and 2014, the median household income in D.C. increased by about $10,000, but growth remained flat for Black households.[5] Similarly, in 2018 the District of Columbia Chamber of Commerce published its "State of the Business" report, which described the "unique" impact of affluent white families driving low- and middle-income Black and brown families out of the city, since these families are not being displaced "by young persons, artists, or other groups typically associated with gentrification but by wealthier families."[6] Progressive shifts in politics and policies over the past forty years have not led to much change. Rapid gentrification in D.C. functions as a perfect rejoinder to segregation and other forms of systemic inequality in ways that continue to economically marginalize and displace Black people in the city. In fact, a 2019 study released by the National Community Reinvestment Coalition (NCRC) claims that Washington, D.C., experienced the greatest intensity of gentrification in the United States between 2000–2013.[7] An excess of 20,000 Black residents have been displaced by mostly affluent, white newcomers. This violent demographic shift is having a profound impact on the physical, cultural, and political memory of Black D.C. that is too often obscured. Black Washingtonians now live in the space between being too much (in terms of their bodies, things, cultures, intensities), and having too little (services, infrastructure, accessibility).

But D.C. is also a place where blackness has been memorialized. With the 2016 arrival of the Smithsonian National Museum of African American History and Culture, colloquially known as the "Blacksonian," it seems appropriate that Black culture and history are preserved in this manner—memorialized and institutionalized as artifact. It makes Black history American history, something Black people have been striving for: an opportunity to be included, incorporated, visible, and in place.

Acknowledgments

Many people have been instrumental in the development of this project. My journey to its completion was not without bumps, jumps, twists, and turns, but I am very grateful for the people in my life who have exhibited incredible patience and support over these many years. This project started when I was in the Sociology graduate program at the University of California, Santa Cruz, and while the book is not my dissertation, the themes and questions that animate it began while I was writing. I wish to express the deepest and sincerest gratitude to my dissertation advisor, mentor, and friend, Herman Gray. Herman is one of the kindest, wisest, most brilliant, and most generous people I have ever met. I am grateful for his patience and encouragement that provided me with the drive to abandon my fears, take risks, and write, or as he would say, "come off the ledge and head to the shed"— both inside and outside of the academy. Without Herman's guidance and persistence, this book would not have been possible. I would also like to acknowledge faculty in the Sociology Department at the UC Santa Cruz, like Deb Gould who generously took the time to share their wisdom and candor with me while I was in graduate school. I am grateful for Dana Takagi's encouragement throughout my entire graduate career, especially her enthusiastic confidence in my messy, complicated, nuanced vision. I am particularly indebted to Miriam Greenberg for her generosity and support throughout the course of my graduate career and beyond. Miriam is a fantastic role model as a scholar, mentor, and teacher.

While at UC Santa Cruz, I developed strong relationships with my fellow graduate students. I would like to thank my comrade Claudia Lopez for her humor, brilliance, honesty, and energy. Claudia, I am honored to consider you a sister-friend. To my beloved "little sister," Sheela Cheong: I certainly would not have made it through the program without you. Sheela is an exquisite individual, and her friendship and support have been vital to me both personally and professionally. I would also like to acknowledge Jimi Valiente-Neighbors, Tracy Perkins, Darren Willett, Alexis Kargl, and Christie McCullen for their encouragement and invaluable intellectual support.

Since joining the faculty at Virginia Commonwealth University (VCU), I have been fortunate to connect with an incredible group of colleagues who have helped me wade through the murky waters of this manuscript writing process. I want to thank Melanie Buffington, Nicole Turner, and Ana Edwards for their warmth, collegiality, and the robust intellectual exchange we had. To the original "First Book" writing group, Chris Cynn, Myrl Beam, and Cristina Stanciu, thank you for your superb feedback, candor, and encouragement. My writing crew, Jenny Rhee and Michael Hall, are both brilliant, incredibly genuine, honest scholars who have offered me enriching, stimulating, unforgettable dialogue. I owe much of my success and sanity to you both. To my coauthor and friend, Kathryn Howell, I am grateful for your wit, consistency, intellectual curiosity, and comparable love for D.C. I am thankful for the support of my colleagues in the African American Studies Department at VCU, but my partner-in-crime, "work spouse" Chioke I'Anson, deserves special recognition for maintaining faith in my project and pedagogy and for being an all-around incredible human being. I also want to acknowledge my research assistant, Haley Tucker, for her dedication to the project; and my mentees, Shayla Diggs and Christopher Robinson, for helping make my transition to VCU so effortless and full of joy. You are both remarkable examples of why I love VCU students so much.

Research and writing for this project could not have happened without the help of archives and libraries and without the generosity of several foundations, institutes, centers, and universities. Thanks to the staff at the DC Public Library's Washingtoniana Collection and the DC Historical Society. Much appreciation to the Woodrow Wilson Foundation, the Summer Institute on Tenure and Professional Advancement at Duke University, the Social Science Research Council, the Mellon Mays Undergraduate Fellowship Program, and the University of California Center for New Racial Studies. I am grateful for the research and travel support of the College of Humanities and Sciences and Humanities Research Center at VCU. I am also indebted to Aashir Nasim, vice president for Inclusive Excellence and director of the Institute for Inclusion, Inquiry, and Innovation at VCU. Thank you for your guidance, leadership, and vision, despite your insistence on proclaiming "I hired her!" at every possible moment.

This project has gone through several iterations, and I have been fortunate to present my research to several audiences. I am grateful for the kindness and generosity of faculty and staff at American University, Johns Hopkins University, Howard University, UC Berkeley, New York University, University of Pennsylvania, City University of New York, ArtCenter College of Design, University of Oregon, Virginia Tech, and Georgetown University. I have benefited from the questions, comments, and provocations from audience members at the American Studies Association, American Sociological Association, American Association of Geographers, Association of Black Sociologists, Society for Cinema and Media Studies, National Council for Black Studies, Association for the Study of African American Life and History, National Women's Studies Association, Modern Languages Association, and the DC Historical Society annual conferences. Portions of chapters 2 and 5 were published in earlier form in *Capital Dilemma: Growth and Inequality in Washington, D.C.*, edited by Derek Hyra and Sabiyha Prince (New York: Routledge, 2015). I am grateful to you both for your constructive feedback and unwavering support. It is such a pleasure to have lived and worked on this project in Washington, D.C. The District is full of life and love, and I have met some of the most incredible, supportive people here. I want to acknowledge and thank Kimberly Driggins, Brian Kenner, Chris Jenkins, and Anwar Saleem for their patience and insight on all things related to D.C.

The book benefited greatly from two external, blind reviewers who offered thoughtful, nuanced, and critical commentary that helped me refine the book. I am grateful for your consistently supportive feedback and belief in the project. The University of North Carolina Press took on this project in its infancy and stuck with me all the way through. For that, I want to thank my editor at UNC Press, Lucas Church. I appreciate your patience and willingness to chat with me about the tiniest, most mundane elements of the process.

There is a collection of dear friends and scholars across institutions and fields who have provided intellectual support, guidance, and inspiration over many, many years: Nathan Connolly, Deva Woodly-Davis, Minh-Ha Pham, Kwami Coleman, Leslie Hinkson, Jennifer Christine Nash, Natalie Hopkinson, Aimee Meredith Cox, Ariana Curtis, Laura-Anne Minkoff-Zern, Jovan Scott Lewis, Tanisha Ford, Siobhan Carter-David, and Tamara Walker. Thanks to Michael Ralph for reading the complete manuscript and offering such generative comments. To all of you, I am eternally grateful for your compassion, wisdom, and faith in me and my work. There were also several brilliant scholars who lent me their ear and provided valuable counsel throughout the course of this project. These allies provided me with both a community and a platform for my work, while exhibiting patience and compassion along the way: Derek Hyra, Sabiyha Prince, Jordanna Matlon, Malini Ranganathan, Samir Meghelli, Willow

Lung-Amam, Marya McQuirter, Anthony Kwame Harrison, Sonya Grier, and Amber Wiley.

There is a group of people who deserve special acknowledgment. To Ashanté Reese, you make me a better writer and a more thoughtful scholar. The passion you have for your work is stunning as well as your commitment to integrity. Our daily chats and messages have sustained me through this process. You remind me to be bold and brave. Thank you for coming into my life at the perfect time and inviting me to remain in yours. To Nicole Fleetwood, I am constantly in awe of your depth, talent, and brilliance. Your work and your life continue to inspire me. Thank you for the gift of your friendship, humor, and professional guidance. You are unlike any other, so exquisite and prolific in life and love. To Marcia Chatelain, the hardest-working woman in the academy, your generosity and tenacity are unmatched. I am still not certain how you do all you do. Your commitment to your family, friends, students, and community motivate me. I am very grateful for your genuine and honest friendship. To Shannon King, my brother from another mother, thank you for keeping me on task and being such an amazing source of encouragement. I deeply appreciate your infectious laugh and commitment to brilliance. Our chats and visits have been a source of great joy for me, and I am so grateful for our friendship. To Nadine Mathis, I am so grateful to you for your vision, wisdom, and spirit. When I first came to Easton's Nook to complete the manuscript, I had no idea I would be supported and uplifted by such an exquisite soul. Thank you for giving me the space to breathe and look within. And to my mentor and friend, Karla Slocum, a tireless professional without whom I would not have gotten as far as I have: I don't think I can find the words to express how thankful I am to have had your guidance and incredible leadership throughout the writing and publication process. You've helped me navigate the academy in immeasurable ways. You are an inspiration to me and many others. Thank you for your confidence, your candor, and your wisdom.

I am grateful to many friends and family members, who often remark that they have no clue what in the world I am doing, but love and support me unconditionally. Thank you to my friends, near and far, who have helped keep me sane and who have offered abundant patience and energy along the way: Myrada Benjamin, Johnny Wright, Dayle Davenport, Shawan Worsley, Rhonda Wright, Rachel Skerritt, Leila Akahloun, Yuriel Layne, Tom Warner, Shauna Brown, Telesa Via, and Jovonne Bickerstaff. A special thanks to Shawn Theodore and Lekan Jeyifous for your contributions to the book, but for also being such brilliant, generous, and inspiring artists and friends.

To my grandmother, Lorena "Lucille" Taylor, you have always been my biggest cheerleader and best sounding board. Your generous love, compassion, and keen sensibility have helped me weather even the most torrential storms, and enable me to dance in the sunlight. I acknowledge with tremendous gratitude my partner, Rob Summers. It has been because of his patience that I was able to complete this book. I am eternally grateful for his trust and support. I must give ultimate thanks to my mother, Debra Taylor Johnson, who taught me to be persistent, independent, honest, and hardworking. All I am is a result of her tireless efforts to raise and love me completely. I am in awe of her selflessness and dedication, and I hope I can adequately honor her for the many sacrifices she bore on my behalf. Words could never express how grateful I am for who she is and who she raised me to become.

Finally, I want to acknowledge my beautiful daughter, Cameron January Summers, to whom I dedicate this book. Cameron is the most precious, delicious being I have ever laid my eyes upon. I never knew I could love anything or anyone as completely and deeply as I love her. It is my greatest joy to be her mommy. She is fierce and fearless and she inspires me every single day. Cameron is my reason for living and I hope to make her as proud of me as I am of her.

Abbreviations in the Text

AMI	Area's Median Income
ANC	Advisory Neighborhood Committee
BID	Business improvement district
DDOT	D.C. Department of Transportation
DHCD	Department of Housing and Community Development
DMPED	Deputy Mayor for Planning and Economic Development
DSLBD	Department of Small and Local Business Development
DTLR	Downtown Locker Room
FHA	Federal Highway Administration
HSMS	H Street Main Street
MPD	Metropolitan Police Department
NCPC	National Capital Planning Commission
NCRC	National Community Reinvestment Coalition
NTHP	National Trust for Historic Preservation
RDC	Reconstruction and Development Corporation
RFA	Request for Application
RLA	Redevelopment Land Agency
RPAG	Retail Priority Area Grant
SCLC	Southern Christian Leadership Conference
SNCC	Student Nonviolent Coordinating Committee
TIF	Tax increment financing
TOD	Transit-oriented development
WDCEP	Washington, D.C., Economic Partnership

Introduction

Black Space Matters

. . . .

What are we to make of this image of a clinched, raised fist? (figure 1). For those familiar with the D.C. flag, this logo directly references the emblematic "stars and bars." But the clinched fist is widely recognized as a radical leftist symbol of solidarity, defiance, unity, and most notably, resistance among oppressed people. While the redness of the fist might lead us to consider its relationship to the "red salute"—a symbolic marker of power and solidarity among communists and socialists—its association with Washington, D.C., invokes us to see the fist as a nod to Black freedom movement tradition. It conjures memories of the Black Power salute, of John Carlos and Tommie Smith raising their fists at the 1968 Olympics in Mexico City, of power to the people. Nevertheless, the Chocolate City Beer logo projects blackness as edgy, cool, creative, resistant, unruly, *and* commercial. The absence of an actual black fist allows the red fist to operate in aesthetic proximity to blackness. While the red fist asks us to imagine its symbolic universality, the image need not be black in order to signify blackness. What are we to make of this image? It is one that resonates with a distinct global history, an image that the Chocolate City Beer brewery's owners said derives from their desire to represent Washington, D.C., the first "Chocolate City," as a neighborhood and not merely the nation's capital.[1]

A new *post*-Chocolate City can be exemplified by the 2011 establishment of Chocolate City Beer. The small brewery opened in a gentrifying neighborhood in the northeast quadrant of Washington, D.C., at a time when craft breweries were popping up all over the country in historic, neglected neighborhoods undergoing economic "revitalization." In order to situate their products within the context of Washington, D.C.'s diverse history, the brewers named their ales after local cultural artifacts, locations, and events. For example, the "1814 ESB" brew, made from English ingredients, was named after the year British troops stormed the city and set the Capitol and the White House ablaze. "Big Chair IPA" was named after a well-known landmark, a large chair that stands nearly twenty feet tall, located on Martin Luther King Jr. Blvd., SE, in the overwhelmingly Black, economically

FIGURE 1 Chocolate City Beer brewery logo.

depressed Anacostia neighborhood. The "Mister Mayor" brew, made with marionberries (blackberries created by the U.S. Department of Agriculture and scientists at Oregon State University in the 1950s), was a direct reference to Mayor Marion Barry, the infamous and embattled former mayor and city councilperson for Ward 8, where Anacostia is located.[2] While the owners make a clear effort to remain thematically consistent with their D.C. location, the Chocolate City Beer brewers literally connect their products to an overall history of Washington, D.C., a place and a space that are recognizably distinct from Chocolate City.

When it was discovered that the now defunct Chocolate City Beer was the brainchild of two white men, Jay Irizarry and Ben Matz, who invited two Black men to join the partnership by preparing the company's business plan and becoming major investors, critics openly complained about the name of the company: "Two white guys running a brewery named Chocolate City is ridiculous."[3] In response to this scrutiny, Irizarry explained that the decision to use the clenched fist as a logo came from their desire to use "iconic images" rather than any direct reference to race or Black political history.[4] The company's appropriation of the clenched-fist imagery capitalizes on Black political resistance that was brutally repressed by the state but is now edgy and "cool."

Blackness has been theorized by scholars in a myriad of ways. While "Black" is a category of self-identity, it is also one that is imposed and resisted. Blackness connotes symbolisms and significations of Black subjectivity and identification.[5] Furthermore, blackness has salience across different time periods and geographies.[6] The evolution of blackness as an engine of profit represents one of the most remarkable transformations of the modern era. An economy of symbols built on anti-Black caricature cultivated the world of golliwogs, Aunt Jemima Pancake Flour, and blackface minstrelsy. Since the mid-twentieth century, however, the incorporation and appropriation of Black self-fashioning, blackness-as-taste, blackness-as-style, blackness-as-struggle, and blackness-as-nostalgia into mainstream markets have created a new medium of racial representation, consumption, and commercial growth, which conceal the violence of dispossession and highlight the illusion of inclusion within the culture of modern capital.[7] The owners of Chocolate City Beer continue this tradition by deploying what I call *black aesthetic emplacement*, a mode of representing blackness in urban capitalist simulacra, which exposes how blackness accrues a value that is not necessarily extended to Black bodies. The brewers seamlessly incorporate Black cultural imagery as part of their logo, which explicitly depoliticizes and aestheticizes an important history of resistance, while also opting out of using Black bodies in the process.

Black aesthetic emplacement accounts for this kind of active dissociation of blackness from Black embodiment, and its re-presentation in the form of words, objects, images, and performances.[8] The projection of blackness invoked by the fist and the "Chocolate City Beer" name is a trope, disarticulated from the complex, nuanced histories of Black life, and is instead used as a site to celebrate difference. As an aesthetic, blackness does not rely on the presence of Black people, or in this case, Black limbs, for social traction. Black aesthetic emplacement opens up a space to play with the fluidity and instability of blackness when Black bodies are both present and absented. The intent of the brewers to represent D.C. as a city of neighborhoods rather than the nation's capital certainly demonstrates that they recognize the importance of the city's cultural geography. However, their decision to use a name and a symbol for their brand that conjure but do not confirm blackness reflects the privilege of whiteness to take Black space and anchor its connection to blackness for profit. The red fist allows the viewer to plausibly deny its association with blackness and thereby keep the viewer from thinking about consuming blackness.

The founding of Chocolate City Beer is both an illustration and a symptom of the significant changes taking place in many urban centers gripped by the hold of gentrification. Washington, D.C., is a crucial site where blackness has historically shaped and defined political, social, and economic relations. For the first time since the 1950s, Black residents no longer represent the majority in Washington, D.C., and areas that were popularly considered off-limits because of high rates of poverty, criminal activity, and economic depression now boast new upscale restaurants, bars, and art galleries. Especially since the 2008 election of President Barack Obama, Washington has become a strategic location to examine the impact of postracial discourses and neoliberal urban development strategies in a city long defined by its celebration *and* abjection of blackness.

Black in Place explores how blackness became a prized aesthetic along the H Street, NE corridor, one of Washington, D.C.'s most rapidly gentrifying commercial districts. Documenting the city's shift from a Chocolate City to a "post-chocolate" cosmopolitan metropolis, I focus on the continuing significance of blackness in a place like Washington, D.C., how it contributes to our understanding of race and the city, and how it laid an important foundation for how Black people were thought to exist in the city. The book also analyzes how blackness—an indicator of diversity—is marketed to sell a progressive, "cool," and authentic experience of being in and moving through the city. I ask, how does blackness, as an aesthetic infrastructure of gentrification in D.C., complement emerging discourses of American racial and cultural diversity? Examining various practices of black aesthetic emplacement, I consider how blackness is aestheticized and deployed to fortify public order, organize landscapes, and foster capital. I theorize black aesthetic emplacement as part of the white hegemonic structuring and signifying of notions of blackness to increase the desirability of a particular location. Therefore, I chart how and where blackness and Black culture are represented through aesthetic emplacement and ascribed to geography. Ultimately, black aesthetic emplacement incorporates spatial projections of blackness that obscure the processes and practices of excessive policing, predatory lending, evictions, and increased tax burdens that accompany gentrification.

Displaced Race and Neoliberal World-Making

Within the domain of twenty-first-century urban development and commercial real estate, practices of blatant discrimination operate alongside racialized discourses of choice, taste, safety, style, convention, nostalgia, and heritage that appear value neutral. In other words, through a series of carefully orchestrated projections of blackness, urban development can take on the appearance of neutrality. These dynamics matter more than ever, as they reveal the limits of how scholars have theorized race and racism in the context of twenty-first-century capitalism. In fact, commercial real estate is arguably one of the few domains that has been strengthened rather than undone by the 2008 economic crisis. I explore the tensions between a post–Chocolate City and constructions of blackness within the context of contemporary neoliberalism—a hegemonic, economic rationality that deploys market logic as a way to protect and promote social equality and individual liberties.[9]

Neoliberalism has become a contentious and overwrought (some say overused) term in several scholarly circles, with its meaning changing over time and varying according to who uses it. Nevertheless, I attempt to clarify the meaning and stakes of neoliberalism within the context of each chapter. Broadly speaking, neoliberalism is a set of economic politics based on the superiority of free markets to foster social mobility and prosperity. Where classical and neoclassical liberalism of nineteenth-century Western Europe and the United States primarily emphasized small government and the individual liberty of white men to own property and vote, neoliberalism proposes that men and women, regardless of creed or color, can enjoy these same rights—despite the fact that wealthy, white men benefit from it most.

As an outgrowth of post–World War II regulatory politics, and white racial privilege masked as colorblindness, neoliberalism evolved into an expressly political project with its emphasis on a minimized state, decentralization, and the affirmation of individual rights. As a result, several major policies that have been implemented due to neoliberalism include privatization, laissez-faire capitalism, deregulation, and significant cuts to welfare spending. Most important to this project, neoliberalism also comprises cultural elements. Neoliberal principles expose putative knowledges that are saturated with logics of class, race, gender, and sexuality. Rather than suppressing cultural and racial difference, neoliberalism produces difference. Notions of diversity and multiculturalism get stitched onto narratives of renewal, globalization, and American progress. Neoliberal discourse has reconstituted and radically inverted concepts of justice, agency, and self-reliance in ways that hold people responsible for their circumstances rather than recognizing these conditions as the result of greater structural forces, like racial and economic inequality. By reframing conversations about gentrification, displacement, and the work of diversity in terms of the relationship between race, space, aesthetics, and value, I detail how blackness is dispatched by different individuals and institutions within a neoliberal framework that furthers the depoliticization of diversity.

Within the context of postindustrial neighborhood change, various initiatives to reconfigure urban space are organized around neoliberal logics, which undergird the rearrangement of some Black people in urban spaces, as well as the displacement of others, while erecting a racist discourse of blackness intended to invoke the inclusion and aesthetic cool of blackness, whether Black people are present or not. Neoliberalism embeds a particular logic about blackness as an aesthetic of commodification and consumption that ought to be examined as racial aesthetics. In other words, race operates as an aesthetic language and a visual logic within the neoliberal episteme. Blackness assumes the form of a distinct aesthetic that is influenced by, but not reduced to, race relations. This is how blackness, but not necessarily Black people, can be cool.

The "Atlas District": D.C.'s H Street, Northeast Corridor

While much of the scholarship on D.C.'s unique cultural history has focused on areas like the Fourteenth Street–U Street corridor, Shaw, Columbia Heights, and Mt. Pleasant, H Street, NE has received considerably less scholarly attention but is well known in the region.[10] H Street of the early and mid-twentieth century was different from Shaw and U Street because of its everydayness. The other corridors were hotbeds for Black political activity, education, and entertainment. H Street was a lively commercial center, but it met the needs of Black consumers, especially when they were barred from shopping downtown. It is this quotidian element of the space that I want to highlight and that I think is missing from scholarship on the topic, and what makes H Street's story relatable to other urban spaces around the United States.

H Street, NE (Northeast) (figure 2) was originally constructed in 1849, and like several neighborhoods in the District, was home to large working-class immigrant populations. Developments in transportation stimulated the growth of commercial activity; however, the construction of Union Station in 1907, with its accompanying cluster of railroad tracks, created a physical boundary between the corridor and downtown D.C. By the 1950s, H Street had already begun to follow representative patterns of urban suc-

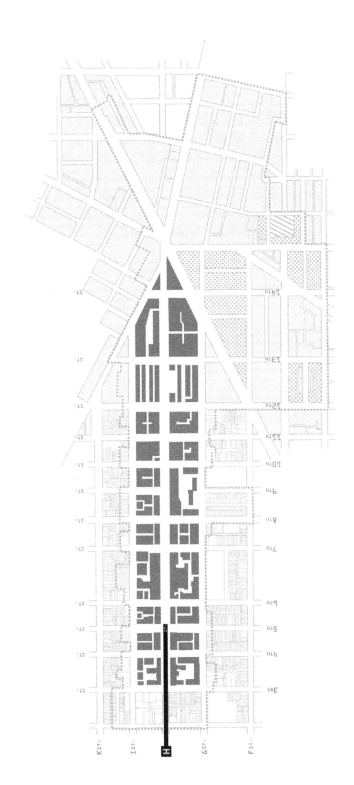

H STREET CORRIDOR
DISTRICT OF COLUMBIA
APRIL 2018   [SCALE 1" = 200']

FIGURE 2 Map of the H Street, NE corridor, 2018. Map courtesy of Olalekan Jeyifous.

cession: additional changes in transportation and the construction of free-ways during the postwar period meant that middle-class white (immigrant and native-born) and middle-class Black residents moved away from the city center, leaving poor Black residents in the blighted, neglected urban core characterized as poor, dangerous, and unlivable. The 1954 *Bolling v. Sharpe* decision legalizing integration in Washington, D.C., resulted in white flight. Furthermore, a combination of state and corporate divestment, abandon-ment, and disparaging representations of urban markets and Black consum-ers left urban commercial corridors like H Street to falter. As a result, local governments were able to strategically develop images and narratives of these isolated communities as "ghettos," "blighted," and "slums" to ratio-nalize the displacement of businesses and residents.[11]

Demographic and economic shifts in areas like the H Street, NE corridor did not occur simply because of benign neglect or the out-migration of wealthier residents but also because of changes to the built environment that enhanced the local government's strategic deployment of damaging narratives that contributed to the devaluation of struggling neighborhoods. An article from 1974 in the *Washington Star* foreshadowed the changes that eventually came to the area. One man, fifty-five-year-old Prince Edwards, sat in front of a laundromat at Sixth Street and H Street, NE proclaiming an end to affordability for the poor and working-class residents who lived in the neighborhood: "If the Lord spares me, I bet that within a year, you will see them over in here. Jogging everyday, walking their dogs, and even us-ing this place to wash their clothes. You and me won't be sitting here talk-ing about nothing, cause we won't be living over here."[12]

Whites (and upper-income Blacks) are returning to the city as products, progenitors, and proliferators of gentrification. In 2014, the *New York Times* describes the H Street, NE corridor as "increasingly mixed, racially and eco-nomically, as row houses within a block or two of the corridor undergo upscale renovations, property values rise and ethnic restaurants and fash-ionable pubs proliferate."[13] Yet in the not-too-recent past, it was a predomi-nantly low-income, Black neighborhood. Linked to these designations has been a gradual demographic shift in the area's population. According to the U.S. Census, the Black population around H Street has been falling since 1990, when African Americans made up nearly 77 percent of the popula-tion. Black residents dropped from 73 percent in 2000 to 45.2 percent in 2010, while the white population has jumped from 22.4 percent in 2000 to 47.7 percent in 2010. Now, the location of the H Street, NE corridor is recog-nized as a particularly attractive space for commercial and residential development because of its proximity to Union Station and because it is within commuting distance of Penn Quarter, Downtown, and other popular neighborhoods. The corridor is a hub of transition and transference as the Metro buses that ride along H Street and those that stop at the high traffic corner of Eighth and H Streets connect the commercial corridor with other destinations in the District as well as other cities in the region.

The H Street, NE corridor is not unlike many other neighborhoods that have been a target for capital reinvestment through urban policies like public-private partnerships, and public subsidies and incentives for private developers, that secure a neoliberal order in urban redevelopment.[14] However, in contrast to those newly (re)developed spaces that are advertised as transcending past historical race and class divisions to welcome social difference, institutional narratives about the H Street corridor promote the area's cosmopolitanism as a necessary and fundamental feature of its historical roots.[15]

The transition of the H Street, NE corridor is not just about an implicit (or explicit) branding of stereotypical representations of blackness for the pleasure of young, white professionals. Instead, there is a retooling of blackness to fit into the corridor's narrative. The grit and danger evoked by the mere mention of blackness do not coalesce with the harmonious cultural diversity that the corridor's success hinges upon. So, we must see stereotypical representations of blackness (negative), iconic representations of blackness (positive), and tangible, material elements (actual Black people) continuing to exist within the space.

Boundaries of Blackness

In June 2012, staff from the D.C. office of the Deputy Mayor for Planning and Economic Development (DMPED) spoke to a racially diverse crowd of business owners at a local church on H Street, NE. The purpose of the meeting was to discuss a retail grant program launched the year before. According to DMPED's Request for Application (RFA), the Retail Priority Area Grant (RPAG) provided up to $85,000 to small businesses along the H Street, NE commercial corridor "for the purposes of improving the subject property or purchasing equipment that will be used onsite," especially for those retail businesses that "include entrepreneurial and innovative retail elements."[16] The program was proposed by D.C. city councilmember Tommy Wells in response to the "H Street, N.E., Retail Priority Area Incentive Amendment Act of 2010," which was enacted as part of an effort to improve the appearance of the corridor. The legislation and language of the RFA had already caused a bit of consternation among area business owners. The grant explicitly excluded *certain* service-oriented and retail businesses from applying: liquor stores, restaurants, nightclubs, phone stores, barbershops, and hair salons. This was of particular concern because most of the businesses on H Street at the time, especially those owned by Black shopkeepers, were service-oriented enterprises. H Street is known as a historically Black commercial district that not only served the needs of its overwhelmingly Black, working-class residents but also featured several Black-owned businesses from the mid- to late twentieth century. Nevertheless, over the past decade, the cultural and commercial landscape of H Street has shifted, making room for lifestyle-oriented businesses that cater to wealthier residents and tourists moving into and through the nation's capital. The language of the legislation provides evidence of a neighborhood in transition, as the grant program that was developed in response to the act effectively excludes Black businesses.

After members of the DMPED staff provided the audience with details about the program, its application process, and parameters, they opened up the meeting for discussion and questions from the audience. One of the first questions was from a white woman who asked for clarity on how the agency defines a "hair salon," since barbershops and hair salons were not eligible for grant funds. The DMPED representative appeared befuddled. After a tense delay, she asked one of her colleagues for assistance in defining the term. They concluded that a hair salon is a business that has dryers and sinks to wash hair. The audience member explained that she wanted additional clarity because she owns a holistic wellness center and wanted to be certain she could apply for the funds. The DMPED representative explained that the decision to exclude certain businesses was based on "legislation," so DMPED has no power to make changes; instead, the DMPED is simply "administering what has been handed down." By the end of this discussion, the DMPED representatives concluded that the inquiring business owner's holistic wellness center would not be considered a hair salon, and she was therefore encouraged to apply for a grant.

I knew immediately that the white woman recognized that the policy was anti-Black in its exclusion of hair salons since she was trying to make certain her business did not fall victim to it by labeling it a holistic wellness center. Any cursory knowledge of the city and the corridor's commercial landscape points to the designation of hair salons as Black. Hair salons (more often called "beauty salons" or "beauty shops") have been important mainstays in Black communities, as they provide wide access to entrepreneurial opportunities, especially for Black women.[17] With its large, niche consumer base, the hair and beauty industry is one of the easier fields to which Black women can gain access. Establishing entrepreneurial ventures like these becomes especially relevant in times of economic decline when unemployment is high and as Black women encounter overall disadvantages in the labor market, social constraints, and racialized gender oppression. Nevertheless, Black entrepreneurs, including salon owners, are often denied access to resources to build and maintain successful businesses. This speaks to a broader context in which Black people face specific resource disadvantages in capitalist economies. In addition to the opportunities for financial autonomy, similar to barbershops, Black hair salons have provided Black women opportunities to create independent, safe, exclusive spaces in which Black women can socialize, build community, and engage in political activity and organization.[18] Black entrepreneurs, including salon owners, are often denied access to resources to build and maintain successful businesses. Historically, the management of Black urban spaces and a segregated economy, from the early- to mid-twentieth century, prevented Black people from developing the range of businesses necessary for interlinking economic structures. More importantly, the segregated Black economy limited entrepreneurs to "body-oriented services," like barbershops and hair salons. Whites didn't have any interest in competing with or patronizing Black salons because the industry lacked prestige. As Bobby Wilson explains, "whites distanced themselves from the nurturing and [a]estheticizing of the black body."[19] What happens when these particular enterprises not only face the imminent threat of displacement but also are deemed unworthy of capital that could be instrumental to protecting them in the face of such threat?

As the conversation in the church that sunny afternoon was unfolding, I thought about the work that is required to pull apart associations of race, place, space, and belonging. Everyone knows what a hair salon is, until a white woman asks how to define it. In this case, a hair salon repackaged as a "holistic wellness center" meets the demands of neoliberal privatization logics that require culture "to be ordered and orderly, as in commercially packaged or aesthetically pleasing to audiences."[20] Furthermore, this trendy, marketable business concept is aesthetically pleasing not only to consumers but also to funders, which maintains racial inequity. The wellness center joins the demand and increasing presence of local-organic-vintage-handmade-sustainable businesses that are appearing in cities all over the country. The corridor, and others like it, are starting to experience higher prices coupled with shrinking retail and service options. New restaurants, bars, and cafés/work spaces have opened, while galleries, boutiques, and yoga studios are replacing salons, drug stores, shoe repair shops, and dry cleaner businesses.

Not only do the amendment and RPAG actively prepare the corridor for aesthetic improvements to the streetscape, they foster an updated commercial landscape featuring trendy, marketable businesses that cater to a more upscale, "diverse" clientele. The erasure of Black space is the condition under which such upscaling occurs, and changes in taste reify this erasure. That the befuddled DMPED staff members were African American made the interaction more intriguing, thereby signaling how policies and legislation are structurally embedded. The race of the person delivering the message does not prevent the erasure of Black space. When it comes to gentrifying Black spaces, the enforcement and implantation of neoliberal capitalist development knows no bounds—neither in place nor in delivery.

I use this example because it demonstrates how market-driven "creative placemaking" and displacement operate within the same space. In gentrifying neighborhoods, poor and working-class Black residents experience cultural displacement, in which they feel unwelcome and uncomfortable in areas where they have lived and roamed for years. Placemaking is an urban planning practice that incorporates design elements of streets and other public spaces to revitalize downtown districts. As Alesia Montgomery points out, placemaking is a strategy adopted by several cities in the United States aimed at "increasing commerce and rents in an area by crafting vibrant streetscapes."[21] Placemaking is imagined as a collective and community-based practice used to transform public space; however, in gentrifying areas, placemaking involves aesthetic upgrades to the streetscape that catalyze economic and cultural displacement. Placemaking is also driven by those who have the most power to shape the tastes that are reflected in the built environment. These actors organize public spaces according to their own desires and modes of living. Using the model of placemaking, cities tie nostalgia, memory, and narratives of history to particular places and promote these spatial identities, regardless of who is living there and their relationship to the space. The impetus to "make places" in the modern, postindustrial, information-driven city is to produce a livable, walkable, entertaining, and "cool" city.

But for whom?

Spatial Realities of Race

In many ways, symbolic representations of difference and diversity encourage consumption, while at the same time they precipitate development strategies that privilege middle-class activities and values. These representations substantiate investment decisions and policies that lead to the displacement of poor and working-class people (particularly Black people). At the same time, representations of urban landscapes, which have an impact on popular knowledge of the space, help construct the meaning of the space and place. Urban landscapes must be made deviant or problematic in order to justify their restructuring as middle class, whereby social issues are framed as spatial issues. H Street underwent systematic disinvestment following turmoil in the mid-twentieth century and subsequent devaluation by real estate investors, developers, and state actors. Through this process, the geographic space was rendered unlivable, lifeless, without history, racially condemned, and in need of "capitalist life-support systems."[22] For H Street, investment (or disinvestment) in blackness drove this shift through designating blackness as problematic, enfeebled, unruly, and incapable.

The story of H Street is not necessarily about a bounded, territorial space. Instead, it speaks to the ways the corridor joins the larger geographic landscape of the city. On H Street, "revitalization" opens up the neighborhood to transition from a container for deviancy to a corridor that links the economic engines of society. As George Lipsitz articulates, "the lived experience of race has a spatial dimension, and the lived experience of space has a racial dimension."[23] To spatialize race speaks to the production of "social relations, institutions, representations and practices in space" within the context of race.[24] In other words, racial inequities have historically been spatialized, or implanted and maintained through geography. Similarly, the racialization of space underscores "the process by which racialized groups are identified, given stereotypical characteristics, and coerced into specific living conditions, often involving social/spatial segregation and always constituting racialized places."[25] The racialization of space is the organizing principle through which unequal and uneven development takes place, rather than the results of this development. In D.C., even attempts to make race less salient and more neutral in these environments demonstrate clear processes of racialization in which cultural narratives about the rise, fall, and resurrection of the historic commercial corridor dominate strategies for how the space is to be developed.

The racialization of space involves the intimate relationship between bodies and landscapes where, as Setha Low argues, human beings "create space through their bodies and the mobility of those bodies, giving meaning, form and, ultimately, patterning of everyday movements and trajectories that result in place and landscape."[26] It is not just the mobility of these bodies that produces space but also their immobility that shapes their surrounding landscapes.

As a sociologist, I often struggle to make blackness legible to a field that makes it singular. I am in a conversation where blackness is the foreground through which I am writing, rather than blackness being the case (as in sociology). Furthermore, some sociologists take space for granted. Many conceive of space as simply where we conduct our research. Therefore, I look to recent scholarship on Black geographies, which troubles modes of thought related to racialization and spatialization, particularly how knowledge is produced about space and the ways people use and produce it. As they address the historical dimensions of Black geographies, Katherine McKittrick and Clyde Adrian Woods suggest that this approach is a useful way to examine the historical struggles over space with which Black people have had to contend.[27] In particular, McKittrick begins with the assumption that "Black lives are necessarily geographic," yet Black people must constantly contend with "discourses that erase and despatialize their sense of place."[28] A Black sense of place involves "the process of materially and imaginatively *situating* historical and contemporary struggles against practices of domination *and* the difficult entanglements of racial encounter."[29] Fights against racism do not wholly define a Black sense of place but highlight the ways in which struggle is a foundational condition of being Black in the Americas.[30] To imagine a Black sense of place expands George Lipsitz's framing of a Black spatial imaginary, defined by Black "spaces of mutuality, community," and "radical" solidarity, as well as "new democratic imaginations and aspirations" that foster communal survival as opposed to individual privilege.[31] A Black sense of place pushes against the notion of blackness being ungeographic, and both hypervisible and placeless.[32]

Black geographic thought imagines cities as contested spaces despite abstract representations of space used by various institutions to envision and develop the built environment.[33] As will be discussed later in chapter 1, a Black geographic lens enables H Street to be seen as a battleground, especially while Black residents and business owners fought over adequate living conditions and plans to rebuild after the April 1968 uprisings. This lens is especially relevant within the context of a transitioning Chocolate City, since Washington, D.C., is a city "fundamentally shaped as much by Black spatialities as by anti-Black racism."[34] Nevertheless, it is equally important to acknowledge that geographies of gentrification, displacement, and market-oriented urbanism are just as racially inflected as the racialized geographies of segregated communities, and divested urban cores of the Jim Crow through post–Civil Rights eras.

Genuflection to Gentrification

Black in Place joins a vast collection of popular and scholarly conversations about gentrification. Rather than discussing gentrification generally, I look at practices of gentrification that are tied up in aesthetic conventions and influence how we see urban space and the function of people within those spaces. Therefore, I examine the dual processes of racialization and aestheticization of bodies and spaces in a postindustrial, cultural, and economic climate. The intention of this book is not to necessarily outline the processes of gentrification in Washington, D.C. However, I do document the historical development of phenomena that resulted in the aestheticization of race—specifically, the stylization and commoditization of blackness in the District.

The transformation of H Street, in many ways, has followed a common model of gentrification that has taken place in urban centers across the United States. It coincides with the proliferation of a neoliberal climate, advanced technology, and creative city movements. Popular conceptions of gentrification involve the replacement of poor and working-class urban residents with middle- and upper-middle-class households.[35] Adding race to this equation, gentrification is also understood as involving the displacement of lower-income Blacks and other people of color with white newcomers who possess higher incomes. Despite multiple definitions of gentrification, most scholars and the general public can abstractly account for feelings of neighborhood change. It is when revitalization and reinvestment strategies are accompanied by gentrification that the overall impact on communities becomes more complicated, since most residents see the benefits of improved physical and economic conditions and services.[36]

In Washington, D.C., gentrification impacts the land and its population similarly to other metropolitan areas in the United States, but it shows up in unique ways. As *Washington Post* columnist Petula Dvorak claims in her

July 2017 editorial, gentrification in D.C. today looks much different than gentrification of yesterday. Black and brown people are not necessarily being displaced and replaced by fancy, rich people; instead, the gentrification of today feels accessible as it revamps and reinvents common, traditional, and popular items: donuts, cupcakes, coffee, beer, burgers, fried chicken, and others.[37] As it will be discussed in chapter 4, the current hyperinvestment in lifestyle amenities has very little to do with simply increasing the value of the space. A new dog spa or craft brewery does not necessarily generate more capital than a beauty salon or local drug store. This is gentrification in the age of neoliberalism: visual consumption enacted by the aestheticization of culture and public space.[38]

The gentrified landscape is decidedly urban, but with aesthetic "upgrades" as it reflects the coupling of the new economy with new urbanism. Gentrification is in part a middle-class desire for authenticity that emphasizes an urban aesthetic of the past.[39] I view gentrification as the investment of public and private capital into previously disinvested neighborhoods, primarily inhabited by poor and working-class Black people, and that which precipitates the social and physical transformation of the built environment.[40] Gentrification is a logic of urban renewal characterized by privatization of formerly public services, multimillion-dollar development projects, physical transformation of spaces, development of new industries, emphasis on the city center, unequal access to the city by the marginalized poor whose homes have been reappropriated to cater to the desires of an elite class of residents and consumers. These "new" urban spaces are actively and "radically transformed as the affluent classes invest millions to live there themselves at the expense of displacing a population that has nowhere else to go. It is this process of displacement that is often termed 'renewal' or 'revitalization.'"[41] As a result of this shift and the neoliberal restructuring of cities, the varnished terrain excludes longtime residents in favor of richer tourists and newcomers. Gentrification is about struggles over land use— how people use space and create place. Therefore, it is important to understand how the design of public space impacts people's sense of community and community identity issues.

Scholars have primarily considered urban gentrification an inevitable economic phenomenon; that gentrification is about exclusion—the invisible hand of the market coming in and taking things that were previously accessible and making them too expensive and therefore unavailable to working-class residents and consumers. They focus primarily on displacement; unregulated, market-driven development that pushes out current residents, renters, and landowners. There is, however, less emphasis on the devaluation and revaluation of physical assets and communities within the context of gentrification through public policy. Urban renewal (or what James Baldwin famously named "Negro removal"[42]), redlining, and uneven development congealed the seemingly natural link between blackness, underdevelopment, place, and poverty as notions of "urban" almost always signify Black.

I focus on the practices of gentrification defined as those activities that reflect the process of moving investment capital into urban areas to commodify space. This framework allows me to examine the effects on the marginalized and displaced populations affected by gentrification, rather than focusing on the motivations and experiences of the gentrifiers, which many scholarly texts do.[43] This book examines the role of the state and movement of capital in cities like Washington, with gentrified and gentrifying neighborhoods—specifically, the city's implication in multiple modes of sociospatial inequality. Therefore, I identify one of the main challenges of gentrification as not simply an issue of physical displacement but also an affective state of being in precarity, not knowing what will come next.

Again, much of the impact of gentrification and urban change is what we see and feel. The aesthetics of gentrification become clear especially when we examine the built environment. The street has become a place where minimalist monoculture is popular: an aesthetics of locality, place-making through aesthetic details (exposed brick, repurposed signage, chalkboards, rusty metal), and a hipster retro aesthetic that ironically signified a kind of working-class authenticity through its presentation of old but new businesses. These aesthetics go hand-in-hand with an emerging ecology of boutiques, coffee shops, expensive restaurants, and other establishments. The aesthetic is decidedly anticorporate, but signals something welcoming to newcomers as a local, inviting space to discover. Cities become spaces that cultivate "sanitized razzmatazz," in which feelings of "urban danger, deviance or desire" disappear, as gentrifiers want the benefits of the city without "the problems that accompany urban life: poverty, crime, racial conflict."[44] Some elements from the past remain and remind you that D.C. is a waning Chocolate City. Ultimately, the aesthetic and affective dimensions of this work have profound impacts on those of us who move through these different spaces. The look of a place, the people who surround you, the sights, the structures, and the landscape all reflect time and change.

Enacting Authenticity and "Post-Chocolate" Cool

A vital component of understanding how blackness figures into the "revitalization" of the H Street corridor is how culture and authenticity work as instruments of urban development. Given the prominence of culture as a key resource for postindustrial cities to attract tourists and residents, several have implemented strategies to promote urban branding. Racialized expressions are more marketable in the emerging "creative city" that emphasizes cultural consumption and creative, aesthetic practices.[45] Producing authenticity through black aesthetic emplacement, marketing both blackness and diversity, and blackness *as* diversity, facilitates gentrification and revitalization on the basis of design and architectural projects. Therefore, analyzing the built environment, especially the spatial organization of streetscapes, sheds light on how the aesthetics of blackness figure into the way the street looks and how Black people move through the corridor. On the other hand, in an urban context, authenticity shows up in the form of cultural values—namely, historic preservation. Restoring and preserving historical styles of architecture are in direct contrast to decades of state-sponsored urban renewal, which demolished and devastated Black neighborhoods, and hyper-redevelopment efforts via large-scale, public-private construction projects.

Creating authenticity is an integral process to the sociospatial organization of gentrifying cities. Several scholars have addressed the role authenticity plays in the making of spaces,[46] especially the role of power in integrating exclusionary practices.[47] Authenticity inherently involves value and how people value a particular place. Furthermore, authenticity structures a sense of belonging by producing, protecting, and celebrating spatial narratives. Mobility is a privilege that is attached to whiteness, so it is those who possess whiteness who are more likely to call a neighborhood authentic or boast its "authentic" qualities as desirable.

As authenticity points to the look and feel of a particular place, I identify an explicit link between aesthetics and authenticity, where designations of authentic spaces are understood in aesthetic terms. This explores how the aesthetics of authenticity get inscribed in the built environment (through historic and cultural preservation, naming privatized public spaces, architecture, and food cultures). I also show how it draws upon the aesthetics of race as the city increasingly caters to "diverse" lifestyles. The politics of this relationship between authenticity and race play out as the city attempts to market this authentic diversity (as we will see with the colorful "DC Cool" campaign in chapter 4). Ultimately, the city and new residents and tourists who come to D.C. have complementary investments in authenticity. From the perspective of the city, creating authenticity through branding strategies spurs economic growth and encourages tourism. Newer, white, upper-middle-class residents produce authenticity through preservation, which helps them to value and find meaning in certain people, places, and communities.[48]

Authenticity requires reinterpretation of a space or social body that draws on an idealized vision of the past.[49] Modern appeals to authenticity purportedly deliver alternative options for pleasure, consumption, and entertainment for upper-middle-class tourists and residents but further limit multiple uses of these "revitalized" urban spaces for working-class residents.[50] I relate these practices of branding and producing authenticity to the transformation and reimagination of the H Street, NE corridor. In conjunction with efforts to rebrand the former "riot corridor" as a distinct cultural, culinary, and entertainment destination come increased police surveillance, higher-priced restaurants, streetcar track construction, bike lanes, and exorbitant parking meter fees that disinvite patrons and customers of the service businesses that once overwhelmingly populated the corridor.

Deindustrialization, gentrification, residential and commercial revitalization, and large-scale development create conditions for the displacement of older and poorer Black residents, as well as Black small businesses, leading to a shrinking Black population in D.C. But why have I chosen to describe Washington, D.C., as a "post-chocolate" city? "Post" shifts one's thinking to "after" or "beyond" a particular condition or situation. In this context, "post" incorporates temporality when discussing spatial matters. "Post" speaks to a shift, a waning of sorts. Acknowledging D.C. as transitioning into a "post–Chocolate City" is a way to examine the intricacies of who and what are often left out, or what is incorporated. In other words, "post–Chocolate City" signals the afterlife of a fiercely and firmly recognized Black place.[51] But what still remains? Certainly, there are other cities around the country that have large Black populations, but the "chocolate" moniker means much more than just having a lot of Black residents.

While Washington, D.C., was the first Chocolate City—the first large, majority Black city in the United States—it is analogous to so many other cities that experienced racism, segregation, high unemployment, and disproportionate incarceration rates but that also have prolific music, food culture, politics, and play. Chocolate City metaphorically undergirds "the relationships among history, politics, culture, inequality, knowledge, and

FIGURE 3 Antigentrification post. Photograph taken at the 1300 block of H Street, NE, Washington, D.C., 2018. © Joseph Young.

Blackness."[52] Where some of the culinary metaphors (latte, cappuccino, s'mores, etc.) used to describe D.C.'s changing demographic landscape signal a shift to whiteness, "post-chocolate" is open-ended; the term doesn't postulate what color or colors are next. D.C. is now a decidedly international city, so the divide between Black and white becomes more complicated. Post–Chocolate City does not specify what exists beyond chocolate; it simply designates a period after chocolate. The post–Chocolate City exemplifies a disappearing mode of social and cultural life that has been revised by an aesthetic infrastructure (figure 3).

Connecting racial discourses with renewal efforts along the H Street, NE corridor, *Black in Place* explores the contemporary operation of race. I identify the way blackness is produced, inscribed, and apprehended in urban environments. In the process, I demonstrate how an ostensible demographic characterization operates as an aesthetic, as well as a politics. The production and circulation of meaning in urban development relies on aesthetics, or visual and affective judgments of taste, to assign value to individual and collective bodies and spaces. Aesthetics are used in urban planning and development through the use of branding strategies, heritage tourism, and lifestyle programs.[53] They are used to attract commerce, customers, and residents. Therefore I consider the function of race as an aesthetic feature and illustrate how (and why) blackness, in particular, is mobilized as style. More specifically, the book situates the "revitalization" of D.C.'s "Atlas District" within a broader context of urban change and focuses on the ways Black aesthetic emplacement inscribes blackness in the built environment during an economic and political moment hailed as postracial.

Conceptually, I argue that blackness is integral to the production of spaces. I imagine a definition of blackness that is capacious enough to speak to shifts in the urban terrain. Through representations of blackness we experience the circulation and articulation of blackness in aesthetic form. To imagine a definition of blackness in this way speaks to, as media studies theorist Lauren Cramer puts it, "the de-corporealization of blackness."[54]

Central to this argument is understanding blackness as an aestheticized social and cultural continuum. Blackness lends itself to the process of urban aestheticization through the paradoxical incorporation and exclusion of blackness. The blackness that people's bodies and culture index in multiple domains becomes part of the aesthetic infrastructure of gentrification. This form of urbanization happens through a violent calibration of blackness that leads cities to ultimately face how Black do they want a place to be. Extending Katherine McKittrick's assertion that "Black matters are spatial matters," I say that spatial matters are also aesthetic matters. This relationship provides the foundation for an urban theory of aesthetics that accounts for what Black studies brings to bear on material processes of urbanization, namely the precarity of always *becoming*. Drawing on bell hooks's insistence that aesthetics is "more than a philosophy or theory of art and beauty; it is a way of inhabiting space, a particular location, a way of looking and *becoming*"—framing gentrification as both aestheticized and racialized is necessary to theorize contemporary urban transformation.[55] Relatedly, AbdouMaliq Simone writes, "urbanization is the possibility of incessant *becoming*, the intersection and constitution of heterogeneities whose trajectories, dispositions can never be definitively mapped or controlled."[56] Elites and state actors use physical structures within urban landscapes as abstract, neutral sites for architectural redesign and reinvention. Therefore, development is heralded as a necessary process in the city remaking itself and its perpetual state of *becoming* modern.

It is important to think about not only how aesthetics ground our experiences but also how aesthetics shape the way we come to see, know, and practice race. Through aesthetics we can explore how the visual logic of race—specifically, blackness—operates in this current landscape. There is a direct relationship between aesthetics and the ways that racial knowledge about blackness is organized today—an assumed knowingness related to how blackness is expressed, recognized, and visualized.[57] Rather than merely operating as a political and cultural identity, Black in Place explores the ways that blackness is used as an aesthetic to draw in tourists, customers, capital, and authenticity to urban spaces. Ultimately, I am arguing that blackness as an aesthetic infrastructure of gentrification is about controlling, defining, and naming space for the benefit of white people.

To aestheticize blackness makes room for subtle shifts in the terrain. Most often when looking at urban planning, design, architecture, and even community development, discussions of aesthetics have much to do with beautification of the city and the built environment, but oftentimes have very little to do with the people who inhabit or use the space. To think of blackness in aesthetic ways (blackness is an inherently aesthetic term—saturation with color) helps us understand how Black people were tied to urban space, and were thought to *belong* in urban space. Considering the many terms used to connote blackness—urban (sociological), inner city (geographic), minority (statistical), poor (economic)—adding an aesthetic dimension explores the traces of blackness that exist long after the last Black body moves on.

Aestheticizing Diversity

Black in Place examines how blackness factors into the interests of the state, developers, boosters, and elite actors in a diverse and progressive society. What do "diverse" and "progressive" mean in this context? From a space impacted by state-sponsored urban renewal that has transitioned to adopt market-based revitalization, I explain how "diversity" in appearance actually encourages neoliberal exploitation. As Shannon Winnubst explains, neoliberal social rationalities spawned a language of multiculturalism and "its even more aestheticized child, diversity, in the late 1990s as the new, preferred vocabulary for social difference."[58] "Diversity" and "development" are buzzwords that allay fears about displacement and inequality. Yet, while the diversity project was aligned with social justice, the two ideas are sometimes presented as synonymous, if not interchangeable.

Where diversity was once invoked to emphasize the need for federal programs that enhanced the life chances of an entire demographic, the concept of diversity is now frequently used to emphasize opportunities for individuals to accrue cherished commodities and individual advantages.[59] As Sara Ahmed writes, diversity is "imagined as a form of repair, a way of mending or fixing histories of being broken."[60] Diversity is a salve used to assuage the rupture and violence associated with gentrification and displacement. Diversity today involves an appeal to difference, eschewing any focus on material inequalities or commitment to action, thereby operating as an aesthetic approach to equality. The consequence of this widespread shift in the value of diversity is that people can associate themselves with the nobility that derives from the term's social justice origins, while partaking in its more recent iterations of what it means to be "cool" and "hip."[61] In the context of diversity's shift from a social justice ethic to an aesthetic lifestyle amenity, blackness enhances, rather than threatens, the esteem of a given neighborhood. It moves beyond compliance and legal redress to adopt a more celebratory approach to equity.

Changes to the commercial landscape of H Street resemble other contemporary "revitalized" urban spaces that can be paradoxically described by the concurrent celebration of diversity and the increasing separation and isolation of different social groups. This shift can be explained, in part, by the infiltration of diversity discourses and by practices of aestheticization that work to naturalize lifestyle and landscape tastes as well as concretize neighborhood forms and cultural difference.[62] Ultimately, diversity draws on the legibility of race especially in terms of urban development, despite the fact that it "diminishes the distinctiveness of race by couching it as one of the many cultural identities that make up America's valued pluralism."[63]

A Brief Note on Methodology

My analysis of race and space specifically emphasizes Washington, D.C., as a post–Chocolate City rather than focusing on commercial revitalization in general. Commercial revitalization is a term that is often used to describe the resurrection of retail activities in communities that were previously considered blighted, unwelcoming, and dangerous. I examine the ramifications of changing demographics and how blackness continues to figure into the reimagining and remaking of a neighborhood in conjunction with the discursive production and institutionalization of a postracial ideology. This market calculus calls for the increasing use of space organized around efficiency and individual responsibility to care for, clean, and cultivate neighborhoods, streets, and blocks. The reimagining of the H Street, NE corridor involves contestations over the meaning of a space in terms of race—belonging and memory—and what the neighborhood should look like.

I turn to an explicit examination of a physical, urban space to demonstrate how race is aestheticized, but the racial logic of blackness is organized in ways that subtly transform the space both symbolically and materially. To explain, I use various qualitative navigational tools to explore this rich space, which resulted in a triangulation of findings: I use archival research (thanks to the extensive records in the Washingtoniana Collection at the DC Public Library and the Historical Society of Washington, D.C.) to gain insight into H Street's rich history. After moving to D.C. in 2011, I spent several days per week over the course of nine months (between 2011 and 2012) observing activities on and around H Street to learn how the stylization of blackness works. I scoured newspapers, planning documents, zoning laws and hearing transcripts, neighborhood blogs, and listservs to discover how diversity was framed and discussed and how the attachment of race to space takes place. Between 2012 and 2015, I continued to speak to current residents, past residents, bartenders, waitstaff, and casual visitors to understand how diversity on H Street operates. Finally, I joined restaurant tours of the corridor alongside several local hotel concierges to see how they explained changing social and economic dynamics involving businesses along the corridor, as well as the importance of food trends in the neighborhood.

I use categories like cuisine, transportation, security, and historic preservation as anchors to demonstrate how stylized blackness is deployed to make the space palatable to newcomers. Throughout the course of my time spent on and around H Street, talking to residents, business owners, customers, planners, and government agency leaders, these themes were most often invoked in relation to the changing landscape of the corridor. While on the surface some of the themes align with those of various gentrifying neighborhoods, my analysis is specifically concerned with the way they are deployed in the post–Chocolate City.

When I arrived in D.C., Vincent Gray was mayor. Muriel Bowser succeeded him in a messy, drama-filled political fight in 2014. With a change in leadership came a different set of priorities. The Bowser administration promoted strategies to open up "pathways to the middle class" that would presumably target African American residents given the wide wealth disparity among Blacks and whites in the District. Yet, these strategies have buttressed the unequal conditions longtime Black residents continue to face in D.C. A 2018 lawsuit filed by D.C. residents Paulette Matthews, Greta Fuller, and Shanifinne Ball against the District of Columbia in the U.S. District

Court alleges these policies served to "attract younger, more affluent professionals" and effectively "discriminated against poor and working-class African Americans who lived [in D.C.] for generations," thereby breaking up "long-established communities."[64] Arguably, since the Fenty administration (2007–2011), the D.C. government has prioritized a "creative economy" that could transition the city's identity from a "government town" to one that provides exclusive opportunities for innovative, entrepreneurial businesses in the fields of art, culture, and technology. While the Bowser administration touts its successful growth of affordable and mixed-income housing opportunities, at the same time it celebrates large-scale projects like the upscale redevelopment of the Southwest Waterfront—paving over the enduring stain of its history as ground zero for urban renewal in the mid-twentieth century.

Summary of Chapters

Black in Place is organized thematically but begins with a brief history of the H Street corridor and its inhabitants. Chapter 1 focuses on the D.C. uprisings and their aftermath of urban renewal and commercial redevelopment. I map the changes in the built environment on H Street onto changes in how blackness and capital intersected. This chapter charts the unique history of the H Street, NE corridor to illustrate how the meaning of blackness has changed since the mid-twentieth century as well as the development and designation of H Street as a Black space. I also examine the intersection of urban development, Black capitalism, local policy, and the racialization of public space on H Street placed within the context of national urban divestment from the 1970s to the 1990s. This devaluation of Black H Street and the strategic deployment of visual rhetoric depicting the space as "blighted," a "slum," and a "ghetto" prepared the space for its eventual revaluation and reelevation for neoliberal times. Ultimately, this first chapter tracks the long march of blackness to become diversity and considers how, through policy and media narratives, blackness became synonymous with the urban ghetto—in other words, how the ghetto "blackened" urbanity.

Chapter 2 highlights the relationship between race, diversity, belonging, and urban development in the historical devaluation of H Street as a Black space, and its revaluation as an emerging multicultural neighborhood. Here, I highlight the remaking of blackness as a thread in the multicultural fabric. H Street acts as a neoliberal zone that affirms blackness by using it as an entrepreneurial machine of development. Employing Brenda Weber's formulation of post-Katrina New Orleans as a body in distress that can be "healed" only by makeover television design experts, I position the post-"riot" H Street, NE corridor as an afflicted Black social body that is restored only by the mobilization of "diversity."[65] In other words, diversity acts as the antidote to blackness. I use this chapter to conceptualize how the old *Black* H Street, as a site of chaos, disorder, and pathology, involved the rehabilitation not only of the physical space but also of symbolic codes of blackness through the lens of a postracial, neoliberal project. What manifests in the remaking of blackness on H Street is that the area has not been purged of symbols of blackness; instead, blackness is rendered palatable and consumable, while some of the constructed "edginess" is deliberately constructed as a form of nostalgia that signifies a suppressed and domesticated Black past.

With its complex history as the site of racial violence, civil disobedience, and police repression during the 1960s, urban blight, and later commercial revitalization, the H Street corridor is an ideal site for examining the interrelatedness of race, nostalgia, and memory in the production of space. In chapter 3, I show how institutionally driven archival and tourism projects help "reclaim" diversity as a way to attract the wealthy and middle classes back to the city. Through an analysis of a neighborhood historical survey, a cultural tourism brochure, and a preservation-based community revitalization program on H Street, I show that this process occurs through the production of official narratives about the area, which involves a devaluing of H Street's undesirable Black history and a rebranding and revaluation of H Street as historically diverse—only momentarily Black. Blackness, in these narratives, shows up as an aesthetic component of multiculturalism.

Chapter 4 explores how authenticity became a way to attach meaning to things and experiences rather than people—hence the proliferation of boutiques, craft breweries, and cafés alongside the practice of branding neighborhoods in terms of distinctive cultural identities. In particular, this chapter examines how tempered exoticism in restaurants is used as a discourse of cultural diversity on H Street and how, through neoliberal urbanism, governance practices that favor "market mechanisms, including limiting state oversight and regulation of the private sector, reducing expenditures on social welfare, and forming entrepreneurial public-private growth partnerships, to create conditions favorable to capital reinvestment,"[66] link culture, race, and authenticity to cuisine. Unlike ethnic-themed neighborhoods like Little Italy, Chinatown, Greektown, or Little Ethiopia that provide commercially constructed forms of diversity and ethnicity, the H Street, NE corridor produces diversity and authenticity through creative-food establishments that offer variations of local, organic, seasonal, "ethnic," and/or fusion cuisine.

Chapter 5 focuses on public space, describing how various forms of power and the aestheticization of everyday life are linked to the control of space and place. The chapter also considers the production of racial aesthetics through the management of Black excess on H Street. This chapter investigates how public space is transformed by private acts often deemed aberrant when Black bodies inhabit the street in an intimate manner. Where physical imaginations of the street are enforced as linear, blackness renders the street a site of paranoia, crime, danger, and excitement.

My concluding chapter draws together the frailties and negotiations that the meaning of blackness endures across multiple sites, and what blackness means in the context of neoliberal imperatives in the post-Obama era.

1   Capital Reinvestment

Riot, Renewal, and the Rise of a Black Ghetto

. . . .

Hey, uh, we didn't get our forty acres and a mule
But we did get you CC, heh, yeah
Gainin' on ya / Movin' in and around ya
God bless CC and its vanilla suburbs

—Parliament (1975), "Chocolate City"

In the post–World War II period, population growth exploded in the suburbs of several major U.S. cities. Politicians and planners used suburbanization as a solution to address the declining conditions of cities in the 1940s and 1950s.[1] For them, weakened economies on both a local and a national level could be strengthened by geographical restructuring, which could effectively address capitalist anxieties. There were several contributing factors that led to the exodus of white middle-class residents from the central city to the suburbs. Newly available credit, federal subsidies (like bank and mortgage insurance, and defense contracts), and high wages led to the drastic population shift of middle- and upper-middle-class white residents from cities to the outlying suburbs. Therefore, cities became disproportionately populated with poor immigrants and African Americans who were left to survive in a rapidly decaying urban landscape. White families wanted to flee to the suburbs in order to leave behind the deteriorating conditions of the city. Because of the rapid and exponential in-migration of Black residents from the South, plummeting property values, growing crime rates, poor school choices, and congestion, white families looked for more space and a modernized landscape. Of course, the departure of white people from the central city helped accelerate its devolving conditions, and as a result of these broader geographical restructurings of the economy, the Black ghetto emerged.

Washington experienced white flight following the 1954 *Brown v. Board of Education of Topeka, Kansas* ruling leading to the desegregation of America's public schools—overturning the "separate but equal" doctrine. Prior to 1965, Blacks and whites equally populated the city and lived side by side in several neighborhoods, including Georgetown, Capitol Hill, and Anacostia.[2] While Congress passed multiple laws guaranteeing civil and voting rights protections for Black Americans, they still experienced significant forms of discrimination in housing, employment, and income and other injustices. Blacks and other marginalized racial and ethnic groups were, in many cases, prohibited from moving to the outlying suburbs and were therefore spatially confined to the city. First, the exclusion was enacted through restrictive racial covenants that were included in property deeds. Then, once these covenants were deemed unconstitutional and no longer enforced, discriminatory and predatory practices like steering (by real estate agents) and redlining (by banks and insurance companies) prevented the construction of federally subsidized housing. Furthermore, exclusionary zoning inhibited the development of higher-density multifamily units that were much more affordable than the pricey single-family, suburban homes. Naturally, the suburbs of Maryland and Virginia experienced incredible development and expansion to attract and accommodate all of the people who were moving there in the 1950s and 1960s.

This chapter takes Washington, D.C.'s history of racial and spatial neglect into account, as well as the city's disinvestment using suburbanization as a tool to later accrue capital. I focus on the 1968 uprisings in D.C., and their aftermath of urban renewal and commercial redevelopment on H Street. Here, I chronicle the history of the corridor to illustrate how the meaning of blackness shifted over time as well as the development and designation of H Street as a Black space. I also examine the intersection of urban development, Black capitalism, local policy, and the racialization of public space on H Street placed within the context of national urban divestment between the 1970s and 1990s. Finally, I chart how this place was allowed to degenerate in order to make way for its eventual regeneration, allowing the capitalist agenda to commodify space to prevail.

Black American Life, Legacy, and Degeneracy

White exodus from American cities was taking place at the same time that scholars and politicians like Daniel Patrick Moynihan (who became an advisor to Richard Nixon during his presidency) generated studies about the culture and status of Black people in the United States. In their pinnacle study on race relations in America during the mid-twentieth century, Nathaniel Glazer and Moynihan perpetuated the idea introduced by Chicago School sociologist Robert Park that Black Americans lack a definitive culture.

Reflecting the importance of "ethnicity" in self-identification and perhaps recognition, the authors suggest that ethnic identities helped direct "the task in self-definition and in definition by others that occupational identities, particularly working-class occupational identities have generally played . . . the status of being an ethnic, a member of an ethnic group has been upgraded."[3] Although they attempted to cast Blacks as having the unique potential of transcending their social and economic challenges because of their lack of historical and cultural ties to the past, Glazer and Moynihan only propagated falsehoods of Black subjectivity that were inconsistent with their intentions. Their narrative of assimilation paralleled concurrent liberal appeals to integration at the beginning of the civil rights movement. Fitness for citizenship and belonging was dependent on the ability to conform to normative conceptions of middle-class (and overwhelmingly white) familial and gender relations. This was just another way to mark the difference of Black Americans.

On a similar note, in the 1965 report aptly titled *The Negro Family: A Case for National Action*, or more popularly, "The Moynihan Report," Daniel Patrick Moynihan argued that the experience of slavery irreparably damaged the Black family structure and therefore Blacks were at a distinct disadvantage since stable, healthy, male-headed families are the key to achieving social mobility. In this text, he effectively placed the Black family at the center of national policy discourse. He attributed the pathologized beliefs and practices of Black Americans to culture and concluded that Black culture led to poverty and inequality. Moynihan (re)introduces notions of Black family structure as dysfunctional because it is primarily headed by Black women. Moynihan's analysis of the pathological nature of female-headed homes demonstrated his interest in policing or disciplining Black sexuality, in addition to shifting the blame away from structural and institutional forms of racism. This narrative constructed both Black men and women as sexually perverse, since, according to the report, they did not follow the normative patterns of American domestic habits and violated established gender roles and sexual standards. The Black American family was the site of deviant sexual formations. In his previous research with Glazer, Moynihan acknowledged the distinction between Blacks and white ethnic immigrants in terms of culture—specifically, family structure. However, in "The Moynihan Report," he makes a stronger claim about the weakness of the Black family structure as the cause of "the deterioration of the fabric of Negro society."[4]

Not only do Moynihan and Glazer provide an ideological framework that develops a pathological and dependent Black subject, they also imagine a proper (moral) liberal citizen. This framework assumes a version of American society in which culturally and economically impoverished communities of color require assistance in achieving equal opportunity and an introduction into mainstream culture. This is especially evident in Moynihan's later work and his long-standing commitment to vocational training and education programs for the Black community as well as his influence in the development of the War on Poverty. In the end, the projections about Black subjectivity proposed by Glazer and Moynihan effectively permeated theories of race and racial difference that continued throughout the rest of the twentieth century.[5] Moynihan and Glazer promote what George Lipsitz calls the "white spatial imaginary," which reinforces structured advantages of whiteness through restrictive spatial exclusivity. According to this approach, "whites viewed inner-city residents not as fellow citizens denied the subsidies freely offered whites, but as people whose alleged failures to save, invest, and take care of their homes forced the government to intervene on their behalf, to build housing projects that were then ruined by alleged Black neglect."[6] In other words, it was the particular practices and culture of Black Americans that served as a fundamental hurdle to actively participating in the liberal capitalist society. The social, cultural, and economic consequences of the white spatial imaginary led to Black Americans being spatially confined, as it not only justified white exodus to the suburbs but also structured the development of the Black "inner city."

Consumption and Containment on H Street, NE

Washington, D.C.'s H Street, NE corridor was a central location for Black social and economic life prior to the 1950s. The popular commercial corridor provided numerous retail options, eateries, and public spaces for Black Washingtonians. H Street was the most significant commercial activity center within the greater Capitol East area; it was second only to downtown D.C. in the production of jobs and tax revenue. Retail anchors included Morton's, Sears & Roebuck, McBride's, and Hechinger's. However, by the 1960s, H Street suffered at the hands of suburbanization in America, when middle-class residents left the cities for the suburbs and utilized malls as their main shopping source. A combination of state and corporate divestment, abandonment, and disparaging representations of urban markets and Black consumers left commercial corridors like H Street to falter.[7] Exclusionary and racist laws regulated by the federal government disproportionately impacted Black families from accumulating wealth from equity in their homes. In several neighboring Maryland and Virginia suburbs, Black families were prohibited from purchasing homes throughout much of the 1940s, 1950s, and 1960s; therefore, Black people were unable to benefit from the burgeoning growth and development in the suburbs like white families. It was not until the passage of the Fair Housing Act in 1968 that some Blacks were able to move to the suburbs with the hopes of finding affordable homes. Nevertheless, the majority were relegated to a crumbling urban core that began to provide fewer services and amenities to allow residents to thrive.

Washington, D.C., was unique in that Blacks constituted a significant portion of the city by the 1950s and had been visibly present since the nineteenth century. By 1968, the Black population of the city was estimated at 67 percent, higher than any other major U.S. city. Despite the shiny veneer of the tourist regions in Washington, the city's everyday life exposed significant fractures in the picture: rat-infested slums; failing education systems and public health; deficient, unsafe housing conditions; disease; and poverty (measured by overwhelming welfare caseloads). The economic situation for Black Americans was dire before the rebellion. Black residents, especially those living in impoverished areas, were often barred from standard retail outlets and therefore had to patronize local shops where they were charged exorbitant prices and credit premiums. On H Street, most of the customers came from the eastern regions of the city, adjacent to the corridor, where Black residents lived in substandard, congested, slum-like dwellings.[8]

Furthermore, in the popular commercial corridors where Black patrons shopped, there was a greater emphasis on goods rather than services. According to a Federal Trade Commission study, at several D.C. stores specializing in selling furniture and appliances to low-income households, approximately "92 percent of the sales of these stores were credit sales involving installment purchases, as compared to 27 percent of the sales in general retail outlets handling the same merchandise."[9] These businesses that catered specifically to poor Black patrons "charged significantly higher prices than general merchandise outlets in the Washington area. . . . The customers of these outlets were paying an average price premium of about 52 percent."[10] The magnitude of these exploitative business practices was exacerbated by the fact that Black customers had limited alternatives. There was a myriad of ways Black consumers were both encouraged to buy things and charged higher fees for goods like electronics and furniture, through TV and radio ads on Black radio stations.[11] Because most of the "ghetto" dwellers have low income and cannot afford the goods outright and must get credit, customers use installment plans that end up charging more than the original price. The importance of identifying the ways that the Black poor were targeted as consumers resists the notion that Black people were economically irresponsible and independently trying to live beyond their means. Instead, as anthropologist Ulf Hannerz points out, a desire for expensive items is directly connected to "the general affluence of the society surrounding them."[12] Thematically, consumption and containment are important to consider when thinking about the meaning of blackness in Washington, D.C. These concepts become particularly relevant when discussing the period before the uprisings, especially along commercial corridors like H Street. The consumption of goods and spatial containment are interrelated with blackness because of the ways that Black residents were encouraged to consume at high levels, while being spatially contained within impoverished areas due to segregation.

Black Washingtonians had the highest unemployment rate in the city, and the jobs they held did not pay well. These conditions were exacerbated by the fact that large sections of the city had inadequate public transportation, which precluded many African Americans from seeking employment in the white suburbs. Although Washington, D.C., was legally integrated, in practice, the city was largely segregated with whites living in affluent areas (a few affluent Blacks also lived in previously white, upscale neighborhoods), some "gray" areas where whites and Blacks lived in the same vicinity, and poor neighborhoods that were mostly composed of Blacks where high rent, congestion, and substandard living conditions for residents prevailed. After the 1950s, the H Street, NE corridor, in particular, provided its Black inhabitants with limited retail options, in contrast to whites living in more affluent areas. Former *Washington Post* journalist Ben Gilbert described the condition of the corridor up to 1968 as "a compact replica of the ghetto commercial strips along 7th and 14th streets, N.W." Like these neighborhoods, Gilbert remarked that H Street was filled with "liquor stores, groceries, carry-outs, and cheap cut-rate stores, as well as smaller and less imposing branches of the variety, clothing, and specialty-shop chains represented on 14th Street."[13] The conditions of ghetto business districts reflect deeply rooted social and economic trends, but the makeup of these spaces also exacerbates the issues customers and residents experience under poverty and underemployment. Once a thriving commercial corridor that provided mostly Black patrons with fundamental retail options, the H Street, NE corridor eventually became a stagnant and marginalized space, and a logical target for social unrest.

Temperature's Rising: Simmering Tensions in a "Riotproof" City

Hundreds of urban rebellions took place all over the country in the mid-twentieth century, but particularly in neighborhoods where Blacks were a majority or in neighborhoods that had been neglected for significant periods of time.[14] Within a two-year period between 1964 and 1966, dozens of violent outbreaks occurred throughout the country in New York City, Cleveland, Chicago, Philadelphia, Watts, Jersey City, and many more places. By 1967, more than 120 uprisings had been registered by the federal government, with over eighty people—mostly African Americans—killed as a result of the outbreaks.[15] The 1968 National Advisory Commission on Civil Disorders, or the Kerner Report's famous statement that America "is moving toward two societies, one Black, one white—separate and unequal," and conclusion that the collective tension resulted from the racist attitudes and behavior of white Americans toward Black Americans spoke to the racial climate of the period. As Janet Abu-Lughod surmises, this oft-cited statement from the Kerner Report did not offer much in terms of new information, and if anything, it signals how out of touch politicians and researchers were in 1968 if they concluded the nation was *becoming* separate rather than having always been that way.[16] This tone-deafness speaks to why these neighborhoods took so long to recover. There was no true assessment of the conditions and motivations for the scores of rebellions that took place in urban areas during the course of the twentieth century, no accounting for what structural inequalities did to Black families and individuals, despite the successes of the Black elite in Washington.

In the five years following the 1963 March on Washington and Martin Luther King Jr.'s famous "I Have a Dream" speech, Black people in Washington, D.C., and across the rest of the United States experienced a profound sense of optimism due to landmark court decisions and legislation, a sympathetic president, and newfound forms of political power. However, by 1968, it became clear that conditions had not shifted and instances of housing and job discrimination remained at significantly high levels. While militant Black leaders called for direct action to challenge the status quo, King maintained his belief in the power of nonviolence. Nevertheless, there was a clear shift from the nonviolent civil rights activism of the Southern Christian Leadership Conference (SCLC) to a more radical brand of Black Power organized by Stokely Carmichael and the Student Nonviolent Coordinating Committee (SNCC) as a result of these conditions of struggle for Black people. Washington was a hotbed for political activity among Black activists and organizers. Chapters of several national organizations and active local groups worked toward social, political, and economic equality for Black people, including SCLC, SNCC, and Marion Barry's Pride, Inc. The intersection of Fourteenth and U Streets, NW (Northwest), in particular, was a central location, as multiple organizations were headquartered along the Northwest corridor. Political changes were taking place amid calls for home rule via the "Free D.C." campaign, which several H Street businesses openly supported. Local activists like the local SNCC chapter president, Marion Barry, believed that without home rule, deplorable housing, school, employment, and overall living conditions for Black people in D.C. would continue indefinitely.[17]

Because D.C. was geographically isolated from the upheaval taking place across the country during the peak of "riot season," there was a commonly held belief that the city was riotproof. Some believed it was because the federal government provided steady employment, in contrast to cities experiencing a postindustrial decline. These federal job opportunities provided the climate for a growing Black middle class. Dana Schaffer, who conducted multiple oral histories with current and former residents of the damaged corridors, discovered that according to the 1960 census, Black families in Washington, D.C., had substantially high income levels compared with those in other major cities, with 22,000 having incomes of greater than $8,000 and 10,800 having incomes greater than $10,000.[18] Additional reasons why D.C. was thought to be riotproof included (1) the existence of a Black mayor; (2) high-ranking Black police officers; (3) its status as the Federal city, in which there was a strong belief that employment was more stable for Black residents in D.C. than other areas of the country; (4) also because it is the Federal city, there was more access to military-grade protection and surveillance.[19] In fact, *Washington Post* reporter William Raspberry, the first Black columnist for the *Washington Post*, wrote in an article one month prior to King's assassination that rioting had not reached the capital city prior to this moment because Washington displayed more "intelligence" than other cities experiencing turmoil. He writes: "Washington has escaped serious summer trouble so far, which may lead to a more balanced view of things. It has a Negro 'mayor' who understands ghetto unrest. It has a most remarkable director of public safety at the top of the Police Department. It must be said, too, that Washington, as a Federal city, has in reserve another level of response and easy availability of Federal troops (and tanks). Since Washington, the Federal city, is already powerfully armed, it makes it possible for Washington, the local city, to exercise a good deal of restraint.

Perhaps most important, the city has intelligent leaders who have seen that police power has triggered more riots than it has prevented."[20] Perceptions of a contented middle class, the existence of a large Black population, and a Black mayor fueled ideas that Blacks enjoyed a better quality of life than Black folk in other U.S. cities. Nevertheless, D.C. experienced racial tensions due to significant economic discrepancies between Black and white residents.

Despite the popular belief that the end of federally mandated segregation combined with a stable social and economic climate for Black Washingtonians would effectively quell tensions, integration and imaginations of peaceful cohabitation in the city were deceptive. Washington faced political and social turmoil in the aftermath of integration efforts. As *Washington Post* journalist Ben Gilbert writes in 1968, "Tensions had developed out of official and unofficial moves to remove racial barriers and integrate public facilities." Gilbert explains that most of these encounters took place without disorder, "but in the 1960's, as the fight for Negro rights took on increased militancy, public confrontations between the police and groups of Blacks became more frequent and less orderly. Washington was becoming less riotproof."[21] In other words, an increase in Black activism, police surveillance, and crumbling conditions made Washington, D.C., ripe for social and economic disorder.

As the 1960s drew to an end, more and more Black residents imagined the benefits of "militant" civil protest.[22] For example, in 1966, following a music concert at the Washington Coliseum, a group of young people stormed H Street, NE, damaging store windows along the way.[23] Given the increasing civil unrest in Washington, President Johnson decided to reorganize D.C.'s city government. He proposed a plan to Congress allowing for the appointment of a mayor and a city council. Once passed, Walter E. Washington was installed as the first mayor of D.C., on November 3, 1967, alongside a Black majority city council. President Johnson's assumption was that a Black mayor could reduce tensions and "improve relationships between the police and citizenry" far better than the three-man board of commissioners that managed D.C. for the ninety-three years prior to Washington's installation.[24]

Fear of increased violence spread in anticipation of King's proposed Poor People's Campaign, planned for April 22, 1968, in Washington. While the March on Washington in 1963 proved to be a peaceful event that spanned several days, concerns over more militant and radical involvement caused local and federal law enforcement officials to enact simplified plans for arrest, detainment, and the quelling of any uprisings. King spoke to a crowd of 4,000 people at the National Cathedral on March 31, 1968: "We are not coming to Washington to engage in any histrionic action, nor are we coming to tear up Washington. I don't like to predict violence, but if nothing is done between now and June to raise ghetto hope, I feel this summer will not only be as bad, but worse than last year."[25] King died four days later.

· · · · · ·

Over the course of several days, Washington, D.C., experienced a series of protests in three major hubs of Black commercial and residential activity: the Fourteenth Street, NW corridor, the Shaw district (Seventh Street, NW), and the H Street, NE corridor. The uprisings were sparked in heavily populated, majority Black areas of Fourteenth and U Streets, NW, and then spread to other neighborhoods. The events began as an organized effort by Stokely Carmichael to encourage local businesses to close out of respect. Nevertheless, by the night of April 4, the situation escalated in dramatic fashion through the destruction of mostly white-owned businesses—specifically, along the Fourteenth Street, NW corridor and in the Shaw district.

Once news had spread of Dr. King's assassination, the activity began on the evening of Thursday, April 4, 1968, at People's Drug Store at Fourteenth and U Streets, NW, a popular bus transfer hub and congested intersection. By Friday afternoon, April 5, tensions flourished and crowds began to gather on H Street, NE. As Ben Gilbert recounts, excitement and tension filled the growing crowds on H Street, NE when a liquor store at Fifth and H burst into flames, leading to the establishment of the H Street, NE corridor as a "section of the city [that] was added to the list of those requiring extraordinary attention."[26] Large groups of people, primarily young Black residents, migrated from Shaw and the eastern part of downtown and started to gather on H Street after 1:00 P.M. The co-owner of Ben's Chili Bowl, Virginia Ali, characterized the uprisings of D.C. as a "commercial riot," since D.C. had the most commercial damage compared with other cities that experienced turmoil after King's assassination.[27] The police were significantly outnumbered as they tried to protect stores from crowds of over 1,000 people. Nevertheless, participants burned and looted, leaving the carcasses of several structures behind (figure 4).

Sam Smith, a white journalist in Washington, D.C., and founder of the *East Capitol Gazette*, lived a few blocks away from the H Street corridor on

FIGURE 4 Front page of the Sunday morning *Evening Star* newspaper, April 6, 1968.

D Street, NE, and was home when the outbreak began. In his book *Captive Capital*, he described the scene:

> My wife and I lived then a few blocks south of H Street, a major Black commercial strip. The next morning [after King's assassination], however, things were still quiet enough that we went about our business as usual. I came home that afternoon to find a slow stream of people walking down the street with liberated objects: hangers full of clothes, a Naugahyde hassock, a television set. There were only a few whites living on the block, but I felt little tension or hostility from those I passed. I mainly noticed the black smoke pouring down from H Street. My wife was out back working

in our foot-wide strip of garden, listening to reports of looting and arson on a portable radio as the black fog settled in. We decided to go up on the roof for a better look. H Street was burning. Other areas had gone first and there were reports of a lack of fire equipment to deal with the situation a few blocks to the north. I tried to count the fires but they congealed under the curtain of smoke. A picture I had seen of blocks of burned-out buildings in Detroit came to my mind and I suggested that we better pack a few things in case we had to leave. For about ten minutes we did so but our instinctive selection—nostalgic items, favorite photos—the unvaluable but irreplaceable—made us laugh. Like loyal children of our generation, we settled down in our smoky living room to watch it all on television. At six-thirty the next morning a white friend from around the corner rang our doorbell. He wasn't in trouble; he just wanted company on a tour of the area. We got into his car and drove to H, Seventh and Fourteenth Streets. As I looked at the smoldering carcass of Washington and observed the troops marching down the street past storefronts that no longer had any backs, I thought, so this is what war is like.[28]

King's assassination prompted hundreds of Black Washingtonians from the most disinvested areas of the city to channel their frustration over their continuing social, political, and economic marginalization. Although the H Street corridor had been identified as a problem neighborhood before the uprisings commenced, patterns of destruction on the street followed a path similar to what had happened the previous day in the Shaw neighborhood and on U Street.

Police officers employed different tactics on H Street to contain the participants than those used in the other two corridors. Rather than use tear gas "freely," as reported in the *Evening Star*, police officers arrested participants. Nevertheless, on H Street, they used more tear gas on assailants than what was used on Seventh and Fourteenth Streets. As part of an effort to curb violence and avoid fatalities, Mayor Washington instructed the D.C. police to avoid excessive force—guns—on the protestors and looters. Mayor Washington and the police were also intent on preserving businesses that existed along the path of destruction. Two dozen police officers faced crowds of over 1,000 people descending upon the neighborhood. In order to protect businesses along the corridor, police officers, "in twos and threes, stood in the middle of intersections and fired grenades at anyone moving."[29] Impressive fires (presumably started by firebombs and Molotov cocktails) engulfed and destroyed several buildings along H Street, including Morton's at Seventh and H. It was there that a thirteen-year-old boy, Vernon Marlowe, burned to death.[30] Another casualty was Harold Bentley, a thirty-four-year-old construction worker who was killed on Friday afternoon by a fire at the I-C Furniture Company near Fifth and H.

The National Guard was called in to quell the tensions and worked with the local police to end the riots after five days (in conjunction with the deliberate withdrawal of uprising participants). The 1968 Washington Civil Disturbance Survey report revealed that the total cost of the damage between April 4 and April 15 reached $57.6 million (which included the value of destroyed inventories of goods and property damage), about double the previous estimates. The revised estimates indicate the rebellion caused nearly $33 million in damage to businesses, displaced nearly 5,000 people from their jobs, and left 2,000 homeless.[31] Furthermore, the uprisings resulted in a total of thirteen deaths and $24 million insured property damage. In the end, D.C. experienced more widespread physical destruction than any other riot-stricken city in the United States.[32] On H Street, in particular, 103 businesses and ninety buildings containing fifty-one residential units were damaged. Forty-one of the ninety buildings sustained more than 50 percent damage.

In comparison to Fourteenth Street and Seventh Street, H Street experienced the least amount of destruction, with total damage to the street estimated at $1.8 million, compared with $6.6 million on Fourteenth Street and $4.3 million on Seventh Street, respectively.[33] The south side of the street saw the most damage—specifically, the blocks at Fifth, Eighth, Ninth, Eleventh, and Twelfth Streets. Despite having less damage, business on H Street was decimated following the uprisings, and several stores that were not completely destroyed never reopened.[34] Accordingly, most of the damage on H Street was done to commercial businesses rather than homes. The poor and marginal condition of homes seemed to have little to do with the uprisings and more to do with the conditions of the area in general. Ultimately, a primary outcome of the upheaval was the destruction of the economy of a retail destination for Black shoppers along H Street, NE. H Street used to be the primary shopping corridor for Black Washingtonians, and a location that employed thousands of Black workers. After the uprisings, there was no central area for them to shop.

Reflection on the Roots of Rebellion

The uprisings in D.C. followed the "Long Hot Summers" between 1964 and 1967, in which violence and turmoil erupted in various U.S. cities, like Detroit, Los Angeles, and Newark. The aggravation Black Washingtonians experienced was part of the national discontent felt by Blacks in various major cities over the stagnant progress of the civil rights movement and unrelenting racial injustice. Feelings of isolation and abandonment reached their climax in 1968. While the horrifying assassination of King prompted the uprisings, the events were also, according to William Raspberry, "a lashing out at an amorphous 'Whitey'—not just the white man who had fired the fatal shot, but the whites who didn't want Blacks in their neighborhoods or schools, who treated them unfairly at the job, who seemed to value them primarily as captive customers for overpriced merchandise."[35] The uprisings took place amid high levels of economic disparity, housing and employment discrimination, and instances of racism that were rampant in social and professional arenas for Black Washingtonians. They also occurred amid tense relations between Black residents and the federal government, since urban policy had experienced a dramatic shift. Historian Howard Gillette explains that the federal government's efforts to implement its "War on Poverty" led to capital being directed "to neighborhood-based organizations with the intent of enabling local residents to improve their own lives."[36] In other words, rather than acknowledging its responsibility in the systemic poverty and oppression of poor and working-class Black residents, the federal government framed the problems facing these residents as an issue of inadequate funding.

Media accounts of the uprisings focused on property "devastated by burning, looting bands of rebellious citizens" rather than analyzing the roots of the disturbances.[37] One D.C. resident, Reuben M. Jackson, interviewed for an oral history project focusing on the 1968 uprisings, explained that most people do not concern themselves with the root of problems, but instead focus on particular actions and behavior. Discussing why he believed the uprisings occurred, Jackson said: "I think, it's just anger over a specific incident, but I think it's like a crock pot. It's like the steam sort of builds up and builds up and builds up. Yeah, one can say there were some opportunists who just took things. It was a good time to get a good TV or something. But 'why' does not seem to be part of the American lexicon, like 'why things happen.'"[38] Several participants in the uprisings possessed a political shrewdness, underestimated by the mainstream media, that characterized the uprisings as irrational destruction generated solely because of the violent assassination of Dr. King. Some participants used the opportunity to take items like clothing, shoes, alcohol, and whatever other goods they could carry from these establishments because of what they felt was owed to them due to continued neglect from the federal government, job discrimination, underemployment, and residential price-gouging.[39] The looting was part of a symbolic action to challenge the status quo. In fact, some of the participants distributed the goods they collected if anyone asked for them.[40]

Black residents in several other urban cities similarly destroyed property and looted goods in response to years of systematic inequalities. For example, as George Lipsitz finds, Black residents of Watts, California, responded to the culmination of systemic racism in matters of housing, education, and employment, as well as state-sanctioned violence. But like D.C., "while the community lashed out, it did not do so blindly."[41] Several Black-owned businesses and organizations remained untouched in areas where every other structure had been destroyed. He continues, "A furniture store owned by whites was looted and burned to the ground, but the storefront next door housing an Urban League employment project remain untouched by the rioters. Inside stores known for charging deceptively high interest rates for installment purchases, looters first demolished the establishments' credit record sections before helping themselves to the clothing, furniture and appliances on display. The riot demolished many commercial buildings, but almost no private homes, libraries, or churches."[42] Despite a clear history of looting activities taking place in reaction to oppressive urban conditions, media narratives of urban rebellions and uprisings identify participants as irresponsible, thoughtless thugs who irrationally destroy "their own" communities.

Much of the destruction that took place during uprisings in Black neighborhoods around the country throughout the 1960s targeted small businesses owned by white shopkeepers and avoided those stores labeled "Soul Brother Managed," those businesses owned by Black people.[43] Along H Street, entire rows of buildings were completely destroyed by fires, while nearby stores remained untouched. Some images show the stark contrast of Black-owned barbershops standing untouched amid the ruins of a furniture store or a dry cleaner. Several businesses owned by "White soul brothers"—white shopkeepers who treated Black customers and employees favorably—were also spared. Buildings that housed public agencies and schools also went unscathed as the participants overwhelmingly targeted white-owned businesses that were known to discriminate against Black customers and practiced a form of surveillance over Black individuals who patronized their establishments.

Sam Smith reflected on his experiences during the uprisings as a business owner. He wrote, "I expected to find our newspaper office smashed and looted. It didn't happen, despite the inviting plate glass storefront. I was inclined, with normal self-delusion, to attribute this to having paid my dues. It was more likely, however, that our second-hand electric typewriters weren't worth the candle when there was a whole Safeway up the street and a cleaners on the corner."[44] Smith's observation about the selective nature of looting activities during the rebellion, and later in conversation with me, explained that the uprisings were less ideological, and more about class than race. He suggests that because he was a white business owner, his office could be subject to destruction if the uprisings were framed as a backlash against white people and white establishments. Instead, he concludes that rebellion participants, mostly poor and working-class Black residents, were more interested in targeting businesses that provided valuable goods that could improve their lives. While class was a significant factor driving the impulses and raw emotions that fueled the events of April 1968, it was the intersection of race and class, political and economic conditions, that explained the outbreak.

The substandard conditions Black people experienced in Washington and other major cities was just as much about their blackness as it was about their poverty. Nevertheless, while Washington, D.C., had an unprecedented number of Black elites and middle-class residents, class alone did not prevent them from experiencing employment discrimination or poor treatment in retail establishments. Smith acknowledges the persistence of racism, especially as it related to urban planning and commercial enterprise. "Those stores in downtown that were dying were in trouble because they continued to cater to a dwindling white market. Morton's department store chain, which marketed to Blacks, had four outlets before the 1968 riots. Two of them were destroyed in what a local Black newspaper editor called 'the great consumer rebellion of April 1968.'"[45] Here, Smith points to consumerism and a lack of access to proper services for Black people. On the one hand, he calls for a distinction between the Black middle class and the Black poor. On the other hand, he admits that the Black middle class still faced discrimination in contrast to white people generally. What this demonstrates is that Black Washingtonians were not a monolith, contrary to popular perception, but most Black Washingtonians in the mid-twentieth century were directly impacted by various forms of systemic and structural inequality.

Scholars and journalists who have written about the D.C. uprisings over the years emphasize the role of surveillance and excessive policing as some of the challenges Black Washingtonians experienced.[46] Ulf Hannerz provides an important link between the discontent in ghettos around the country in the 1960s (namely, Harlem in 1964, Watts in 1965, Chicago and Cleveland in 1966, Detroit in 1967) and what was occurring in D.C. with regard to substandard conditions and services for Black urban dwellers. Hannerz focuses his analysis on policing and ghetto merchant practices since, he says, they are "those outsiders who become most directly involved in the insurrection itself."[47] Similarly, *Washington Post* journalists Harry Jaffe and Tom Sherwood described the "roots of anger" precipitating the 1968 uprisings as connected to political and social turmoil caused by a fractured relationship between the D.C. police and Black Washingtonians. They document the extent to which D.C. police officers terrorized the Black community: "In 1967 and part of 1968 city police killed thirteen African-Americans, including one whose offense was as petty as stealing a bag of cookies. It was called 'justifiable homicide.' The Black community had complained about police brutality for years, but little had changed except for the mounting rage."[48] Since the population in D.C. was 65 percent Black and the police force in D.C. was over 80 percent white, the D.C. police were perceived as a deadly occupation army by Black residents.

Katherine McKittrick's theorization of a Black sense of place, in which she identifies the intimate connection between blackness and geography, is useful here. Even though Washington was thought to be riotproof (despite the fact that disturbances had occurred in D.C. during the "red summer" of 1919), as McKittrick argues, "relational violences of modernity produce a condition of being Black in the Americas that is predicated on struggle."[49] Acts of racial violence shape Black life and Black worlds. In particular, the "ghetto" operates as a site for racial entanglement.[50] Like other cities, the D.C. uprisings occurred as a result of mounting anger over unfulfilled expectations of civil rights legislation, feelings of hopelessness and powerlessness in the aftermath of segregation, spatial containment, a repressive police apparatus, neglect, and an emerging sense of Black pride and militancy.[51] The pervasiveness of the uprisings reflected frustrations related to multiple forms of violence enacted against Black communities in D.C.[52] Some of these include price gouging and discriminatory treatment by white business owners, inferior physical conditions of ghetto buildings, legacies of police surveillance and brutality, the colonial relationship between D.C. and the federal government (with D.C. not allowed to govern itself), and federal disinvestment of the urban core. All in all, the uprisings of April 1968 changed Washington, D.C., from a sleepy, southern town to a burgeoning social and political hotbed.

First Steps to Recovery and the Black Spatial Imaginary

Of the three "riot corridors," none was as slow to redevelop as the H Street, NE corridor. In May 1968, congressional hearings were held to determine what had caused the riots. Various Black D.C. residents spoke about the political, economic, and social assault on Black people by the federal government as worse than the damage inflicted by the riots, highlighting "the Plan"—a conspiracy to forcibly push Black Washingtonians out of D.C. city limits and D.C. politics (by way of gentrification, economic and social policies, etc.) that has been a popular narrative among long-term residents since the 1960s. Testimony stressed that Black residents had not been adequately involved in the process of planning and rebuilding their communities.[53] Racial tensions continued to plague the neighborhood as merchants and residents attempted to recover from the damage inflicted upon the area. The white merchants, who mostly lived outside of D.C., expressed a belief that there was a deep sense of resentment toward whites in the area. Several of these merchants believed "they had friends in their neighborhoods—until the riots."[54] Nevertheless, according to Marion Barry, then director of operations at Pride Inc., a Black-run job-training program founded in 1967 sponsored by the U.S. Labor Department, "the nation was divided into two cultures, one white, one Black, and if the city was rebuilt the way it was for whites, it would be burned down again," echoing findings generated by the Kerner Report.[55]

That same month, the National Capital Planning Commission (NCPC) released the *Civil Disturbances in Washington, D.C., April 4–8, 1968, A Preliminary Damage Report* to assess city conditions after the rebellion and provide suggestions to assist in the city's rebuilding. By August 28, 1968, the NCPC in cooperation with District of Columbia agencies published a second report, *Alternative Approaches to Rebuilding*, which specifically discussed the three major corridors. The Metropolitan Washington Board of Trade also conducted a survey of the damage. The reports acknowledged less about the roots of the turmoil and focused on plans for rebuilding the damaged corridors. Nevertheless, the NCPC study did emphasize the need for improved physical, as well as social and economic, conditions in the damaged areas, which included higher levels of home and business ownership, and improved access to healthcare, education, police protection, and job opportunities. The second NCPC report focused on proper assessment of physical damage caused by the uprisings. Specifically referencing conditions on H Street, the report identified the significance of the space as a "major retail center," second only to D.C.'s downtown Central Business District. And while there was less damage on H Street than on Seventh Street or Fourteenth Street, a significant portion of stores (approximately one-third) were completely destroyed.[56]

A cluster of mostly Jewish business owners organized a group they called "We the People" and sued the city and the federal government, seeking compensation as victims of the uprisings. As one *Washington Post* reporter explained, "Many businessmen in the primary riot areas of the city have complained that neither the city nor the federal government provided adequate protection for private property during the height of the looting and burning."[57] Despite evidence to the contrary, these shop owners openly challenged the argument that ghetto business owners were swindling the poor. They argued, "While there are undoubtedly some merchants whose practices are questionable, we can submit positive proof that the great majority of merchants affected by violence operated their business with absolute integrity."[58] This perspective adds fuel to the argument that rebellion participants were indiscriminate with their destructive activities, and that, therefore, white shopkeepers on H Street should have been better protected from the violence. The grievances lodged by this group reflect the white spatial imaginary, which "views space as a locus for the generation of exchange value."[59] The privilege of white business owners to sue the city and federal government on the basis of property (accruing value) when Black residents and consumers lived under deplorable conditions that were well documented shows how "the lives and property of some people [are] worth more than the lives and property of others."[60]

While many of the white business owners on H Street blamed the local government and authorities for not providing adequate protections, others saw the destruction of H Street as an opportunity to rebuild this space using Black developers and filling the corridor with businesses owned by Black entrepreneurs to serve the overwhelmingly Black residential population.[61] Black activists, business owners, and residents proposed that the rebuilding of the decimated corridors be an opportunity for Black stakeholders to transform the space to suit to their needs.[62] They, in essence, used a "Black spatial imaginary" to envision spaces that were Black built and Black run. According to Lipsitz, the Black spatial imaginary has been used by African Americans as a way to turn "dehumanizing segregation into exhilarating and rehumanizing congregation."[63] In particular, representatives from Pride, Inc. called for the city government to cease rebuilding efforts along the riot corridors and instead implement their plan, which included (1) the U.S. Small Business Administration (SBA) to stop processing disaster loans for businesses destroyed by the riots; (2) the SBA and local lending institutions to provide loans only to businesses that are at least 51 percent owned by Blacks, since the loans are "economically unfeasible" because they will only be burned and destroyed again; (3) Black contractors to be hired to convert burned sections of the neighborhoods into parks. They also advised that the city government and lending institutions establish a $5 million fund to provide Black residents with long-term, low-interest loans in order for them to gain economic security. They proposed job training in business management and accounting and implored the city to limit the number of liquor stores in Black neighborhoods with the intention of controlling "quality, price, and credit exploitation." Finally, they called for the closing of stores that sell "inferior merchandise."[64] Pride, Inc. hoped to address several of the systemic challenges that prompted the riots and that continued to plague the H Street, NE corridor and its surrounding neighborhoods.

In addition to Pride, Inc.'s proposed plan for these neighborhoods to be rebuilt by the Black residents and businesspeople who lived within them, Black architects also joined the conversation by proposing development plans. Several Black architects, many trained at Howard University, made demands to the overwhelmingly white leadership in D.C. and the federal government, who were still unable to properly assess the conditions Black people faced in D.C. specifically and in the United States generally.[65] One of these Black architects, Robert J. Nash, wrote angrily in 1968:

Whites can no longer be the paternalistic stumbling, confused stepparents of blacks. Blacks, in turn, are now at the point where it is necessary for them to take a massive, collective, objective look at themselves . . . with black people doing the defining.

It's tough, and what may be tougher is that whites have to understand that *any* role they play in rebuilding and planning for black ghettos has to be defined by black people! Whites can participate, but no longer at the leadership or decision-making levels to which they are so accustomed.

At this very moment, blacks are establishing their own "design criteria," a good portion of which dictates who is to do what and when. Obviously, these standards will insist on maximum involvement of blacks, from layman through professional. This is but one element of the insurance policy against the distrust that has mounted over centuries.[66]

Nash's indignation speaks to recognition of blackness as central in determining the direction of development along the damaged corridors but also called for an equal recognition of whiteness and its role in the oppression of Black Washingtonians. Consistent with much of the Black empowerment rhetoric that had begun to surface in the years leading up to the uprisings, Black architects spoke of their desire for full-scale change. Similarly, Black residents and business owners saw the aftermath of the rebellion as an opportunity to establish thriving Black communities in spaces that had been abandoned by white people and white capital.[67]

Ultimately, Mayor Walter E. Washington decided that a nongovernment entity should be charged with rebuilding efforts, so his administration established the Reconstruction and Development Corporation (RDC) with a $600,000 grant from the Ford Foundation.[68] Progress toward rebuilding stalled because most insurance companies refused to sell policies in the damaged areas. For example, on H Street, prior to the uprisings, insurance companies would have been willing to provide fire insurance for business owners up to $20,000. After the uprisings, that number went down to $10,000.[69] Immediately after the uprisings, within the same month, speculations arose over the value of the damaged property and claims about "natural market forces" making it difficult to find insurance companies to invest in the "riot corridors."[70] It was not until the summer of 1968 that Congress passed legislation creating a mandatory pool of insurance money to guarantee coverage to these merchants. The insurance policy did not cover acts of vandalism or broken plate glass, so many of the shopkeepers were unable to benefit from the legislation.[71] In terms of value, real estate that sits for a long time without any movement detracts from the attractiveness of the space as an investment instrument.[72] Therefore, the refusal of insurance companies to sell policies to business owners on H Street had profound impact on the space and its ability to thrive.

The Inner City Planning Associates, Inc. was formed in February 1969 and led by Rev. Walter E. Fauntroy, founder of the Model Inner City Community Organization (MICCO). The organization was established at the request of Mayor Washington and the Nixon administration to organize efforts to rebuild the commercial corridors most impacted by the uprisings. Washington offered Fauntroy's group a $200,000 grant to initiate efforts. The initial funds came from the Ford Foundation's original grant to the RDC that was established to provide the relief Fauntroy's new group was then charged to do. In other words, since the RDC did not accomplish much, Mayor Washington and federal officials from the Nixon administration appointed Fauntroy to do the job. Reverend Fauntroy, who proposed H Street, Seventh Street, and Fourteenth Street as urban renewal sites (figure 5), met significant opposition from organizations (including MICCO) that claimed he was not a good representative for the Black community.[73]

Another plan developed in April 1969 by the National Capital Planning Commission (NCPC), the Redevelopment Land Agency (RLA), and the RDC proposed a complete overhaul of H Street with retail stores on the ground floors of buildings and residences directly above, and additional mixed-income housing.[74] Because the RLA had sole authority to clear and sell land, it did not have the capital to help struggling businesses repair damage.[75] As a result, more businesses closed and buildings were boarded up. The Model City Commission, along with city councilmembers from Stanton Park (an area adjacent to H Street), protested federal and local government efforts and argued that residents and true stakeholders were being left out of the process. Although the NCPC, the RLA, and the RDC claimed to seek citizen input through the distribution of surveys, neighborhood activists resisted these efforts and claimed that they did not represent the interests of the H Street residents.[76] The NCPC plan was revised several times and then languished. For years, developers found it to be nearly impossible to find financing for construction of commercial and residential projects along H Street. There were several plans to rebuild, but most were stalled or never got off the ground.[77]

Eventually, the D.C. government through the RLA began buying land along H Street wholesale, a total of ten acres, with the intention of selling the parcels to developers who would in turn receive government assistance to revitalize the corridor. As a result of these purchases, residents were pushed out of their homes and the market for businesses plummeted. "The purchase left the area with empty lots and boarded-up buildings, looking like a ghetto, repelling young home buyers who might have revitalized H Street."[78] The city made several attempts to make the H Street corridor more desirable and worthy of investment by designating it as a Capitol Hill neighborhood—a respectable, safe, tony area that had a growing population of

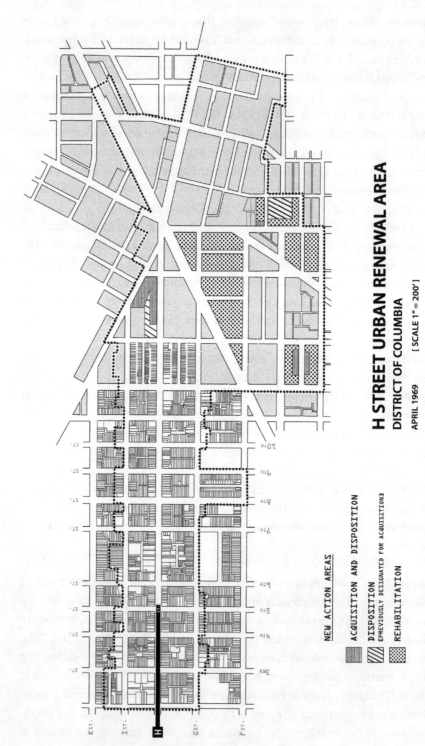

H STREET URBAN RENEWAL AREA
DISTRICT OF COLUMBIA
APRIL 1969   [SCALE 1" = 200']

NEW ACTION AREAS

ACQUISITION AND DISPOSITION

DISPOSITION
(PREVIOUSLY DESIGNATED FOR ACQUISITION)

REHABILITATION

FIGURE 5 Map of H Street urban renewal area. Map courtesy of Olalekan Jeyifous.

young, white, upper-middle-class families who had replaced its longtime Black, working-class residents. These efforts to rename the space were largely unsuccessful: "This bank officer also said he is skeptical of persons who come to him seeking loans to refurbish their business or houses in the H Street area and who try to tell him that the area is part of the Capitol Hill expansion. He thinks that the area is too far from the Hill to be described this way, and that such a description is basically a psychological trick designed by speculators and real estate people to build up the area." In the 1970s, a comparison to Capitol Hill was necessary to garner interest in the area.[79] Government administrators proposed multiple programs throughout the 1970s, yet "the casual stroller down H Street [in the late 1970s would] see basically a scene of decay, even devastation."[80] As one resident in 1977 lamented, city officials "talk around circles rather than getting to the point of what really needs to be done on H Street. Since 1968 there hasn't been any improvement around here (as far as I can see). You'd think that the government would take an interest in the welfare of the people, but after the politicians get (elected), they turn their backs on the people. Here you have a community that's been like this since 1968, but yet they can go across the sea and bring up Germany in 10 years (through the Marshall Plan following World War II)."[81] While the site of charred buildings was cleared away by the city, the families who shopped along the corridor remained—ignored and unsatisfied. Then city councilperson Marion Barry chose an H Street, NE location to outline his program for job opportunities and economic development during his run for mayor, a position he won in 1978. Barry claimed that the H Street corridor, "which has a number of boarded-up stores, a supermarket and several small business shops, reflected the 'gross neglect' of the mayor [Washington]."[82] Although H Street was not as heavily damaged as Seventh Street or Fourteenth Street by the mid-1970s, virtually no work had been done. Progress and change on H Street were particularly slow. The same conversations about urban renewal plans that began in 1969 remained unfinished and unfulfilled by 1974.[83] One key factor to the delay in reconstruction was the Nixon administration's freezing of federal funds for urban renewal in the wake of several major program failures. It was not until 1974 that the funds were again released, and central projects on the riot corridors were able to continue. Despite receiving limited support from the federal government, the image of H Street created a unique challenge for finding developers. When city officials were able to locate compliant developers, inadequate financing and incomplete planning stalled construction plans—sometimes indefinitely.[84]

Where the city proposed but did not implement plans to improve the corridor, the bulk of responsibility was left up to small business owners and nearby residents. From organizing fundraisers to sponsoring street cleanups, business owners along H Street sought their own plans to revive the corridor despite marginal assistance from the local and federal government.[85] Having been contained within a neighborhood "where zoning, policing, and investment practices make it impossible for them to control the exchange value of their property," these community members were committed to restoring the area and encouraging Black businesses, thereby generating "a spatial imaginary that favors public cooperation in solving public problems."[86]

The H Street corridor was especially disadvantaged not only because of the economic challenges but also the architectural ones. Another major project, this time by the federal government, that served to further isolate the H Street corridor, was the construction of the H Street Bridge, colloquially known as the "Hopscotch Bridge" for the decorative mural that adorns it, which connects North Capitol Street to H Street, NE. The Hopscotch Bridge was built in 1977 as part of the Federal Highway Administration's inner beltway system for D.C., and it replaced the underpass that once carried the street beneath the railroad tracks.[87] Plans for the bridge were opposed by residents and Black business owners along the corridor.[88] As one neighborhood resident and business owner explained, "When they built that bridge, you didn't have that traffic flow. People had to go around about to come down here to do business."[89] Even today, the bridge serves to visually isolate the northeast neighborhood. The bridge narrowed traffic and created a visual and physical obstruction to views of downtown, and some believe it was constructed as a strategic move to keep the predominantly Black and poor dwellers of the H Street away from downtown neighborhoods. While the overpass did not involve the demolition of homes that displaced thousands of Black residents like in some urban centers, it did serve a similar purpose; the physical isolation of H Street was significant to its devaluation as it cut off economic growth and is a hindrance as a physical and visual barrier to downtown.

A decade after the uprisings, H Street still struggled. Popular media accounts of the neighborhood described it as a destitute space, hopeless and stagnant. As written in the *Washington Post* in 1978, "the once riot-torn H Street NE area that was referred to by police in 1968 as a 'hot spot' [is] now frustratingly called a 'concentration of the miserable.'"[90] Economic and physical abandonment, coupled with disparaging images of overwhelmingly Black and poor areas like the H Street corridor, as urban studies scholar Christopher Mele argues, effectively "reinforce each other, creating a seemingly intractable stereotype of the ghetto as an oppressive and unredeemable space."[91]

Economic Downturn and the Rise of a Black Ghetto

By the 1980s, H Street was firmly recognized as what Elijah Anderson might call an "iconic ghetto."[92] The corridor resembled many other "blighted" sections of major urban centers that were disproportionally disadvantaged after economic downturns in the early 1980s and the gradual shrinking of government services for the poor and disenfranchised. H Street experienced challenges from the economy, and the residual impact of the uprisings stalled its growth. While the Hopscotch Bridge physically isolated the area, conditions of buildings along the corridor and surrounding neighborhood were still only marginally improved by the 1980s. Property values around H Street, NE (and D.C. as a whole) reached rock bottom, and violent crime and drug use depressed the area. It was during the period of the late 1980s and early 1990s that Washington, D.C.'s homicide rate climbed, earning the city the name "Murder Capital." H Street, NE became a symbolic space for mayoral candidates to promise to help spur growth and improve conditions in the city as a whole. Plans to designate the area as a space where Black entrepreneurs and developers could bring the corridor back to life were abandoned because of changes in the economic market, according to former housing director James E. Clay.[93] Many of the troubles that plagued the area before the uprisings continued to do so two decades after they occurred—underemployment, inadequate outlets for youths, poor residential conditions, and poor commercial options.[94] Very little had been done to the H Street corridor despite constant planning efforts by city officials, consultants, local merchants, and citizens. As one *Washington Post* reporter wrote in 1982, "Fifteen years of city planning have so far produced 738 units of federally subsidized housing and long stretches of cleared land."[95] The RLA ultimately reclaimed five city-owned parcels along H Street because developers did not follow through on their plans due to several years of inaction or financial instability.[96]

In 1983, the *Washington Post* reprinted an editorial from 1971 that emphasized the inactivity on H Street and other riot corridors. Stating that the article "could have run almost any day in the last 15 years,"[97] the *Post* lamented the stagnant progress taking place in all three corridors. H Street was not alone in its ruin, since both Seventh Street and Fourteenth Street were also filled with boarded-up storefronts, "hookers, and junkies."[98] In the following year, 1984, the local government retooled its fifteen-year-old strategies for reviving the H Street corridor, since a shift in economic conditions had "made the original proposals unworkable."[99] Also, in 1983, the D.C. government proposed yet another renewal plan for the H Street corridor that would involve the development of seven vacant lots owned by the RLA and would emphasize "its potential as a neighborhood shopping area rather than one that could attract shoppers from around the region."[100] This plan opted for movie theaters and casual restaurants, as opposed to fast-food outlets, to draw traffic to the area. The plan also called for $1 million toward aesthetic improvements to the streets—new sidewalks, curbs, benches, lighting, and other amenities.[101] Like most of the other redevelopment plans proposed by the government, this strategy failed to take hold in the midst of continuing controversies surrounding a misuse of funds by the H Street Business Community Association (HBCA), which was tasked to distribute loans and grants to businesses for renovations along the corridor.

The area was overrepresented by the prototypical urban businesses that are part of a ghetto economy, like liquor stores, convenience stores, barbershops, beauty salons, nail salons, check-cashing facilities, and carryout restaurants. When the Hechinger Mall was first built in the late 1970s, just a few blocks away from the heart of the H Street corridor, residents and community leaders saw it as a positive change that would offer residents retail options following the uprisings. By the early 1980s, the thirty-store mall was seen as a hindrance to the developing corridor as it was siphoning off businesses and customers from H Street. For example, one of the anchor stores at the mall was a Safeway grocery store that was the largest of the supermarket chain on the East Coast. Eventually, this location led to the closing of a small Safeway store at Sixth and H Streets, NE in 1984. With Safeway closing, revitalization efforts stalled even more and the building joined a collection of several vacant lots and struggling small businesses.[102]

The impact of Safeway closing had not only economic repercussions but social ones as well. To many residents around the H Street corridor, especially elderly men, the Safeway, like many other businesses on H Street, served as an informal communication space where friends would gather out front to socialize, or in some cases attempt to make a few dollars by guiding customers home from the store.[103] The reduction of public space that serves as sites for social gathering, like this one, is a common outcome of the privatization of space and signals what Arlene Dávila calls "a decline of opportunities for where alternative economic activities can take place."[104] As Hylan Lewis wrote in the introduction to Elliot Liebow's pioneering ethnography *Tally's Corner*, detailing Black men's relationships with their families, work, and each other in the Shaw neighborhood of Washington, D.C., urban businesses like small grocery stores, carryout restaurants, record stores, and laundromats act as "part of a distinctive complex of urban institutions" that speak to the needs, desires, and limited choices of urban dwellers.[105] Following the departure of Safeway, several more stores closed, and by 1985, more than sixty stores had closed along the H Street corridor since 1968. Approximately 150 businesses remained boarded up or were among the many vacant city-owned lots.[106]

In the aftermath of the D.C. rebellion, Black entrepreneurs attempted to build, grow, and maintain small businesses throughout the H Street corridor, but several failed. Stores were left in limbo because of urban renewal plans that were unclear and, in some cases, unfulfilled. Aside from facing challenges in getting loans because of the rising costs of affording them, Black business owners struggled to physically maintain buildings in various states of deterioration.[107] The physical environment of the H Street corridor featured a declining commercial infrastructure, boarded-up homes and storefronts, and vacant lots. Buildings abandoned due to disinvestment had a profound impact on the built environment, producing an atmosphere of decline and decay. Small Black-owned businesses struggled to find their footing along the corridor, as the building stock literally deteriorated. Some shop owners expressed their reservations about making significant improvements, for fear of RLA purchasing and demolishing the buildings.[108] Those Black businesses that survived the uprisings bore the imprint of destruction, especially since few businesses were adequately renovated and rebuilt decades after the disturbances.

During the 1980s and 1990s, while neighborhood residents attempted to reconstruct the decimated retail corridor, informal and often extralegal economic activities developed along and around H Street. With this introduction of what Natalie Hopkinson calls a "go-go economy" came a diverse system composed of "geographically dispersed clothing lines [and] graphic shops that create event fliers and press T-shirts."[109] "Go-go" is not only a style of music. It also describes the space where musicians and their fans would gather—in backyards, street corners, parks, restaurants, nightclubs, skating rinks, firehouses, community centers, and college campuses. Go-go is often characterized as a style of music that is endemic to Black residents in the Washington, D.C., area and is a deeply rooted culture that developed because of the challenges young Black men and women faced in the region. Go-go culture emerged from a decaying landscape and was used as a place-making device for those who felt disenfranchised, even in a chocolate city. It makes sense that it found a home along the H Street, NE corridor.

For the young Black men and women who lived around H Street, go-gos and street corners were sites of refuge, since many complained "that they don't have anywhere else to go or anything else to do."[110] In particular, the intersection at Eighth and H Streets was for many years and continues to be a center of activity and a meeting place along the corridor.[111] In the 1980s, the corner housed a "dismal, trash-littered park [that was] used by neighborhood residents, young and old, as a place to play cards, to shoot the breeze, smoke, drink and talk."[112] It was from this intersection that the "Eighth and H Street Crew" got its name. Seventeen members of the "crew" were charged with the October 1, 1984, slaying of forty-nine-year-old Catherine Fuller—often described as the most brutal murder in the city's history. Although only seven of the young men were tried and later convicted of Mrs. Fuller's murder, the unprecedented arrest of the seventeen youths allegedly involved in Ms. Fuller's murder reflected the criminalization of young Black males that took place at alarming rates in urban centers during this violent era. As one twenty-year-old resident of the area told the *Washington Post*, "What the police are calling gangs is really just groups of guys who know each other and hang out together, mainly at the go-gos."[113]

The economic and social infrastructure that collapsed prior to the riots continued to falter twenty and thirty years later. "There ain't no community organization building—nothing out here to keep everybody busy and help us make no money," one resident proclaimed. "So what are we supposed to do? Some youths are weak and dumb and don't know how to get what they want. So, they just try to get what the next guy has."[114] In 1987 a new mall, the H Street Connection—which was eventually demolished in 2017 to prepare for a high-rise, mixed-use building—was erected on H Street between Eighth and Tenth Streets, and a Dart Drug Store sat on the site of the park where the Eighth and H Street Crew gathered prior to the murder of Catherine Fuller. In addition to the drugstore, the mall featured a police substation and several clothing stores. While many residents hailed the new economic activity along the corridor as a result of the new mall and future plans for a $23 million, five-story office building set to accommodate 900 employees of the D.C. Department of Human Services, the extensive "street crime and drug trafficking associated with H Street NE" caused neighborhood merchants and residents to still be "concerned about the safety of their customers and about shoplifting in their stores."[115]

Despite efforts to bring stability to the neighborhood through business ventures that would support the health of the community, the 1990s ushered in a new set of challenges toward the redevelopment of H Street, NE with an economic downturn that affected the region. Notably, the federal government cut aid for economic and community development in 1990 because of mismanagement by city officials (the funds were later restored in 1992). The corridor's only remaining supermarket, Mega Foods (the largest Black-owned supermarket in D.C.), also closed its doors in 1990 as well as the National Bank of Washington, and Fantles, a local drugstore. The shuttering of these businesses, especially Mega Foods, slowed down commercial activity on H Street and further limited access to quality services and goods. But it was also in the 1990s that the corridor began to experience some of the first signs of gentrification, with an increase in the number of Asian and Latin American immigrants moving to the area as well as some young white families who could not afford property on Capitol Hill. According to the *Washington Post*, "Many H Street NE shoppers resent the gentrification, just as many Black Washingtonians said in a *Washington Post* poll last year that they bristle at Hispanic and Asian immigrants who have taken over small businesses in black areas."[116] In the face of these challenges, throughout the 1980s and 1990s, there were several additional efforts to spur Black entrepreneurialism and pride along the corridor. City officials, merchants, and residents organized a festival to celebrate the impending revitalization of the H Street, NE corridor. The *Washington Post* described the 1992 event: "The contrast between the reality of the Northeast Washington business corridor and the long-promised revitalization could not have been stronger. Almost a quarter-century after the 1968 riots, one of the city's main commercial strips of black-owned businesses yesterday again found itself looking forward by looking back."[117]

The festival along H Street was planned as a way to bring positive attention to the area that was populated with a mixture of new and old retail and service businesses, as well as several vacant storefronts, people drinking alcoholic beverages from paper bags, and shopkeepers conducting business from behind bulletproof glass windows. The festival took a four-year hiatus between 1995 and 1999 because of a lack of funding. With its reputation as a problematic, enfeebled, decimated space, H Street became one of those neighborhoods that politicians, particularly mayoral candidates, used to symbolically foreshadow their positive impact on the city. In other words, if one can successfully turn H Street around, one can do anything—especially make D.C. better.

· · · · · ·

On April 4, 1998, thirty years after Dr. King's assassination and the outbreak of civil disturbances in Washington, CNN published an online article that discussed the ways in which Washington, D.C., is still recovering from the 1968 uprisings.[118] H Street is highlighted as one of the places that continued to struggle. While H Street received federal and local funds toward its rebuilding, the construction of the Hopscotch Bridge divided H Street from the rest of the city. In the story, former resident, business owner, and current H Street Main Street executive director Anwar Saleem noted that several of the businesses along H Street struggled and lost business due to the bridge. H Street was a location where the working poor resided and roamed. But according to Bill Barrows of the H Street Community Development Corporation, rocky race relations still contributed to the inequities many Black people faced in the area.[119]

The rebuilding of Washington was a direct result of the uprisings. Black mayors, a Black police chief, and other Black leaders came into power after the D.C. uprisings. Many believed change would come in favor of Black residents with strong Black leadership. In the years following the uprisings, the federal and local government, developers, and neighborhood organizations made strident efforts to rebuild H Street. Nevertheless, redeveloping the commercial corridor proved to be a challenge for business leaders and the local government to provide adequate solutions for the rebuilding of D.C. despite the fact that initial planning for the reconstruction of the damaged areas began almost immediately. The federal government provided funds to the new independent local government, which then empowered nongovernment organizations to oversee the rebuilding—a plan that drew ire from neighborhood residents. Failed collaboration between these entities eventually led to the precipitous decline in H Street's economic value.

Over several years of miscommunication, mismanagement of funds, and unfulfilled plans, all compounded by increasing inequities that gave rise to exceptional violence in inner-city neighborhoods, the radical spirit conveyed in the 1960s had been effectively muted. Multiple examples of Black businessmen and businesswomen attempting to revive the corridor were overshadowed by the increasing violence and poverty taking over the neighborhood. Even their attempts to rebuild the corridor were often thwarted due to bureaucratic hurdles. To think that a resurgence of Black businesses and Black developers could save the corridor without systemic overhaul was naive. Black people in U.S. cities, including Washington, D.C., were facing conditions that made their success that much more difficult to achieve. That the push for all-Black business opportunity growth took place at the same time as Nixon's usurping of "Black Capitalism" as an economic strategy meant that the structural conditions would not change. Attempts by Black residents to spur revitalization by patronizing Black-owned businesses proved to be a toothless strategy in the face of a local government that had not fully committed to the needs of the community. As one Black resident surmised, the D.C. government "puts simple development over here, rather than investing real money. They build enough to keep the community satisfied. I think the community deserves a little better."[120]

The uprisings brought into view the notion that struggles against oppression are ultimately struggles over space.[121] A year before his assassination in 1968, Martin Luther King Jr. spoke openly about violence and feelings of disillusionment in Black, urban spaces. His articulation of riots as "the language of the unheard" underscores the importance of acknowledging and condemning the circumstances that produce these conditions. The uprisings represented a significant turning point for H Street, in terms of not only the space itself but also the spatial and racial formation of blackness. Racialized geography reproduced on and through the built environment (via slums, urban renewal, highways, public transportation, and suburbanization) contributes to the organization and value of race and space.[122] In Washington, D.C., like in many other U.S. cities that experienced turmoil in the late 1960s, the uprisings are commonly understood as a definitive moment of change leading to the city's steady degeneration. The events are also recognized as the "catalytic moment" of the exodus of whites from D.C. With this exodus came a cycle of disinvestment and reinvestment precipitated by a significant event. "The decline of the H Street area, which was once a bustling commercial center that drew shoppers from all over the region, began about 1960, according to a study for the city by the Real Estate Research Corporation. Average income dropped substantially below that for the city as a whole and the area's overall population declined from 75,000 in 1960 to 62,000 in 1975."[123] Ultimately, the uprisings had multiple effects, not the least of which was the eventual denouement of H Street's cultural landscape.

As this chapter demonstrates, commercial revitalization became a significant part of urban renewal in Washington, D.C., and various community organizations, Black architects, and contractors concerned with cultural empowerment wanted to rebuild their neighborhoods by using public funds to benefit Black residents and shoppers. Recognizing urban rebellions as important sociospatial events allows us to see how they inherently shaped the spatial practices of Black people in U.S. cities. Considering the attention bestowed upon the H Street, NE corridor following the uprisings, it would seem that they helped Black Washingtonians secure an authoritative voice in the urban renewal process, as federal legislators started including Black community organizers and politicians in the decision-making coalitions tasked with rebuilding communities that were destroyed. However, plans to refurbish H Street as a Black-developed and Black-operated commercial corridor were deemed economically impractical and unfeasible. Following the failure of lukewarm government-led efforts to revive the area, H Street NE, *devalued* as a poverty-stricken, Black space, was considered hopeless and stagnant by lending institutions, developers, small business owners, local government officials, and media outlets. The area was not worthy of investment or habitation. Ultimately, this devaluation of Black H Street and the strategic deployment of visual rhetoric depicting the space as "blighted," a "slum," or a "ghetto" prepared the space for its twenty-first-century revaluation and reelevation.

The uprisings of April 1968 were not only in reaction to Dr. King's assassination. They represented a movement against widespread social, economic, and political injustices experienced by Black residents. Even today, Black Washingtonians continue to experience the legacy of the riots as they combat various issues related to social and economic development in their neighborhoods.[124] In many ways, D.C. never recovered from the uprisings. As Jaffe and Sherwood note, "People will always define the city's history as 'before the riots' and 'after the riots.'"[125]

2 Washington's Atlas District

Inequality, Cultural Vibrancy, and the New Regime of Diversity

. . . .

They only want certain kinds of businesses on H Street now.

—Daniel, H Street business owner

Several years of failed investment schemes plagued the H Street, NE corridor after the 1968 uprisings through the beginning of the twenty-first century. As the neighborhood grew poorer and blacker, the closure of several key retail stores in the thirty years following the rebellion left large gaps in its streetscape. Narratives about H Street's revival point to an ineffectual local government and unruly people who were unable to fix the neighborhood's problems. Ineptitude, absence, and neglect from the local government would require the involvement of private sources, sometimes in collaboration with public sources. Since the 1980s, there has been a marked shift in how important participation by the private sector has become. In particular, the role of the government has been to support the efforts and encourage private investment in urban development. This is especially relevant in terms of business ownership on H Street as small Black businesses have increasingly struggled to remain in the area.

The absence of a welfare state and the minimized role of the state as protector and provider require people to learn to govern themselves. The state no longer supports groups against oppressive conditions, since the revised role of the state is to support individuals and monitor social responsibility. Therefore, public space becomes a showcase for the entrepreneurial. Furthermore, market-based redevelopment strategies are different from the past in that they emphasize the importance of private-sector investment. While some believe Black business owners must conform and "learn to be like white businesses," as H Street Main Street executive director Anwar Saleem suggests, in order to thrive in the corridor, others recognize that Black businesses are priced out, as the taxes have tripled and quadrupled since H Street has become more popular.

In this chapter, I show how the category *diversity* performs subtle yet significant discursive work in the contemporary development of H Street, NE following the midcentury uprisings. Discourses of "diversity" accompany race-neutral policy, which seeks to replace and revalue the Black space. According to this logic, as Christopher Mele finds, the urban core is then defined as "a post-racial realm hamstrung by the deficiencies of individual self-sufficiency, responsibility for one's social welfare, and participation in the market economy," not as a space "replete with systematic discrimination and exclusion."[1] Furthermore, I highlight the relationship between race, diversity, belonging, and urban development in the historical devaluation of H Street as a Black space, and its revaluation as an emergent multicultural neighborhood. While some scholars have analyzed transformations that lead to the revalorization of devalued landscapes, I claim that the modern, postindustrial city requires ruin to justify the imposition of order.[2] I begin with a discussion of the political and economic climate in D.C. under the leadership of Mayor Marion Barry and his successor, Mayor Anthony Williams, as the city migrated from radical, race-conscious governance strategies to market-oriented, race-neutral, pro-growth urban policy.

Capitalism has a way of creating new spaces and shifting environments that are needed for profit and accumulation. At the same time, capitalism devalorizes the landscapes that it seeks to overhaul.[3] In terms of the racialization of space, I also explore how discourses of diversity shape who and what are desirable and undesirable, and identify how these discourses legitimate practices of racial inequality without naming race explicitly. By using diversity to map the space, the development of H Street places emphasis on a specific ideology of difference as multiculturalism and diversity. Given the history of the neighborhood, this chapter considers the remaking and literal embodiment of H Street as a space of diversity. H Street's remaking requires changes to the prevailing narrative that defines the neighborhood as a Black ghetto, or area of urban blight, to a more desirable narrative of a diverse, multicultural welcoming space. Therefore, I investigate how diversity has been discursively sutured to this neighborhood to produce a brand-new spatial identity.

Political Revisioning and Revitalizing a "Postriot" D.C.

Shifts in the economic and political climate of D.C. began to take shape in the late twentieth century as the city's leadership changed from a more passive form of governance under Mayor Washington to a radical, Black

Power–centered agenda advocated by Mayor Marion Barry. By the 1970s, when various cities around the country were just starting to experience an influx of African Americans winning political office, "the People's Mayor," Marion Barry, continued to advocate the principles of the civil rights and Black Power movements as he led the nation's capital. In particular, Barry's solution for broadening the city's economic base was to emphasize measures that supported Black entrepreneurs.[4] For example, in 1977, the Minority Contracting Act became law in Washington, D.C., which required all D.C. agencies to earmark 35 percent of construction contracts for minority business enterprises. Once Mayor Barry took office in 1979, he advocated the law and made it clear that 35 percent of the city's overall contracts (not just construction contracts) would go to minority businesses, thereby making it "the most ambitious minority-procurement program of any city in the nation."[5] Later, in the 1980s, Barry moved several city offices to H Street (and U Street) in order to spur development along the neglected commercial corridors in the wake of the uprisings.[6]

Despite Barry's efforts to pursue political and economic strategies that empowered Black entrepreneurship in the 1980s and 1990s, his administration operated in direct tension with the movement toward practices of neoliberal urbanism, which prioritized market-oriented urban policy that attempted to raise land value while ignoring the effects of displacement.[7] Barry wanted to grow the size and power of the local government (in many ways, to serve his own interests and those of his associates) and espoused programs and legislation that increased his political control. Later, he paid the price for these tactics.

Amid growing frustration from President Clinton and the Republican-led Congress, in 1995, Congress passed the Financial Responsibility and Management Assistance Authority, which established a five-member Control Board that was charged to "oversee the District budget, wield management authority over District agencies, and hold a veto over local legislation."[8] The creation of the Control Board resulted from Mayor Barry's 1994 announcement that D.C. was $722 million in debt, and his subsequent request for assistance from the federal government. Barry asked Congress to "assume control of essential city services, including courts and prisons, and give the city $250 million in aid to cover Medicaid overspending."[9] This move to manage the economic functions of the D.C. government exacerbated an already tenuous relationship between the federal government and Mayor Barry. The bill also established the position of a chief financial officer who was tasked with running the day-to-day operations of the city. Anthony

Williams became the District's first chief financial officer and later succeeded Barry as elected mayor in 1998.

Since the early 2000s, powerful funding mechanisms have been put in place in D.C. as part of the city's strategy to increase the middle-class population and tax revenue. In 2003, Mayor Anthony Williams introduced a plan to attract 100,000 new middle- and upper-middle-class residents to D.C. in an effort to make the city economically solvent. The trouble was that Williams realized much of the land in D.C. was exempt from taxation (federal lands, schools, churches, etc.) and the millions of Maryland and Virginia residents who worked in the city did not have to pay a commuter tax. So, he implemented pro-growth policies and pro-development practices that irrevocably changed the built environment in order to generate revenue, despite the negative impact on D.C.'s most vulnerable populations.

One of Williams's main plans was to "revitalize" commercial centers like H Street. Commercial spaces hold particular symbolic value because they "take such a central role in building local neighborhood identity [and] they are fundamental to understanding the process of inclusion and exclusion at the neighborhood level."[10] In the past, city leaders had attempted to stimulate economic activity in different neighborhoods by moving central offices to those areas that needed the most attention. Williams's strategy was quite different, as he encouraged private business operations, where Barry saw the value of a larger government to provide services to and hire D.C.'s majority Black population. Nevertheless, Williams's plan successfully brought a more diverse and upper-income population to the city. Williams ultimately faced a distinct challenge in his attempt to balance the city's budget so D.C. would not receive additional oversight by the Control Board or the federal government generally. By encouraging more tourists and affluent residents, Williams successfully shifted the tide and enabled D.C. to (partially) gain control of its finances. Of course, the consequences of these actions proved to be most harmful to the working-class and poor Black population. Thirty years after D.C. fought for and achieved emancipation from the federal government's direct economic and political control, the city remained powerless in many ways. With the federal government maintaining unique oversight of D.C., Black Washingtonians were at a distinct disadvantage. Regardless of his administration's attempt to support lower-income residents, Williams's reliance on market-based strategies, including rapid development and public-private partnerships, disproportionately impacted longtime Black residents.

Since Williams's tenure, the D.C. Office of Planning, the D.C. Department of Transportation (DDOT), the D.C. Department of Small and Local Business Development (DSLBD), the Office of the Deputy Mayor for Planning and Economic Development (DMPED), and subsequent mayoral administrations have had a hand in planning various phases of D.C.'s development. Acting independently and sometimes collaboratively, these agencies and organizations offer developers tax incentives to build upscale facilities and residential units instead of affordable housing units. While private corporations provide the investment capital to fund these projects, local government agencies offer tax abatements, subsidies, and relaxed regulation to support development. These activities undergird the state's entrepreneurial engagement in place marketing, beautification, and tourism efforts.

The Black Social Body and Gentrified Urban Diversity

The late 1990s and early 2000s saw a turning point in the process of gentrification across the country, a particular kind of gentrification that commodified culture and racial and ethnic diversity, transforming it into a feature that brought added symbolic value to living there and added economic value to real estate prices.[11] Cities began to market neighborhoods through a conjured historical identity that was well suited within a new economy where neighborhoods have taken on new values as markers of identity while affluent white residents move to the city. As geographer Eugene McCann argues, "The politics of local *economic* development must, then, be understood as always, simultaneously, the *cultural* politics of making meaning, making a living, and making place."[12] A neighborhood like the H Street, NE corridor is appealing "for the capital that it may attract, never for the value it already represents to residents because of the histories, meanings, and value that it may sustain or help produce."[13] For example, in my interview with Shauna, a young, married white woman in her twenties who moved from northern Virginia to the "Atlas District" in 2010, she explained that she and her husband chose to purchase a home there primarily because they believed they could benefit financially from the increased value that would come as a result of the forthcoming streetcar. They surmised that streetcar service, even the promise of a streetcar, would presumably lead to the success of neighborhood businesses and increased property values. Furthermore, she extolled the increasing diversity that the neighborhood was experiencing as a clear virtue and a sign of positive change.

Renewed energy around the development of H Street in the 2000s—and the process of its revaluation—placed particular emphasis on the corridor as a welcoming space of diversity. These efforts have not gone unrecognized. Besides its designation in *USA Today* as the top U.S. neighborhood to explore, in 2011 *Forbes* magazine ranked H Street number six on its list of "America's Hippest Hipster Neighborhoods" (behind other popular, "diverse," and controversial gentrified neighborhoods like the Mission District in San Francisco and the Williamsburg neighborhood in Brooklyn). Several stories about the transition of H Street suggest that early signs of gentrification—cleaning up the neighborhood, increased property values, implementing various aesthetic improvements to the streets, increased presence of law enforcement—have been understandably welcomed by older Black residents and store owners.[14] Despite national attention and local praise for the transition and aesthetic appeal of H Street, many of the problems that Black residents faced since the 1950s, like poverty, inconsistent and insufficient city services, limited retail options, and a lack of employment opportunities, continue to plague its longtime residents. In fact, some residents complain about the influx of restaurants and bars on H Street and limited retail options for Black (working-class) customers.[15] Others see the changes on H Street as part of a strategic ploy to rid the area of Black residents in favor of whites—who fled the city for the suburbs in the aftermath of the uprisings.[16]

While the rebuilding and transformation of a neighborhood require traditional economic components like labor and capital, as Sharon Zukin argues, "it also depends on how they manipulate symbolic languages of exclusion and entitlement."[17] The aesthetic appearance or "feel" of a city reflects what Zukin identifies as "decisions about what—and who—should be visible and what should not, on concepts of order and disorder, and on uses of aesthetic power."[18] The H Street, NE corridor was once signified by the national media, local officials, and some residents as a poor, Black ghetto but has been reimagined to attract individuals with cosmopolitan tastes who value diversity. Now, "constructed multicultural urbanity"[19] is used to attract new affluent residents, visitors, businesses, and developers.

Similar to Brenda Weber's formulation of post-Katrina New Orleans as a "body in distress that can only be effectively 'healed' through the design ministrations offered by the experts who populate makeover television,"[20] I call attention to the location of blackness in a neoliberal context by positioning the "postriot" H Street, NE corridor as an afflicted Black social body that is only restored by the mobilization of diversity.[21] Blackness is deemed excessive and unwieldy if not disciplined, managed, contained, or deployed for proper use. Despite narratives and representations that equate diversity and equality, the process of (re)valuing H Street reveals the embeddedness of neoliberalism in its transformation, as Weber writes, "where a logic of seemingly [race] neutral market competition in the context of state absolution prevails."[22] The state has no bearing on dismantling systemic racial inequalities that are exacerbated by free-market competition. I find Weber's makeover metaphor useful in conceptualizing how the old "Black" H Street, as a site of chaos, disorder, and pathology, required the rehabilitation not only of the physical space but also of symbolic codes of blackness through the lens of a neoliberal project in the purported age of colorblindness and postracialism. What manifests in the remaking of blackness on H Street is that the area has not been purged of symbols of blackness; instead, through black aesthetic emplacement, the blackness that is located within the space is palatable and consumable while some of the constructed edginess remains to add excitement.

What follows is a conversation about the emerging themes of devaluation and revaluation and the deployment of "diversity" to discursively produce postriot H Street as a multicultural space, rebuilt by innovative entrepreneurial pioneers. Then I highlight two local programs with intended race-neutral policies that have racial consequences. Here I demonstrate how even in the most mundane spaces, as Leland Saito notes, "race is already present in the ideologies and practices of larger society that shaped the formation and implementation of policies."[23] Finally, I explore the ways in which "diversity" is institutionalized as a valuable social commodity to market. In other words, I discuss how the aestheticization of blackness and space contribute to the structuring of H Street as both universal and exclusive.

Devaluing and Practices of Revaluing the H Street, NE Corridor

As discussed in chapter 1, plans for the redevelopment of H Street in the 1970s originally included significant involvement and placed decision-making power in the hands of local groups led by Black residents and community leaders. The rebuilding of H Street was seen as an opportunity for the Black community to control the money, jobs, and political power—an element that many Black leaders felt was missing in D.C.[24] Organizations like the Marion Barry–led Pride, Inc., Model Cities Commission, Near Northeast Community Improvement Corporation, and People's Involvement

Corporation all requested access to local and federal funds to rebuild the tarnished corridor.

Black residents living in the area wanted the corridor to be planned by Black developers, built by Black architects, and refreshed with local Black-owned businesses, who they believed could adequately meet the needs of the predominantly working-class, Black neighborhood that lacked political and economic support from the local and federal governments.[25] Nevertheless, plans to refurbish H Street, NE as a Black-developed and Black-operated commercial corridor were later deemed economically impractical and unfeasible. In a May 1968 statement offered to the press by D.C. City Council chairperson John W. Hechinger, he contends that the council believes the Black community should have a "central and powerful role in the planning and implementation of policies for rebuilding and recovery" of the H Street corridor.[26] However, Hechinger stresses the council's rejection of the idea that Black residents and business owners should be allowed exclusive rights to this rebuilding. He says: "The Council strongly rejects, however, the ideology of two separate societies . . . which was espoused by a number of witnesses who urged that black people *only* be involved in the rebuilding and running of the riot torn areas. At the same time, the Council calls for a sharp and large scale reappraisal of the attitudes and actions of the white community especially business, financial and investment sectors. The talents and energies of all races and economic groups are needed to make this city strong."[27] Hechinger's statement advocates racially integrated efforts to rebuild the corridor after the uprisings and actively admonishes the white business community's anti-Black sentiments and activities. Nevertheless, following the failure of lukewarm government-led efforts to revive the area, H Street, NE, devalued as a Black, poverty-stricken, blighted ghetto, was considered hopeless and stagnant by lending institutions, developers, small business owners, local government officials, and media outlets. The area was not worthy of investment or habitation.

In contrast to the previous three decades, with the dawning of a new millennium, city administrators implemented effective plans that began to transform H Street, NE into a twenty-first-century version of the lively commercial corridor that thrived fifty years prior. For example, in 2010, Councilmember Tommy Wells introduced a bill that would designate $5 million of the $25 million tax increment financing (TIF) bonds toward the mixed-use development project on Third and H Streets (which currently houses a new Giant grocery store) toward the Steuart Investment Company as part of a tax abatement promised to the developer in 2009.[28]

Generally, commercial revitalization utilizes various short-term strategies to aid small businesses in the area like "technical assistance, access to small business capital, corridor beautification, and area marketing,"[29] and race-neutral discourses expedite the directives that support tax abatements, public-private partnerships, and other development practices. Nevertheless, implementation of market-driven policies that emphasize growth (profit for developers and property owners) has disproportionately adverse effects on Black business owners. Commercial revitalization is inherently racialized, even in the absence of overtly racist and discriminatory practices. I agree with Saito's assessment that race-neutral policies and practices in cities contribute to policies that have racialized outcomes and argue that similar practices have taken place, and continue to thrive, in Washington, D.C.[30] In fact, as Christopher Mele argues, "color-blind racial discourse does provide an underlying vocabulary useful to planning, implementation, and promotion of neoliberal urban policies and practices that enhance sociospatial inequality."[31] There is particular significance to supporting race-neutral policies in a city that is known for its Black majority, political leadership, and diversity. Such policies assume benefits of integration for people of color. What underlies emphasis on diversity measures makes a similar assumption. Race is always already present despite efforts to produce race-neutral policy and results.

It was not until the Williams administration in the early 2000s that changes took hold and H Street attracted a number of investors, restauranteurs, and developers to transform the neighborhood. The Williams administration primarily stressed neoliberal development strategies that encouraged economic growth through the proliferation of public-private partnerships. Rather than emphasize an expanded role for the local government, several of the programs introduced by the administration, like the Main Streets and Great Streets initiatives, largely supported entrepreneurial efforts toward the growth of small businesses. These initiatives limited the role of the local government in providing various services for its residents, in favor of free-market approaches to economic development.

In 2004, the D.C. government approved a Strategic Development Plan for H Street, NE, which invested over $300 million (mostly private) from Second Street to Maryland Avenue. The plan called for new retail, housing, and entertainment venues, as well as the establishment of a streetcar system, and more aesthetically pleasing sidewalks and public spaces. In 2007, H Street became the first area to achieve recognition as a Great Street, which means it was eligible to receive local government funds to spur retail growth.

Under the direction of Mayor Williams, the Great Streets Initiative began in 2006 as a commercial revitalization program for gateway commercial corridors with depressed retail. Led by DMPED and in conjunction with the D.C. Office of Planning and the D.C. Department of Transportation (DDOT), the Great Streets Initiative helps with exterior street infrastructure improvement—curbs, gutters, street lighting, and sidewalk widening—and interior space improvement through the dissemination of grants. Also in 2007, the D.C. City Council named H Street one of six neighborhood retail priority areas and set aside up to $25 million in TIF bonds to stimulate develop-ment along the corridor. With the TIF bonds, for those taxes that are generated along the corridor that go above the D.C. Office of the Chief Financial Officer's estimates, the area can capture the excess and use it for spatial improvements.

H Street is a prime example of the TIF funding mechanism being extremely profitable. The corridor generated approximately $25 million in 2010 to be spent solely on efforts along H Street. No other neighborhood has experienced such a high tax increment and financial program success rate. Nevertheless, H Street is also a unique space because it has been designated as the initial location of a renewed streetcar line, surging property and sales tax rates. Through the Great Streets Initiative, the city has paid a tremendous amount of attention and capital for aesthetic improvements.

In early 2008, Councilmember Tommy Wells, joined by Mayor Adrian Fenty, announced the initiation of DDOT's landmark streetscape construction, for which the agency committed $50 million in streetscape, safety, and transportation improvements along the H Street corridor. Mr. Wells spoke about the residents and businesses surrounding H Street, NE waiting patiently for the city to devote much-needed energy and ideas to bolster commercial activity on the corridor. He said, "Today marks the start of an immense city investment in the future of this great street—over $76 million between the streetscape project, new streetcars, TIF financing incentives, neighborhood and business grants, and a new dedicated shuttle bus to this corridor."[32] In addition to the $25 million TIF and the $50 million streetscape renovation, the H Street, NE corridor also received $600,000 for neighborhood investment funding targeting community-based projects; $500,000 toward reimbursable grants for façade and building improvements; and $225,000 toward a dedicated, branded H Street shuttle bus to support small businesses linking passengers to Union Station and Benning Road Metro stations. It was not until 2009 that H Street became a designated "revitalized" corridor—a tourist destination for restaurants and retail.[33]

H Street, NE Retail Priority Area Grant

In 2011, Councilmember Tommy Wells proposed legislation for a grant program to benefit retail businesses along the H Street corridor between Third Street and the Starburst intersection. The act was proposed as part of the local government's effort to improve the aesthetic appearance of the corridor and therefore attract more visitors to the area and to complement the TIF initiative that was already successful on H Street (generating vast sums of money for exclusive use along the corridor). After the "H Street, N.E., Retail Priority Area Incentive Amendment Act of 2010" passed, as part of the Great Streets Initiative, DMPED was charged with enforcing the new legislation. The agency then drafted the rules and regulations and disseminated a Request for Application (RFA) for the Retail Priority Area Grant (RPAG) to provide current H Street business owners and those interested in opening businesses along the corridor.

The grant awards totaled $1.25 million and were to be distributed in increments of up to $85,000 for qualifying businesses. In October 2011, representatives from DMPED hosted their first information session. Similar to the meeting described in the introductory chapter, this meeting was well attended and featured a racially diverse sampling of current and budding entrepreneurs. A great deal of tension also filled the room, primarily because the RFA explicitly excluded certain service-oriented businesses from applying for the grant. At the time, most of the businesses on the H Street corridor, especially those owned by Black shopkeepers, were service oriented. The specific language of the RFA (and the legislation proposed by Councilmember Wells) excluded the following entities from receiving the area grant: liquor stores, restaurants, nightclubs, hair salons, barbershops, and phone stores. Noticeably absent is the exclusion of nail salons, which since the 1990s has been an industry overwhelmingly managed by Korean and Vietnamese immigrants.[34]

While the frustrations many Black business owners expressed were due in large part to the language of the grant, their vocal dissatisfaction reflected previously existing tensions that developed alongside H Street's changing environment. With the introduction of a crop of new bars, lounges, yoga studios, bicycle shops, and eclectic restaurants by local entrepreneur Joe Englert, these longtime business owners recognized the "new and improved" H Street catered to a different demographic. There was a clear divide between existing businesses that withstood the uprisings of 1968 and had served their customers loyally for years, and newer, younger entrepreneurs who saw untapped opportunities in this transitional space. The longtime, and mostly Black, business owners who lived through the uprisings and/or the subsequent decline were also challenged with six years of erratic construction projects on H Street for the streetcar lines. Reminiscent of the postrebellion era when Black business owners attempted to rebuild the corridor and received inadequate support from the local and federal government, these businesses endured the construction too and suffered because of the turmoil. The disruptive streetcar construction was one of the more explicit measures that prevented the businesses from thriving in contrast to the subtle practices of the 1960s through 1980s.

The details and tenor of the meeting were described in an article titled "DC Government Bans Black Businesses from H St Grant," published in the *Afro-American*. The article describes a heated debate among longtime minority business owners and city officials. The reporter claims that the D.C. government's grant program provides little relief for longtime minority-owned businesses along the H Street corridor. During the meeting, participants questioned why barbershops and beauty salons are excluded from consideration, claiming racial discrimination, since most of these shops are owned by Black entrepreneurs. One business owner said he believed the goal of the grant "is highly questionable [because it excluded] certain businesses associated with small black businesses."[35]

The Black business owners along H Street believed that the grant funding process was particularly planned against them and in favor of upwardly mobile newcomers who brought "nightclubs and tiny eateries" to the area. According to the reporter's account, community activist and business owner Pam Johnson argued with Councilmember Wells's chief of staff, Charles Allen, who defended Wells's legislation as being "fully vetted through the public hearing process," thus suggesting that if the disgruntled business owners were unsatisfied, they could have introduced their constructive objections at community hearings. Johnson replied: "Black-owned businesses have weathered the storm via the riots of the 60s and crack epidemic since the 80s. Now with the D.C. government investing over $50 million in the H Street Corridor and enacting policies that expedites the gentrification of H Street, it seems the Council wants to prevent our barber shops and beauty salons from receiving one dime of the assistance that's being given to the gentrifying businesses."[36] The economic, cultural, and social interests of new retail entrepreneurs reflect a particular form of power being used in cities today. These entrepreneurs find ways to accrue economic capital and interests when they discover opportunities as the population shifts to include people with higher social profiles and disposable income. Entrepreneurs open businesses that cater to their tastes (e.g., high-end pet stores, wine shops, and other boutiques). New retail entrepreneurs also open up businesses that speak to a burgeoning culture arriving in these neighborhoods with an emphasis on arts, music, and local cuisine.

Although DMPED officials were charged with implementing the legislation passed by the city council, they received the bulk of the blame for racial undertones embedded in the language of the act. Nevertheless, in reaction to the resistance DMPED faced because of the legislation, in September 2012, Councilmember Wells modified the legislation to remove the language excluding barbershops and beauty shops. The updated amended act reads: "Eligible applicants include retail businesses engaged in the sale of home furnishings, apparel, books, art, groceries, and general merchandise goods to specialized customers or service-oriented businesses providing a direct service to specialized customers or artistic endeavors, such as art galleries, theaters or performing arts centers. Special consideration shall be given to retail businesses that include entrepreneurial and innovative retail elements. *Eligible retail development projects shall not include liquor stores, restaurants, nightclubs, phone stores, or businesses with 20 or more locations in the United States.*" Although applicants were required to have a storefront on H Street, NE, not on the side streets where leasing space was less expensive, changes to the legislation enabled several additional Black business owners to participate in the grant application process. Nevertheless, after three funding cycles, DMPED had significantly more funds than businesses applying for the grant.[37]

One reason for the surplus in grant funds and the low turnout for Black business owners could be the required "Clean Hands Self Certification" form. This document requires that business owners owe less than $100 in outstanding debt to the D.C. government (this includes property taxes, business license taxes, unemployment insurance, and traffic fines). The disciplinary power of this application process is reflected in the solicitation of individual business owners to apply for the grant only if they are financially solvent and had owned up to all of their fiduciary responsibilities, thus regulating themselves and their businesses. Any business owners who are unable to perform these duties would be excluded from consideration.

Another reason for the low application numbers could be the grant's emphasis on "retail businesses that include *entrepreneurial* and *innovative* retail elements" (emphasis mine). The term "innovative," like "creative," might be disinviting to business owners with certain skills, specifically related to invitations by the city government for new businesses on H Street. Interest in "innovative" businesses signals an entrepreneurial turn in urban planning, "one that downplays citizenship and collective identities, and in turn emphasizes capitalist ideologies, encourages people to become entrepreneurial, commercially minded subjects, and which promotes private-sector solutions to social problems."[38]

With the rapidly shifting demographic, preference for "entrepreneurial" and "innovative" businesses have replaced a desire for simply profitable businesses. For instance, the decision to limit highly profitable beauty salons came even after H Street salons were graded an "A" overall in the Office of Planning's Strategic Development Plan for their profitability, sophisticated ownership and management, demonstrated financial acumen, implementation of a marketing strategy, and thorough knowledge of their customer base. The neoliberal turn emphasizes entrepreneurialism as an integral element of economic growth, and therefore shies away from social welfare commitments. Despite the high tax revenue generated by beauty salons, barbershops, and other service-oriented businesses often run by Black entrepreneurs, in a multicultural and economically diverse climate, creative and innovative retail and service offerings are ideally represented by Bikram Yoga and Metro Mutts (a pet supplies and pet-sitting service business).

Performance-Based Parking

In the spring of 2009, the D.C. City Council passed the "Performance Parking Pilot Zone Act of 2008," to be enforced by DDOT, which was enacted to manage curbside parking in high-density areas of the city, particularly newly major retail and entertainment centers. The first two locations for the program were established in the neighborhood surrounding the Nationals' Ballpark/Capitol Hill and in Columbia Heights. The H Street corridor was the third location, established in 2012. The program was piloted on H Street, NE, between Third Street, NE and Fifteenth Street, NE. The program provides protection to residents and businesses by applying strict parking restrictions in residential neighborhoods and brief curbside parking meter limits to encourage high vehicle turnover. With such restrictions in place, the program's intention is to foster a livable, walkable environment that reduces automotive congestion. Nevertheless, to limit the length of time vehicles are able to park on and around H Street disproportionately encumbers certain small businesses, like beauty salons, whose services often require two- to three-hour commitments. Presented as an apparatus of shared governance, Councilmember Tommy Wells, in conjunction with DDOT, hosted several public meetings about the proposed program for community members to review and comment on.

At a February 2012 Advisory Neighborhood Committee (ANC) 6C meeting, representatives from the D.C. Department of Transportation spoke about the implementation of performance-based parking zones on H Street, NE, which attempt to support residents and businesses while discouraging automotive transportation along the very busy and often congested corridor.[39] The DDOT representatives discussed plans to establish "resident only" signs on one side of the streets surrounding H Street, and two-hour parking on the other. Residents on performance-based parking blocks receive one visitor pass per household. White residents who spoke at the meeting praised the department's efforts and plans for implementation, while also asking questions about their ability to receive additional visitor parking passes. The frustrations displayed by Black residents highlighted tensions with the increasing commercialization of the area. These residents complained about parking restrictions, the added presence of tourist traffic, and diminished access to resident parking passes.

One Black business owner, Daniel, who spoke openly at the meeting, has owned a hair salon on H Street for more than fifteen years. The majority of his customers travel from Maryland and Northern Virginia and now have difficulty finding parking in the area. Prior to the implementation of the performance-based parking program, he lost clients because of the construction of the streetcar lines, since his customers faced difficulty finding parking or received tickets for parking in designated construction zones. Transportation and parking issues on H Street were particularly challenging during the construction, which began in 2008. Several months of intermittent disruption meant that many businesses along H Street lost customers because the construction blocked parking spots and the entrances to several businesses. A disproportionate number of these businesses were Black owned. In contrast to the early years of his business when business traffic was sparse on H Street and he "had to step over crackheads," the salon owner expressed his belief that many Black business owners like him were being pushed out, since "poor black businesses don't get allowances and money." The salon owner later shared that his business taxes have increased significantly in the past few years and soon he, and similar business owners, would be unable to maintain their business on H Street.

Daniel's story is particularly compelling when one also considers the Retail Priority Area Grant, discussed above, since many of the individually owned Black businesses along the H Street corridor are service oriented, like beauty salons and barbershops, rather than retail stores. The challenge for these shopkeepers with the implementation of policies that regulate and limit parking is that the policies demonstrate an explicit preference for retail businesses and restaurants, where customers are expected to patronize the establishment for shorter increments of time. Service businesses like beauty salons and barbershops, especially those that cater to Black customers, often have their customers remain in their location for two hours or more. Black beauty salons and barbershops have served as important discursive spaces for Black cultural exchange. They not only provide hair care; salons and barbershops also operate as a cultural and community space for social and political discussion. The relevance of barbershops to the Black community, in particular, has been the subject of multiple scholarly studies and popular films such as *Barbershop* and its two sequels, *Barbershop 2* and *Barbershop 3*.[40] Barbershops and beauty salons are irreplaceable havens where a diversity of Black men and women find social, cultural, and emotional safe spaces.[41]

The effort Daniel's customers exert to travel from outlying areas to his salon speaks to the social importance salons represent for his clients. The parking legislation is advertised as an effective way to protect the interests of both residents and the small businesses along the corridor by ensuring residents maintain adequate parking options (for themselves and their visitors), and by encouraging business patrons to shop quickly and efficiently. Specifically, for the businesses, this plan lays the foundation for encouraging particular kinds of businesses (retail) and eschewing others (service-oriented businesses) that have withstood the previous challenges of the area. Daniel's story highlights tensions between residents and business owners along the corridor.

The Strategic Value of Planned "Diversity"

Multicultural diversity has become a positive characteristic for business and tourism along the H Street, NE corridor. This logic of difference as multiculturalism orders the political economy of the corridor. Culture and economics are not mutually exclusive categories; in fact, in this era of neoliberalism, culture and commerce are co-constitutive. As evidenced by the content and dramatic increase in media attention, commercial development, and financial investment to the corridor, current value on H Street, NE is abstractly conceived through material and symbolic representations of diversity, "hipness" or "coolness," global cultures, and authenticity. These discursive representations affect the resources the area receives. Resources like policing, surveillance, national media attention, and visits by political figures and celebrities increase as the area is deemed more desirable. Various actors (government officials, investors, and residents) rely on representations of a neighborhood to direct funds and development. The importance of diversity and cultural consumption intensifies social and economic inequities by valorizing diversity in particular areas to make previously undesirable spaces popular.

Diversity is incorporated as part of the vision for H Street's future in the District's official strategic plan drafted by the Office of Planning. In the early 2000s, the D.C. Office of Planning held multiple community meetings seeking input from local residents about their vision for the H Street, NE corridor. From these discussions emerged the theme "Respect for History, Heritage, and Diversity" for the purpose of land use, zoning, and development as a "shared vision" between residents and the local agency. According to the report, the neighborhood's history, heritage, and diversity already provide "a strong foundation" for the future of the corridor.[42] Throughout the plan document, the term "unique" is used multiple times to describe the corridor's social and physical environment. In addition to emphasizing the purported economic benefits of historic preservation and heritage tourism, "diverse" is one of the few descriptive terms used to characterize the space.

In her account of how organizations and institutions use the language of diversity as a mode of celebration and value, Sara Ahmed argues that diversity ultimately adds value to what it has been attributed. In particular, she maintains that diversity can be understood in market terms. Ahmed describes this stylization of pluralism as a Benetton mode of diversity, "in which diversity becomes an aesthetic style or way of 'rebranding'" a particular space, institution, or organization.[43] The enactment of diversity on H Street appears in different forms, such as on official statements and in photographs. Branding efforts along the H Street, NE corridor fall in line with the decline of manufacturing in U.S. cities, especially as it relates to the increasing importance of cultural production in the economic growth of urban centers in its ability to attract business and spur tourism.

The 2013 H Street, NE neighborhood profile brochure produced by the Washington, D.C., Economic Partnership (WDCEP), a public-private partnership that specializes in promoting business opportunities in D.C., provides general information about the corridor. In the organization's attempt to attract business, the brochure enumerates the advantages of H Street's cultural diversity and proclaims the street has "returned to its roots as a thriving, commercial hub, and is home to a diverse, cohesive community." The brochure goes on to describe some of H Street's attributes: "A revitalized visual and performing arts scene, hip bars and restaurants, art galleries, music venues and a boom of high-end condos and apartments are quickly reshaping the historic corridor."[44] As historians Christopher Asch and G. Derek Musgrove argue, public-private partnerships like WDCEP are in alignment with investors and hipsters who "highlight H Street's early 20th century heyday as a bustling, working-class commercial strip—a history that sells well as entrepreneurs seek to revive its commercial success by catering to a clientele interested in a gritty 'authentic' experience."[45] Instead of being overlooked, the Black and working-class history of the neighborhood is embraced and commoditized. Therefore, the value of diversity is in the construction of a thriving, "cohesive," hip, and upscale community that supposedly dissolves tensions between longtime residents and newcomers—all while respecting the history of the neighborhood.

The frustrations experienced by some longtime Black residents were highlighted in a February 2012 *Washington Informer* article. The piece describes complaints these residents have with the demographic shift of H Street. Where H Street merchants previously "catered to the tastes of Blacks, [they] now cater to others."[46] Furthermore, some Black residents resent the increasing presence of bars and restaurants along the corridor, since "they are not offering any of the Black men a job."[47] Similarly, Black business owners along the corridor have expressed concerns that the changes to H Street, and the implementation of large-scale projects like the streetcar development plan, lead to "discriminatory tactics aimed at forcing minority operators out of business" in favor of white entrepreneurs.[48] It is important to mention here that I mark the shift away from Black enterprise and aesthetics on H Street not to memorialize a glorious Black past, but instead to indicate the particular ways that governing, markets, and style are now organized around diversity. This matters because narratives about the diversity of the H Street corridor impact how people move through the space. These discourses shape what spaces and people are cool, safe, or unsafe and which establishments and people belong.

In order to retain its new value, H Street must be constructed as an ideal space for investment—a place where people should spend their money, where difference does not threaten the seamless narrative of hip, cool authenticity, and be a potential haven for the upper middle class away from sterile, predominantly white neighborhoods like Georgetown in Northwest D.C. Over the past decade, the H Street, NE corridor has experienced significant growth in entrepreneurial retail capital. Sharon Zukin and colleagues define new entrepreneurial capital as small businesses (local chains or individually owned stores), "with a recognizably hip, chic, or trendy atmosphere, offering innovative or value-added products (e.g., designer furniture or clothing, gourmet food) and enjoying a buzz factor in promotion, including heavy press coverage and online presence."[49] In conversation with Mark Johnson, the co-owner of Hunted House, a now-defunct vintage furniture store that resold unique items from local auctions and estate sales, and was located on H Street between Fifth and Sixth Streets, Johnson stated that he and his business partner decided to move their store from the trendy Fourteenth and U Street Corridor (where several other established vintage furniture stores reside) to H Street, NE in 2012. Mark shared that the rent is significantly higher on H Street; however, they decided to relocate because it was "the place to be." In their two years, business had been relatively steady but not incredibly successful. Mark said he believes there is a solid customer base for the products he sells around the "Atlas Corridor" and his most frequent customers are nearby residents. In contrast to older retail stores, boutique businesses like Hunted House constitute a strong discourse of change and represent a shift to "social" entrepreneurialism, where business owners attempt to draw from the aesthetic tastes of the new residents.

Vestiges of H Street's yesteryear were represented by stores like Murry's, previously located on Sixth and H Streets, NE. Identified on a large placard as "Your neighborhood food store," Murry's survived some of H Street's most challenging times—poverty, gang violence, and illegal drug distribution and abuse. Although customer service was attentive and friendly, Murry's was like many grocery stores in low-income communities that carry a small selection of fresh fruits and vegetables and a wide variety of packaged, processed food choices. The prices were steep compared with the nearby local grocery chain, Giant, or online grocery shopping services like Peapod. The white, one-story building, surrounded by steel gates erected to prevent shoppers and neighborhood dwellers from stealing shopping carts, did not fit the distinctive architectural aesthetic of H Street's refurbished Victorian dwellings (figure 6). Like the Safeway store that inhabited the space before it, the wooden bench in front of Murry's served as a social gathering place for older Black men, and a place of solitude for others who wish to relax and read the daily newspaper.

Ultimately closing its doors in 2014, the building that housed Murry's, its adjacent parking lot, and the neighboring five-story H Street Self-Storage

FIGURE 6 Sunday best at Murry's. Photograph courtesy of Steven Cummings.

facility were demolished and replaced by a 101,000-square-foot, mixed-use development to be anchored by a Whole Foods Market. In the case of the Murry's/H Street Self Storage demolition and construction project, the designated ANC worked with representatives from Insight Development (which bought the land) to "create a design that complements the historic fabric of H Street NE." In a February 2013 letter addressed to the D.C. Zoning Commission secretary, the ANC 6A chairperson emphasized the committee's work with Insight Development and the committee's conditional approval of the construction if the developer agreed to preserve the corridor's "historic building fabric" and support the proposed designation of H Street as a historic district.[50] While ANCs play a large role in the neighborhood's development planning, they do not directly impact policy. Nevertheless, the destruction of the buildings that housed Murry's and H Street

Self-Storage removes an aesthetic that is "incongruous with the spirit of authenticity" the committee hopes to restore in its imaginative reconstruction of H Street's past.[51]

Desire for retail businesses like Whole Foods Market, which replaced Murry's, that serve an upper-middle-class customer base rather than service businesses that cater to a largely working-class Black consumer exposes a clear contradiction of neoliberalism: approval for individual and entrepreneurial endeavors alongside the growth in policing and restricting groups that have historically demonstrated significant levels of entrepreneurialism.[52] Furthermore, changes to the commercial landscape of H Street resemble other contemporary "revitalized" urban spaces that can be characterized by both the concurrent celebration of diversity and increased isolation and separation between groups. This shift can be explained in part by the infiltration of diversity discourses by neoliberal market logics and by processes of aestheticization, which work to normalize architectural and landscape tastes and intensify cultural difference.[53]

Hipster Superheroes

The revaluing of the H Street corridor as a burgeoning and inviting commercial corridor involves the acknowledgment of individual entrepreneurs for the neighborhood's renaissance. Belief in the significant role of entrepreneurs underscores the ostensible ineffectiveness and incompetence of government and signals the need for private enterprise.[54] In other words, only hard-working entrepreneurs had the foresight and creative means to turn H Street around. In this case, the media, local business organizations, and political leaders frame restauranteur Joe Englert and developer Jim Abdo as pioneers and saviors. Englert and Abdo's projects attracted a diverse (particularly white and Asian), upscale clientele and changed the recognition of H Street from a blighted ghetto to an ideal space for urban living, commercial retail, global cuisine, culture, and entertainment. The *New York Times* described Abdo as a catalyst for the renewal of H Street due to his company's renovation of the Children's Museum, which he converted into high-end condominiums—the Landmark Lofts at Senate Square.[55] Before becoming the Capital Children's Museum in 1979, the 140-year-old collection of red brick buildings that house Senate Square was built for the Little Sisters of the Poor and Saint Joseph's Home, which closed in 1977 after 107 years as a direct result of the Hopscotch Bridge construction. Senate Square is positioned at the base of the Hopscotch Bridge, which connects to a large parking facility that was built to serve Union Station. Since its construction in 1977, the bridge has been viewed as a visual barrier between H Street and downtown neighborhoods. The bridge used to be isolated, but now as Senate Square and other condo buildings surround it, the Hopscotch Bridge acts as a connector to downtown and other neighborhoods, rather than as an obstruction. Seemingly, Abdo's initial project spurred tremendous growth, as the construction of more residential buildings continues in order to meet the growing demand for housing.

Joseph Englert has been profiled in several Washington-area publications over the past fifteen years for his commercial development projects in both the U Street and H Street corridors. Englert is known for opening quirky, eclectic bars and lounges in underdeveloped areas. He is credited with transforming both the U Street corridor and H Street into "two of the city's hippest nightlife districts."[56] In fact, one 2012 article in the *Washingtonian* magazine identified Englert as the brains behind the renaming of the east end of the corridor to the "Atlas District"—named after the previously segregated movie theater that reopened as an arts and culture center in 2003. The cover page of the article features an illustrated image of a bespectacled Englert wearing a decorative black T-shirt with the words "Stewed, Screwed, and Tattooed" fancifully adorning it. Englert's glowing body appears to hover above the city below, as his head is level with the billowy clouds in the sky. Bright white rays emanate from behind his body and the brilliant sun shines from behind his back. Englert stands with his hands on his hips, and his chest moderately protruding. He looks like a larger-than-life, middle-aged, hipster superhero. In this image, Englert embodies the anticorporate image that brands H Street.

Brenda Weber offers a useful connection between superheroes and neoliberalism. Weber describes the glorification of (white) designers who have the power to enact "positive" change on the (Black) social body through aesthetic means. She maintains that while their racial identity has nothing to do with their superpowers, superheroes are exceptional beings that are summoned only once governments cease to operate effectively. Weber uses the metaphor of superheroes to demonstrate how white designers are bestowed with the power of exceptionalism, which makes the white designer "a singular being, the only person who might experience such social freedom."[57] Englert's brand of hipster entrepreneurialism reinforces the neoliberal logic that "suggests that if one person can transcend social impediments so as to exist on a level field of achievement, all people can."[58]

The east end of the corridor, branded by the D.C. Department of Planning as the "arts and entertainment" section, features numerous restaurants, lounges, music venues, and bars. Several of these establishments are owned by Englert, including Rock & Roll Hotel, The Pug, and the H Street Country Club. Keeping with the tradition of celebrating the corridor's rebirth, Englert named his first restaurant (with a full-service kitchen) Dr. Granville Moore's Brickyard (later shortened to Dr. Granville Moore's). Dr. Granville Moore's is a Belgian gastropub named after a Black doctor who treated patients on H Street during the mid-twentieth century and as a way to recognize the area as the former location of a brickyard. Back in 2005, when he ventured to open eight bars on H Street concurrently, Englert received heavy backlash from ANC community leaders and residents. In response, he posted a brazen note to a neighborhood listserv characterizing H Street as dangerous and undesirable, then providing his vision for a new and improved corridor. He wrote: "It's the two dozen or so homeless, urinating, yelling, screaming and guzzling malt liquor crazies populating the street corners that no one has the bravery to move along. . . . I have a plan to clean up H St, to recruit not just restaurants, but bakers, chocolate shops, museums, flower shops and more to the strip. What have others been doing except for joining alphabet groups and simply talking, not doing?" Super-Joe exercises his social freedom to rescue H Street from the evil machinations of homeless offenders and drunken (Black), malt-liquor-drinking villains since ineffectual groups like the ANC and government agencies have been unable or uninterested in doing so.

Englert was interviewed in 2013 by the *Washington City Paper* about his thoughts on the intended Whole Foods Market at Sixth and H Streets. He sees the move as "sad" because for him, H Street represents a space that is unfinished, in transition, and he prefers it this way. What he likes most about the corridor is that "it's not yet baked. . . . We don't know what it's going to be yet. You know what 14th Street is going to be. You know what Dupont is. You don't know what H Street is going to be yet. Hopefully, it just remains strange and sort of uncompleted all the time, I think that would be really good." He goes on to say that H Street has a particularly small-town feel and despite his distaste for the word "diverse," it is a great way to describe the area's "mixed bag of people." "It's not smooth, slick. It's just not brand name and perfect yet. It's not Georgetown . . . it's not really corporate."[59] Englert's frustration seems to stem from his desire to prevent H Street from becoming a typical gentrification story like other D.C. neighborhoods. However, his plan to change H Street—rid the neighborhood of its dangerous elements—by incorporating amenities that do not reflect the needs and preferences of the residents reinforces gentrification in meaningful ways.

The complexity of Englert's desires maps perfectly onto the ambivalent struggles over the costs and benefits of gentrification. While Englert expresses his vision for an H Street that remains small and quaint in terms of its "feel"—thus resisting the encroachment of large corporate brands like Whole Foods Market—he still supports the proliferation of amenities that appeal to households with higher income levels. Therefore, the diversity he seeks to maintain does not include an economically diverse population. Rather than acknowledging the clear racial and economic implications of supporting these amenities, he frames the issue as one that pits disingenuous corporations against an authentic, diverse, transitioning community.

In contrast to the transition of the Fourteenth and U Street corridor, which as one writer for the Root.com proclaims has been transformed as a result of "swagger-jacking," the H Street, NE corridor thrives on the discourse of diversity and the potential for a diverse, multicultural space.[60] H Street is thought to have maintained a delicate balance "between hipsterization and its historic African American culture." Former Mayor Vincent Gray emphasized the desire to see the corridor grow, "but we want the diversity and affordability to remain intact."[61]

· · · · · ·

For years, many Black Washingtonians have talked about "the Plan" to remove Black people from D.C., and while there is little evidence to support an *explicit* strategy to do so, changes to the lived environment seem to favor residents with more access to capital. Knowing the shifting political and economic climate in D.C., from an era that was pro-Black and emphasized a large government under Barry to one that advocated race-neutral, market-based revitalization strategies to grow the local economy under Williams (and later Fenty), is important to help one understand the social geographic changes that took place on H Street. Through the redevelopment of the H Street, NE commercial corridor, "diversity" is used to attract businesses, customers, and tourists to the area. Diversity discourse makes blackness one of many inflections, while H Street acts as a neoliberal zone that sustains neoliberal reforms and affirms blackness by using it as an entrepreneurial machine of development. It is through the work of diversity that H Street emerges as a hip, yet edgy, district. Nevertheless, while diversity evokes difference, it does not provide commitment to redistributive justice.

Neoliberal discursive logic stitches race and ethnicity into discourses of market revitalization and progress. Infusing a desire for "diversity" into the reimagining of urban space allows for the local government, developers, entrepreneurs, and new residents to ignore the conditions that made the H Street, NE corridor Black and poor in the first place. While the intentions to redevelop the area are not to displace Black residents, local efforts to construct a "multicultural urbanity"[62] attract a diverse sampling of young, upwardly mobile professionals. Emphasis on diversity replaces social justice issues with the notion that a successful commercial corridor will be universally beneficial despite the fact that the largely poorer, Black residents will no longer be able to afford not only housing but also the retail options along the corridor. A consequence of a diverse space is often the disinviting of Black residents.

H Street is a place where difference acts as an enhancement. It is through statements about diversity (as introduced by the D.C. Office of Planning, Main Streets programs, etc.) that the political economy of the H Street, NE corridor is organized. Racism and other forms of inequality that take place here are not overt, but subtle, where euphemisms like "creativity," "innovative," "diversity," and "cultural vibrancy" are used to disinvite. H Street remains raced, and the management of blackness produces a specific form of inequality in a different guise. It is not simply the production of blackness that has now been claimed in the name of diversity and multiculturalism on H Street; rather, it is the production of Black inequality and disadvantage.

3 The Changing Face of a Black Space

Cultural Tourism and the Spatialization of Nostalgia

Fixity is a function of power. Those who maintain place,
who decide what takes place and dictate what has taken place,
are power brokers of the traditional.

—Houston A. Baker

Nestled prominently at the center of the 1300 block of the H Street, NE corridor stands the Atlas Performing Arts Center. This refurbished site originally closed its doors in 1973 amid urban divestment, neglect, and an overwhelmingly Black poor majority, only to reopen to a highly planned, burgeoning, rapidly gentrifying, culturally diverse arts and entertainment district undergoing significant change. Built in 1938 and previously named the Atlas Theater, this structure was one of four movie houses along the historic commercial corridor. The Atlas operated as a whites-only movie house until 1951, along the commercial corridor known as a "viable black-business downtown district."[1] While H Street was the most significant commercial activity center within the greater Capitol Hill East area, several factors led to the street and the Atlas Theater's eventual demise. As discussed in chapter 1, a combination of state and corporate divestment, abandonment following the uprisings, construction, and disparaging representations of urban markets and Black consumers led to the decline of H Street. The Atlas Theater closed the same year the D.C. Home Rule Act was passed.[2] The facility reopened in 2003 as the Atlas Performing Arts Center after significant capital investment, rebuilding, and renovation of the structure.

The resurrected Atlas Theater later precipitated the designation of the H Street, NE corridor as the "Atlas District." The Atlas Theater was one of several entertainment venues along the corridor and was one of few that prohibited Black patrons. It was the last theater built on H Street, and yet the neighborhood currently bears its name because of its historical significance. While the term "Atlas" directly references the Titan god of astronomy and endurance in Greek mythology, an atlas is most often recognized as a bound collection of maps, one that illustrates the vast global terrain. To maintain the "Atlas" name for the performing arts center, and later the neighborhood, seems particularly purposeful given the center's proposed mission to "bring people together through the arts." In many ways, the neighborhood's naming reflected a desire to push beyond its longtime affiliation as a poor, blighted, urban space to one that invites dwellers from all walks of life. This vision of the Atlas Performing Arts Center as a welcoming space for all exposes a particular narrative about the corridor as a whole. It is an attempt to (re)frame the neighborhood as diverse in public discourse. For example, at the 2010 opening of the Atlas Performing Arts Center's "Intersections" art festival, the festival's artistic director remarked that H Street "has historically been an intersection," listing various ethnic groups—Italian, Jewish, and African American—that lived in the neighborhood.[3] With its complex history as the site of racial violence during the 1960s, urban blight, and later commercial revitalization, the Atlas District is an ideal site for examining the interrelatedness of race, nostalgia, and memory in the discursive production of space.

What history must be effaced in order to brand the neighborhood after a formerly segregated theater? How the past is constructed tells us a great deal about an idealized present and future. Both Fredric Jameson and José Esteban Muñoz argue that a sense of futurity is always bound to nostalgia for an idealized past.[4] I take up nostalgia in this way, and specifically the kind of work nostalgia does to produce authenticity in urban spaces. City governments and developers use narratives and images, alongside policy, to shape how certain spaces and places are understood.[5] In this case, they use nostalgic renderings of a multiethnic, multicultural, multiclass utopia (not a working-class Black space) to make H Street's identity legible and desirable to its intended audience of tourists, private businesses, upwardly mobile residents, and consumers.

In what follows, I analyze a neighborhood historical survey, a cultural tourism brochure, and a preservation-based community revitalization program on H Street to show how the processes of making spaces authentic take place through the production of official (state- and corporate-sanctioned) narratives about the area, which involves a devaluing of H Street's undesirable Black history and a rebranding and revaluation of H Street as historically diverse—only momentarily Black. The revaluation of the built environment not only requires investment, it also entails a discursive shift in how the space is seen. Part of that work involves revising the narrative. The enactment of these narratives bolsters the meaning and impact of the colorblind race strategies discussed in chapter 2. First, my analysis of the D.C. Historic Preservation Office's "Near Northeast Historical Study" enables me to track how the history of the H Street corridor is told and what version of history is told. Second, the Cultural Tourism DC's "Hub, Home, Heart" guide speaks to how tourists, residents, and those in transit can experience the physical space. Finally, the National Trust for Historic Preservation's Main Streets program highlights the multiple ways in which the built environment was ordered to support commercial activity and attract new investments. All three implement the production of nostalgia as memory (by eliminating negative and painful memories), race, and space. These documents and programs, generated to offer present-day narratives of the past, expose the power of the state and elite actors to shape both the perception and development of the space. Together they highlight the many conditions and strategies that undergird the transformation of urban space, and the ways that racialization and capital structure these changes.

During the mid-twentieth century, cities were believed to be suffering from a crisis of image with residents, small businesses, and corporations abandoning the city for its outlying suburbs. By the late twentieth century, city officials became expressly interested in new strategies of growth and development. One of the most popular and effective strategies was to attract tourism by turning derelict spaces into attractive, entertaining centers. Washington is not quite like other postindustrial urban centers like Detroit, Chicago, New Orleans, Philadelphia, and New York that experienced varying levels of Disneyification through the cultural homogenization and sanitization of urban spaces.[6] Instead, D.C. has relied on different forms of capital, namely, the federal government, to keep it running. As the nation's capital, Washington has long been positioned as a relevant tourist destination where the preservation of American political culture appears prominently. Washington's history, politics, memorials, and monuments are what make the city unique and relevant.

Discursive Production of Diverse Abstract Space

As discussed in chapter 2, community organizations and government agencies have placed significant efforts into the rebuilding and rebranding of the H Street, NE corridor, privileging "diversity" as a means to encourage the possibility of a global community. This remaking of the corridor requires changing the vernacular, or popular narrative that defines the H Street neighborhood as a "Black ghetto," to a more desirable narrative of racial and ethnic diversity. The production of contemporary urban nostalgia exists not only to attract visitors to cities but also to create a seamless narrative of interracial cooperation that substantiates the implementation of diversity measures today. Diversity—a color-conscious racial construct that might otherwise deter white residents and patrons—now becomes a cherished asset, because of diversity's shift from a social justice ethic to an aesthetic lifestyle amenity.[7] It is important to consider the performative elements of diversity, and similar to cultural theorist Sara Ahmed, ask what diversity discourse *does* rather than what it *means*.[8]

By implementing a multiethnic, multiracial narrative history of H Street, local government agencies, developers, and planners construct the neighborhood history as racially diverse as part of local economic strategy. They use this approach to attract tourists and consumers—thereby erasing its affiliation as a historically Black space. Presenting the commercial corridor as a socially inclusive space allows for diversity to operate as "an innocuous, sanitized version of ethnic and racial differences, scrubbed clean of their potential anti-development, political or social content."[9] Endorsing diversity is part of the neighborhood's efforts to remake itself as a cultural, tourist, and investment destination.

Blackness was not only economically unmanageable on H Street but also socially undesirable in the redevelopment of the commercial corridor. With the decline of the welfare state and the retooling of government involvement under neoliberalism, the Black cultural milieu, and any potential for it, declined, hence the need for an institutionally supported (and funded) narrative of H Street, NE as a historically diverse neighborhood that was accompanied by recognizable symbols of blackness. In terms of history and rememories of urban spaces, I lean on Sharon Zukin, who emphasizes "origins" as it relates to cities.[10] Rather than trying to determine which group or groups settled in an area first (a challenging task, since cities experience layers of historical migrations), "origins" refers to a "moral right to the city," a right to inhabit a space as opposed to consuming it as a lifestyle experience. Therefore, as it relates to historic preservation and cultural tourism, authenticity involves a continuous process of quotidian experiences, not historic buildings. Zukin explains that the notion of a neighborhood being authentic and true to its origins by encouraging a cohesive community "reflects more about us and our sensibilities than about any city block."[11] The documents and program I discuss below do the work of remembering a past, producing authenticity through the preservation of chosen histories.

Nostalgia, Authenticity, and Urban Life

A longtime white D.C. resident and local blogger spoke to me about her love of H Street and shared her perspective that the H Street corridor is often mischaracterized as historically Black when it has "always" been diverse. She likened H Street to New Orleans, a city that she believes has been historically diverse in terms of race and class. She explains that H Street had a large Jewish population and "to say it was historically Black ignores the history of the area." Furthermore, she claims that Blacks and whites lived side by side in the H Street corridor for years, unlike in other parts of the city that were largely segregated. The diverse history that she refers to was prior to the late 1940s when the neighborhood became majority Black. The blogger invokes ideas of this diverse history as a claim of legitimacy for the demographic changes taking place along the corridor. Her sentiments exemplify nostalgia as a longing for a lost or perhaps forgotten past. While reports funded and organized by the D.C. Office of Planning and the D.C. Department of Transportation highlight the period between the 1870s and 1940s, prior to when it had a Black majority, as H Street's "heyday," H Street Main Street executive director Anwar Saleem (and several media outlets) establish the H Street commercial corridor as a historically Black neighborhood.[12]

Local government agencies, media, urban planners, and developers play crucial roles in shaping urban development trajectories. Several urban scholars have become attuned to the cultural politics that arise over the multiple constructions of diversity in public spaces.[13] In fact, some have argued that developers construct popular representations of ethnic and racial diversity in order to achieve their political and economic goals—and thus attract a favorable group of consumers.[14] Strategies to draw wealthy residents and tourists to the city have become integral to urban planning and redevelopment plans. In many ways, these strategies rely on the romantic notion of an intrinsic connection between diversity, vibrancy, and urban space.[15]

The reclaiming of a nostalgic, diverse past has become a central defining feature of H Street's past, present, and future. The term "nostalgia" originates from the Greek words "nostos," which means return home, and "algia," longing together. Bridging the two terms, "nostalgia" essentially means to long for a distant home that no longer exists, or perhaps never existed. There are both spatial and temporal elements of nostalgia in that it is a longing for another place and another time. While most would attribute diversity to modernity and progress, these renderings evoke a form of nostalgia for a mythic past in which people from different backgrounds lived in a cosmopolitan harmony.

Michael Maly, Heather Dalmage, and Nancy Michaels define nostalgia as "a special type of memory, one that elevates pleasurable experiences and screens out more painful ones."[16] Furthermore, sociologist Janelle Wilson notes that nostalgia involves an "active selection of what to remember and how to remember it."[17] Ultimately, nostalgia is the longing for a particular space, place, and time. In their study of the nostalgic narratives used to construct and maintain white racial identity in Chicago, Maly, Dalmage, and Michaels find that current and former white residents often use the racially coded language of culture, crime, religion, and property maintenance to mourn the loss of a segregated white world. They maintain that the "memories of the loss of the old *white* neighborhood converge with the nostalgia for a time when 'white culture' was unquestionably synonymous with American culture."[18] In the case of H Street, the nostalgic past focuses on a diversity narrative rather than one that emphasizes whiteness; nevertheless, like the neighborhoods studied by Maly, Dalmage, and Michaels, nostalgia for the multicultural past "serves as a culturally sanctioned strategy for shoring up white privilege."[19]

Academic and popular discussions from the 1980s and 1990s about contemporary urban life framed the decline of U.S. cities in particularly nostalgic terms.[20] The discursive production of nostalgia around the H Street corridor generates a contradictory construction of blackness that recognizes and commemorates Black historical and cultural contributions to the neighborhood. Through the recognition of buildings and public spaces that were constructed, developed, and/or patronized by Black slaves and laborers, nostalgic references promulgated Black inferiority, and as historian Lynell Thomas argues, "indict[ed] African Americans for perceived postbellum and post-civil-rights-era social ills of poverty, crime, immorality, educational inadequacy, and political corruption."[21] Unlike the multiple decades when H Street and its surrounding blocks were firmly an overwhelmingly Black space, institutional narratives of H Street's history—supported and promoted by the local government—designate the "good life" as an important part of the past that was damaged and disrupted by racial change.[22]

Responsibility for the disruption of this multiethnic utopia "is generally placed on the shoulders of those labeled the destroyers—blacks."[23] In 1984, for example, H Street corridor business owners hoped to change perceptions of the area as a Black neighborhood in order to attract customers. According to the owner of a Hechinger Mall ice cream parlor, for the H Street corridor to flourish, "the key was changing the perception of the area as a 'black area.' . . . When people hear 'black,' they think low-income, they think negative—like crime and no taste. We had to look beyond the obvious. . . . Ignore the H Street corridor and you will find a tremendous consumer market that has been grossly underserved."[24] More recently, business owners and community leaders emphasized the historical roots of H Street as ethnically and racially diverse. Instead of promoting the superiority of authentic white space, there is a new regime of power from which the idea of "diversity" serves to commodify bodies and spaces. The space cannot be too Black, and instead is valued highly for its ability to maintain diversity. This practice of privileging diverse spaces with diverse history reassigns American culture as multicultural rather than purely white. As Westwood and Williams note, collective memory is produced in and through an "urban imaginary," which includes "literary productions, notions of urban myth, memory and nostalgia in the city and its environment, [and] the sociological imagination re-cast within the changing realm of new technologies and new forms of communications."[25]

The retelling of the H Street history positions it as an ethnically and racially diverse space that was momentarily decimated by an overwhelming wave of Black degeneracy. In other words, blackness does not represent the "truth" of the area; instead, Black bodies are woven into the diverse fabric of the space and their blackness requires discipline in order to fit the seamless narrative of a diverse space that nurtures progress and opportunity for all. It is the discursive production of a nostalgic multicultural past that regulates blackness in this urban space. The diverse story of H Street, preceding the uprisings, requires Black people to have been the passive recipients of the many opportunities and amenities provided by the neighborhood. The narrative suggests that while other neighborhoods were segregated, H Street welcomed people of all backgrounds, including Black people, to take advantage of quality employment opportunities and to patronize shopping and entertainment venues. This story accounts neither for the establishments that remained segregated (or open to whites only), like the Atlas Theater, nor for the abysmal social, political, and economic conditions Black people faced with the advent of Jim Crow.

Complementing this emphasis on diversity and nostalgia is the work of authenticity. Notions of authenticity impact how people move through urban spaces, especially those undergoing significant change. Authenticity today, as Sharon Zukin argues, relates to style rather than origins. Zukin writes that authenticity has conceptually "migrated from a quality of people to a quality of things, and most recently to a quality of experiences."[26] Therefore, narratives that emphasize H Street's diverse cultural heritage allow everyone to have an identifiable piece of this history. An authentic, ethnically diverse past dissolves the guilt of white gentrifiers moving in on sacred territory. If the area was always racially and ethnically diverse, it can stand the presence of more white people, especially white ethnic groups. These narratives of diversity make room for everyone to have a place at the table—making displacement seem much less violent. As they relate to historic preservation and cultural tourism, nostalgia and the practice of remembering the past place are often used as a way to achieve economic growth for cities. City officials take advantage of opportunities to market the preserved histories of neighborhoods in order to attract attention and money. These urban histories become commodities ready for consumption.

Storytelling: The Near Northeast Historical Study

The discursive presentation of the H Street, NE corridor as a historical intersection of ethnic and racially diverse people is plainly illustrated in contemporary documents produced by local government agencies in conjunction with strategic commercial development plans. One such document is a 2002 report titled *Near Northeast Historical Study*, primarily funded by the D.C. Historic Preservation Office, a subsidiary of the D.C. Office of Planning.[27] The D.C. Historic Preservation Office functions as the mayoral administration's agent for historic preservation in Washington, D.C. While the document was not ultimately published, it was freely available to be accessed through the Office of Planning website and was posted online to social media sites, including some popular neighborhood blogs.

Various historic preservation efforts, like establishing landmark status for various commercial and residential buildings, are popular in gentrifying urban areas where newcomers and urban pioneers seek to experience an "authentic" version of a neighborhood's history. The revaluation of urban life coincided with "discovery" or invention of various heritage and urban conservation efforts and emerging postmodern design and architecture. Specifically used as a strategy to attract capital, intangible aesthetic elements of urban space and place are commodified for the purposes of economic growth, heritage, and improved quality of life.[28] Historic preservation operates in defense of the gentrification of urban spaces by "depoliticizing the processes of urban restructuring and working-class displacement through discourses of aesthetics, class and race."[29] Furthermore, historic preservation has played a significant role in the re-presentation of the H Street corridor as a thriving multiethnic commercial and residential space.

The study, written by Nancy Schwartz and Richard Layman, offers a detailed architectural, commercial, and cultural history of the area surrounding the H Street, NE commercial corridor using data obtained from oral histories, newspaper articles, archival materials, and in-depth interviews. It situates the corridor's origins and development within the scope of L'Enfant's planned city. The study provides historical data about early land ownership in the eighteenth century, topographical information, burial grounds, the role and significance of railroad and streetcar transportation, and business development. The study was written at a point in H Street's history when the corridor had an overwhelmingly Black and poor population, and while the study was not used to directly preserve architectural or artistic structures, it asserts a particular narrative of H Street and connects this history with contemporary changes. One of the overarching themes of the study is a narrative of H Street's culturally diverse origins. In particular, the authors highlight the early makeup of the corridor in the late nineteenth century as having an eclectic mix of recent immigrants from Ireland, Germany, Italy, England, and Sweden, as well as the newly freed slaves who helped build the White House and the Capitol. The study frames the neighborhood as a vital, bustling commercial district and transportation corridor that met the needs of its diverse residents.

According to the study, by the early twentieth century, the neighborhood comprised a greater mix of ethnicities. The authors suggest that the Near Northeast area was one of the few neighborhoods in the early twentieth century known for its ethnic plurality. Of those Black inhabitants who lived in the area, by the 1920s, they were able to procure "more substantial jobs" than work as unskilled or domestic laborers. The study confirms that Black Americans on and around H Street, NE worked as "railroad firemen, elevator operators, teachers, letter carriers, clerks in government offices, and skilled laborers at the GPO."[30] The authors then identified neighborhood Black professionals by name and address: "Burton G. Robinson, a Black physician lived at 702 12th Street and Peter Price, another Black doctor, at 1128 G. Harvey Lewis, a D.C. school principal lived at 822 12th Street, and George Lomax at 813 9th Street was a barber with his own shop. Linden Street was an enclave of middle class African Americans whose professions in 1920 included dentist, policeman, music teacher, photograph enlarger, and clerks in the Treasury and Post Office Departments."[31] Although the narrative acknowledges that Blacks continued to lag "behind whites in employment opportunities," Schwartz and Layman write that "there had been a decided improvement in the status of some of those living in the study area in the ten years from 1910 to 1920."[32] Highlighting professional Black residents despite the majority of Black Americans who still suffered in poverty and from underemployment, the study suggests that by living in an ethnically and racially diverse community, these exceptional Black professionals transcended the enduring systemic oppression of segregation and the aftermath of slavery. This delineation also leads the reader to assume poor Blacks (who are later implicated in the destruction of H Street) did not live in or near the corridor. The study goes on to say that at the start of the Depression in the 1930s, H Street "was a middle and working-class neighborhood, more affluent at its western end, with remarkable ethnic diversity along its prosperous local shopping street, and with some businesses that attracted citywide patronage."[33] This designation emphasizes ethnic diversity and prosperity on H Street in contrast to other areas of the city. Nevertheless, it is unclear how and why H Street operated in an economic, political, and cultural bubble, especially during the Depression, where Black and white people prospered together.

With the physical incorporation of Black residents in the area, the study offers a story of interracial cooperation, with Black and white people living, working, and shopping side by side. The report positions H Street, as an inclusive, Black-friendly space, in particular contrast to downtown commercial districts where shop owners exercised their right to discriminate against Black shoppers because of federally mandated segregation laws, even while establishments like the Atlas Theater remained open solely to white patrons. The report states:

> Although H Street did not have the large and exclusive stores to be
> found on F Street downtown, H Street businessmen competed for
> business in several ways. One was by offering longer store hours.
> With their eclectic mix of ethnic backgrounds, the merchants of
> H Street were also less tied to the conservative, southern attitudes
> of the more formal downtown stores. African Americans were
> welcomed to shop on H Street. Merchants would sell on credit and
> keep a running account for good customers. Informal oral history
> interviews with people who shopped on H Street in the 30s, 40s, and
> 50s, yield the same general impressions. A shopper could find almost

anything he wanted on H Street; service was good; and the shop-keepers eager to please.[34]

While writing that Black shoppers "were welcomed" to patronize stores on H Street, the authors insinuate that Black people had a choice of where to shop, rather than having limited options under the social and legal oppression of the Jim Crow racial segregation laws, which were not officially abolished until 1965.

Schwartz and Layman go on to say that in this period, during the 1930s and 1940s, commerce along the corridor was at its peak. "People who knew the street during the late 30s and 40s refer to crowds moving up and down the sidewalks, and describe it as 'like a shopping mall.' It had a neighborhood quality in which people would patronize their favorite merchants, but it was large enough to include all types of businesses. Many people, especially in the Black community, did all their shopping there."[35] Similar to Sharon Zukin, in her critique of Jane Jacobs's view of New York City as an urban imaginary, Schwartz and Layman's descriptions of H Street preserve an image of the corridor "as a microcosm of social diversity."[36]

While this historical narrative suggests that Black patrons were able and invited to shop at all H Street stores like their white counterparts, several accounts of the social and economic conditions leading up to the 1968 uprisings convey that most of the businesses that were burned or looted did not allow Black shoppers or made Black customers feel unwelcome. Nevertheless, the authors characterize Fourteenth and U Streets and the Shaw District (the two other "riot corridors") as the centers of "commercial and social life for the African American residents of Washington," since Black residents were unable to attend movie theaters and other entertainment venues on H Street.[37] By classifying Fourteenth and U Streets (affectionately known as "Black Broadway") and the Shaw District as popular and necessary destinations for Black leisure and entertainment, the narrative allows for H Street to be reinscribed as diverse rather than "Black."[38] Both Shaw and U Street are popularly recognized as important for Black leisure and entertainment, not because they had more Black people in the area compared with H Street, but because Black people had restricted or prohibited access to nearby playgrounds and movie theaters, like the Atlas. "In the segregated world of Washington in the first half of the 20th century, the rich history of movie theater development along H Street . . . benefited only the white residents of the area. For most of their entertainment needs, African Americans living in the Near Northeast had to journey to other parts of the city."[39] Even when the study acknowledges segregation as it relates to the entire city, H Street was still a welcoming place for Black people.

The study glosses over much of the period after the 1968 uprisings and is particularly silent on activities in the area during the 1980s and 1990s. The study details the history by decade in the earlier parts, but provides a short description of activities after the 1968 uprisings (cursory details about urban renewal efforts). In fact, the authors designate one short paragraph to describe the uprisings and a second longer paragraph to discuss planning activities in its aftermath. Neither the structural root causes of the uprisings nor details about grievances expressed by the Black community are addressed. Although the authors acknowledge a demographic shift in the late 1940s, when the Black population became a majority, details about the H Street corridor began to taper with their retelling of the relocation of immigrant families to more affluent areas. The study ends with a fitting reflection of the neighborhood's diverse roots: "Although there are some quite large houses from the late 19th century, the majority of the residences in the study area are the modest homes of the middle- and working-class residents, of many ethnic groups, who made this neighborhood their home from the 1870s on."[40]

Although H Street has been represented as historically a multiethnic, multiclass, diverse space, its semblance to other identifiably Black neighborhoods suggests otherwise. The narrative that a high concentration of Blacks shopped along the H Street corridor because of the discrimination they experienced downtown and in other segregated spaces indicates erroneously that H Street was a utopic, colorblind space. In this way, the progressive narrative of H Street's storied past dissociates the corridor from local, regional, and national patterns of racial discrimination and violence by constructing the idea of a harmonious, multicultural commercial corridor where the racism that was experienced elsewhere was aberrant or absent.[41] Furthermore, characterizing H Street as diverse historically masks the experiences of racialization in the twenty-first century beneath the discourse of cultural celebration and market competition.

Americana 2.0: H Street Main Street

Narratives about the diversity of the H Street corridor impact how people move through the space. These discourses shape what spaces and people are cool, safe, or unsafe and which establishments and individuals belong. To this point, the designation of H Street as a Main Street produces a nostalgic fantasy of Americana with global cultures visibly present. The Main Streets program also impacts the political economy of the neighborhood by designating the area as economically viable and worthy of certain public services (trash collection, parking permits, police surveillance, etc.). Intended to "tell us who we are and who we were, and how the past has shaped us," the program provides a clear example of the intersection of race, culture, profit, and nostalgia, as Main Streets are purportedly the universal "places of shared memory where people still come together to live, work, and play."[42] Longing for shared memories of "the old days" and "the old neighborhood" requires the discursive production of a diverse, welcoming space linked to commercial and residential development.

The Main Streets program is a commercial revitalization strategy developed by the National Trust for Historic Preservation (NTHP) and coordinated by the organization's National Main Street Center. Most often, towns and small cities implement Main Streets programs as an integral part of their downtown development strategies. The program uses historic preservation–based development plans to revitalize commercial districts, with the goal of retaining a unique sense of place. There are currently eight Main Streets programs in Washington, D.C. In 2002, the same year the "Near Northeast Historical Study" emerged, merchants on H Street received one of the city's first urban Main Streets grants to develop the business corridor using the historic building stock as an asset. H Street Main Street (HSMS) is a nonprofit organization that provides funds and technical assistance to businesses along the commercial corridor to spur retail growth and community development. It is a principal organization in the redevelopment and transformation of the H Street, NE commercial corridor. While each D.C. Main Street has its own bylaws and operating procedures, all Main Streets programs are led by an executive director, a board of directors, and community development professionals. Unlike larger-scale business improvement districts (BID), which rely on assessments at the expense of property owners, funds distributed to the H Street Main Street are managed by the taxpayer-funded Department of Small and Local Business Development (DSLBD).

The Main Streets program hinges on commitment from the community on matters of promotion, marketing, and economic restructuring and diversification.[43] Promotion and design are two categories in which the HSMS has been particularly successful and has devoted significant resources and time—from press exposure (local and national), to the H Street Festival, the HSMS website, streetscapes, and signage. H Street, NE has been touted as a thriving Main Street and has been featured in numerous national publications and has won several awards. For instance, HSMS won the NTHP's 2013 Great American Main Street Award—success measured by vacancy rate: 30 percent in 2002, 2 percent in 2013. The Main Streets program strategy was appealing to HSMS executive director Anwar Saleem because it had national recognition, "the most widely used and heralded method of downtown revitalization" even though it was not typically used for urban centers.[44] Despite their initial hesitance to implement the Main Street strategy on H Street because of its "rough" reputation, the NTHP worked with Saleem to promote, redesign, and organize an economic restructuring of the H Street, NE corridor.

Community leaders and business owners perceive Saleem as a particularly effective leader because he not only grew up in the neighborhood (he witnessed the uprisings firsthand and his best friend was one of the few casualties during the uprisings), but he has also owned several businesses on H Street and has a friendly rapport with the business owners and residents along the corridor. Although Saleem no longer lives in the neighborhood, he and his family are still very tied to the neighborhood through his work and his civic duties. Under Saleem's leadership since 2006, H Street has received significant local and national press, and his efforts have resulted in the annual H Street Festival becoming one of the most highly populated events in the city. HSMS is the primary coordinator of the annual H Street Festival, which now draws a crowd of over 50,000 people each September. Like many neighborhood festivals, the ten-block event features a wide sampling of food from food trucks and restaurants along the corridor, music, and other forms of entertainment. The festival is part of the revitalization strategy to bring more attention to the neighborhood. It features a wide array of people, music, fashion, and food. Outside of Washington Redskins games, the H Street Festival is one of the most diverse (racially and economically) events in the area. The festival is slated to become one of the largest street festivals in the city.

Saleem characterizes the neighborhood as predominantly and historically African American and believes the Main Streets program "saved" the neighborhood. He supports a program that ultimately uses a particular narrative to reimagine and package the neighborhood as universal and diverse in order to attract commerce but also wants longtime Black business owners and residents to incorporate their experiences and family histories into the emerging multicultural narrative. In terms of branding efforts, Saleem expresses his desire to promote diversity and identify H Street as different from other corridors to highlight the camaraderie of a multicultural space. "It's a feeling. H Street has always been a warm place."[45] Saleem's affective rhetoric speaks to H Street's authenticity—a way to make claim on the space. As Sharon Zukin argues, "Authenticity refers to the *look* and *feel* of a place as well as the social connectedness that place inspires."[46]

At the same time, Saleem wants to support Black entrepreneurs but believes they need to take cues from successful white business owners. He has worked with Georgetown University to organize business summits to help grow retail on H Street by teaching small business owners useful entrepreneurial strategies. Saleem and others have been quoted as saying that the H Street corridor used to be a shopping haven for Black customers.[47] It was a place where people could find anything they needed. Use of the Main Streets program infrastructure is an attempt to revisit a nostalgic past (whether it was the distant "multicultural" past or the more recent "Black" past). Nevertheless, framing H Street as a Black shopping mecca does not account for the fact that Black activity concentrated on H Street because of the segregationist policy that prevented Blacks from shopping in other areas of the District.

Mr. Saleem's relationship to the corridor is tied up in the complex nexus of racial politics. His ambivalent insistence on the presence of multiculturalism *and* blackness on the corridor is effective in creating a connection between the nostalgic past and a utopian future. Saleem acknowledges the structural challenges Black people have historically faced in their desire to live and work in the neighborhood, but his insistence that Black business owners ought to take on the practices of successful white entrepreneurs denies the structural barriers that limit the success of Black entrepreneurs. Ultimately, despite Saleem's noble intentions, he acts as an ideal Black neoliberal subject—monetizing Black history while at the same time attempting to increase investment dollars toward the growth of the corridor—thereby defining the successes and failures of Black businesses according to the logic of the market.

The Main Streets model serves a particular function in the transition of the Atlas District. That the model has been implemented in an urban space rather than a suburban or rural space, as it generally has been in other U.S. cities, offers a new way to think about this space, locality, economic and social justice, and entrepreneurship. The use of the Main Streets program in an urban locale retools race in strategic ways that privilege a universal, diverse experience of the past to assuage more affluent potential residents. The program allows developers and local government agencies to cast aside the political and economic needs of a community in transition that previously and necessarily served lower-class Black residents and shoppers.

Cultural Touring: Greater H Street, NE Heritage Trail

As part of a new cultural economy to help spur growth and redevelopment in urban locales, heritage tours establish a neighborhood's diverse historical identity for tourist and resident consumption. Cultural tourism plays a significant role in shaping public spaces. It produces racialized narratives about the built environment.[48] The heritage tour for the H Street, NE corridor is organized around themes that make the neighborhood appealing, including the incorporation of Black heritage. The tour is shaped by racial logics that both celebrate diversity and overlook inequalities by emphasizing the neighborhood's "trend towards greater racial and economic diversity."[49] This logic does not necessarily involve a strict adherence to the positive aspects of H Street's history, but the tour and brochure make the negative events seem insignificant to the overall cohesion of the neighborhood.[50] Cultural tourism programs construct particular narratives of a space that incorporate storytelling and visual imagery to provide context and texture. They ultimately shape how people move through the space. The programs generated by Cultural Tourism DC also incorporate walking tours so people can personally experience what it feels like to be in the space, as if they can feel what it was like to be there.

Cultural Tourism DC, the group that established the heritage trail, is a nonprofit organization that works in partnership with local government agencies. The Neighborhood Heritage Trails are self-guided pedestrian routes that use signposts and accompanying brochures to share historical stories, maps, and photographs of Washington, D.C., neighborhoods. The "Hub, Home, Heart: Greater H Street, NE Heritage Trail," established in 2012, is the thirteenth walking tour created by Cultural Tourism DC and includes eighteen signs that span 3.2 miles. Some of the signs identify the location of where Dr. Granville Moore, a Black physician, practiced medicine for fifty years, and the Swampoodle region where working-class Irish immigrants who built the White House and the Capitol lived. The heritage tour brochure engages in a form of respectability politics that highlight the contributions of Black individuals, like Dr. Granville Moore, whose profession and service reflected positively on this sanitized history of H Street. To make H Street a welcoming space does not require the exclusion of Black bodies; instead, the inclusion of contented Black subjects speaks to this narrative.

By visually highlighting these designated moments in the neighborhood's history, Cultural Tourism DC effectively produces heritage by "retrieving the affective significance of places that may easily be ignored by residents—significance that must be ignored by developers, planners and revitalization experts eager for the creation of new land (and, hence, social) values."[51] Furthermore, efforts to preserve structures and spaces associated with the lives of immigrants and racial minorities reflects a shift in historic preservation, a field that privileged the history of white people, notably the work of well-known architects.[52]

Other Cultural Tourism DC heritage trails provide consistent themes throughout the city that explicitly privilege diversity and multicultural cohesion. They include Adams Morgan's "Roads to Diversity," Columbia Heights' "Cultural Convergence," and Downtown's "Civil War to Civil Rights," which boast such sites as the location of the District's "Latino Intelligence Center," and "DC's longest-operating gay bar" (Columbia Heights); the city's "oldest synagogue" and the "hotel where the Reverend Dr. Martin Luther King Jr., put the finishing touches on his 'I Have a Dream' speech" (Downtown). These narratives require a re-presentation of cultural and spatial history in some of Washington, D.C.'s most historically monocultural neighborhoods. They construct approachable histories to which most people can relate. Strategies to incorporate cultural tourism on H Street took place at a later period than that of most of the efforts that took place across the country and in the city. Cultural tourism and historic preservation proliferated in the 1970s as a way to diversify economic activity. Along H Street, the proliferation of these activities coincided with implementation of various neoliberal measures, like the growth of public-private partnerships, as the city transitioned from state-sponsored urban renewal into market-based revitalization.

Funding for the H Street project was provided by the D.C. Department of Transportation, the U.S. Department of Transportation, and Events DC, the official convention, sports, and entertainment organization for the District (formerly known as the Washington Convention and Sports Authority). The trail was developed in collaboration with its three cochairs: Anwar Saleem, restauranteur Joe Englert, and Marqui Lyons (a longtime H Street African American woman resident).

The cover text of the "Hub, Home, Heart: Greater H Street, NE Heritage Trail" brochure characterizes the H Street, NE corridor as a "bustling working-class neighborhood [that] grew up here alongside the railroad and streetcar. Mom-and-pop businesses served all comers in the city's leading African American shopping district." It mythologizes the history of the corridor following the uprisings and invites visitors to "discover how, even after the devastating 1968 civil disturbances, the strong community prevailed to witness H Street's 21st-century revival." By using the nostalgic imagery of H Street as a lively, approachable community with enduring roots, the heritage trail produces the neighborhood surrounding H Street, NE as a space that induces memories about a particular time to be revived, salvaged, relived in the present, and extending the life of the preservationist into the distant past. Although the brochure provides readers with an introduction to the H Street corridor as "the leading African American shopping district," it also identifies the area as historically an ethnically diverse neighborhood since its early beginnings in the mid-nineteenth century, prior to the construction of Union Station.

Like the "Near Northeast Historical Study," the heritage tour brochure depicts a neighborhood filled with active retail stores, restaurants, and professional service offices "run by Jewish, Italian, Lebanese, Greek, Irish, and African American families," where Black shoppers were free to patronize shops "unlike those in downtown DC where African Americans met discrimination." Although the brochure modifies language adopted by the "Near Northeast Historical Study" that suggests Black patrons were encouraged to shop at all of the stores on H Street, the brochure euphemistically implies that H Street was a collaborative, multicultural space where different ethnic groups peacefully lived side by side, despite the racial turmoil and tensions that were taking place within other D.C. neighborhoods and in most other major cities in the United States.

The brochure and the accompanying signposts emphasize the overwhelming influence of entrepreneurialism along the corridor. Nevertheless, early signs of business acumen and savvy entrepreneurialism seemed to benefit white ethnic groups and not Black entrepreneurs; by the 1940s, most of the European immigrants fled the neighborhood for more affluent and less racially diverse neighborhoods. The brochure's neoliberal discourse of immigrant success via dedication and hard work suggests that the challenges Black entrepreneurs faced were problems of "self-care" rather than structural or institutional forces—despite the failure of several insufficient attempts by the local and federal governments to develop the H Street, NE corridor throughout the 1970s, 1980s, and 1990s.

The brochure highlights a demographic shift during the 1940s that saw "the children of H Street's European immigrants [reach] adulthood and [move] on." Since segregation remained in place in that period, "churches found new congregations, and the city switched public schools into the 'colored division' to accommodate their increasing black population."

Following the 1953 Supreme Court decision to outlaw segregation in public accommodations, all the public facilities on H Street integrated; like white residents around the city, whites living on and around H Street fled in droves and for decades, according to the brochure, "Greater H Street was almost completely African American." With the intensification of Black population growth around H Street, the brochure claims that the businesses along the corridor "continued to cater to its neighbors and to commuters." In other words, the businesses began to reflect the poor and working-class Black population, a ghettoized economy that featured liquor stores, secondhand stores, carryouts, and corner stores.

In the years that led up to the 1968 uprisings, after desegregation, Washington, D.C., experienced heightened racial polarization as whites fled the cities for the suburbs and H Street experienced not only a demographic shift but also an economic shift downward as the quality of services began to reflect this change. While the brochure does include a brief entry that quotes a *Capitol East Gazette* journalist claiming that the "riots did not happen in a vacuum," the comprehensive narrative of the brochure focuses more on H Street as a historically inclusive, multicultural space.

The guide and accompanying street marker (figure 7) describe the violent aftermath of Dr. King's assassination as the actions of "grief-stricken, angry men and women [who took] to the streets across the city—looting and burning." While Dr. King's assassination certainly spurred the event, to distort its inception as the emotional catharsis of the protestors repudiates the totalizing oppression that led to the uprisings and absolves the local and federal government of responsibility for this oppression. Adding to the narrative that the "angry" masses who destroyed H Street and other commercial corridors chose to do so out of grief, or perhaps greed, the H Street heritage tour brochure quotes a fireman who claimed that the area behind Morton's Department Store was "'a freeway for looters' carrying 'television sets, clothes, everything.'" Referring to Ben Gilbert's interviews with rioters, the guide offers no context or indication that the looting was a form of symbolic action against the deplorable conditions Black Americans were facing, or that some of the looters gave the goods away. Instead it framed these actions as irrational: "When Morton's first opened downtown in 1933, it was among the few white-owned department stores that did not discriminate in hiring or sales. In fact, owner Mortimer Lebowitz was a former Urban League president who had marched with Dr. King. Nevertheless, looters ransacked and torched his store here." This retelling suggests that the misguided and impractical protestors attacked a white ally who helped

FIGURE 7 Cultural Tourism DC heritage trail marker designating the 1968 uprisings on H Street. Photograph by author.

keep the neighborhood orderly and successful. Despite the mention that the uprisings occurred in conjunction with high levels of Black unemployment and underemployment, the pamphlet's text paints acts of political protest and violence as irrational disorder, thereby undermining the resistance efforts of the disgruntled and underserved Black residents coping with the conditions of inequality.

Emphasizing narratives of a diverse past ignores the reality of structural inequalities that plagued the corridor prior to and following the 1968 uprisings. Furthermore, this practice associates diversity with universality. The pamphlet's ambivalent description of the past celebrates the incorporation of Black heritage by highlighting positive, progressive stories about Black residents and customers, and minimizing less desirable details about H Street's recent past. Using a nostalgic narrative of diversity, the pamphlet, in conjunction with the street markers, discursively foreshadows a contemporary return to diversity in an area that was momentarily designated as Black. To say that the area was historically Black is less desirable in this era. Nevertheless, blackness is disciplined in this story to fit within a harmonious narrative about H Street's ethnically diverse past.

Cultural and heritage tourism, the reintroduction of the streetcar, high-end ethnic restaurants, and boutique stores, which cater to those with considerable social and economic capital, operate as cultural strategies to enhance the visual appeal of H Street (including the renaming of the area to "Atlas" after the historic, whites-only theater). The placement of iconic imagery on and around the corridor works alongside narratives of commercial vitality to promote renaissance and regeneration of the corridor, while masking historical and contemporary inequities. Like historic conservation and historic preservation, heritage tours act as aesthetic discourses about everyday life and institutionalized practices among city planners and developers.[53] As opposed to simply assisting in a nostalgic politics of heritage along the H Street corridor, narratives promoted by local preservation and heritage organizations couple with community development to produce an aesthetic discourse that celebrates the ethnically diverse heritage of the neighborhood.

• • • • • •

Briefly returning to the restored and renovated Atlas Performing Arts Center, its official website briefly describes the center's history in terms of its origins but does not mention the theater was a whites-only establishment for almost half of its original existence. The website reads: "Originally built in 1938, the Atlas was one of four movie theaters in the H Street Northeast corridor. After the riots of 1968, the Atlas, a community icon, ultimately saw its demise and became a dark and silent reminder of the once vibrant H Street." This retelling of the center's history missed an important opportunity to expose the complicated history of the H Street corridor and highlight the ways that diversity and inclusion have become hallmarks of the area. In nearby Fredericksburg, Virginia, a historical marker titled "A Vibrant, but Segregated Community" stands at the intersection of Wolfe Street and Princess Anne Street. Alongside an image of Jason C. Grant, a nineteenth-century African American resident of Fredericksburg and principal of the Fredericksburg Colored School, the inscription reads:

> In the aftermath of the Civil War, numerous former slaves came to Fredericksburg where there was already an established free black community. Many freedmen took work as laborers and servants. Others brought artisan skills they had practiced in slavery. The area in front of you and to your right became one of several African-American neighborhoods in Fredericksburg.
>
> The local economy, however, had been devastated by the war and did not provide many opportunities for skilled workers. Available jobs were primarily in mills and factories. Educational opportunities were limited to a segregated school. Still, many African-American small businesses flourished.
>
> These blocks were Fredericksburg's black center of commerce until the 1970s. Restaurants and boarding houses initially appeared among the residences, catering to the local community as well as to travelers. There were also professional offices, retail stores, barber and beauty shops, a grocery store, a funeral home and two hotels.

Unlike selective versions of H Street's history, this description of the Fredericksburg neighborhood provides a nuanced vision of the area, one that acknowledges its thriving commercial history alongside its troubled racial history.

The history of H Street tells the story of a Black space that underwent significant challenges to achieve the political and economic infrastructure it needed to thrive. The area did not suffer from lack of attention or a commitment of funds, but a lack of sustainable options to adequately support the people who lived there. In the years following the 1968 uprisings, the H Street corridor was deemed by the media, local politicians, and residents blighted, unwelcoming, and teeming with transient people who did not care about their own condition or the condition of their environment. Although the downfall of the corridor was due to a variety of factors, renderings of blackness and the notion of a renewed Black retail space worked discursively to forestall the restoration of H Street, NE. The production of documents and programs like the Near Northeast Study and the H Street Cultural Tourism program provide ways to promote the neighborhood by offering a development narrative in which the neighborhood's commercial past is celebrated "followed by brief mention of urban decline and the challenges it poses, and ending with destination consumption spaces as *the* opportunity for sustained economic revitalization."[54] This practice is in line with the renaming of H Street as the Atlas District to symbolically distance the neighborhood from its violent past and to also create distinction between nearby neighborhoods like Capitol Hill.

The retelling of the H Street's history positions it as a multicultural space that was momentarily decimated by an overwhelming wave of Black degeneracy. Blackness does not represent the truth of the area; instead, Black bodies are woven into the multicultural fabric of the space and their blackness necessitates disciplining or control and revitalization in order to fit the seamless narrative of a diverse space that nurtures progress and opportunity for all. It is the discursive production of a nostalgic multicultural past that regulates blackness in this urban space. The multicultural story of H Street, preceding the uprisings, requires Black people to have been the passive recipients of the many opportunities and amenities provided by the neighborhood. The narrative suggests that while other neighborhoods were segregated, H Street welcomed people of all backgrounds, including Black people, to take advantage of quality employment opportunities and to patronize shopping and entertainment venues. This story accounts for neither the establishments that remained segregated (or open to whites only), like the Atlas Theater, nor the abysmal social, political, and economic conditions Black people faced with the violence of Jim Crow.

The production of nostalgic narratives of H Street as a multicultural space connects to a larger conversation about the interrelatedness of neoliberalism, race, value, and urban space. Particularly troubling is a discourse of nostalgia that paints a racially pluralistic utopia while erasing structural forms of inequality and disenfranchisement. A nostalgia industry is particularly suited for and promoted by developers and local government agencies who have an economic interest in the profitability of the H Street corridor. I find it key to consider the ramifications of changing demographics and how race, and blackness in particular, continue to figure into the reimagining and remaking of a neighborhood. The past is constructed to suit the needs of an imagined future community rather than critically examine the social construction of heritage.

The divested urban core serves as an ideal location for the state to modify historical narratives and create a "blank space" for a new story to get mapped upon it, even in the name of historic and cultural preservation. As John Hannigan writes: "With no overwhelming consensus on how the past is to be used in building a new identity, or even *which past* is to be privileged in doing so, different groups of social actors actively contest the meaning of nostalgia and authenticity."[55] These contested meanings become integrated into the landscape.

Together, the Near Northeast Study, Main Streets program, and H Street Heritage Trail are prime examples of what Lefebvre calls representations of space.[56] For Lefebvre, representations of space are the discursive spaces conceived by planners, bureaucrats, and other urbanists.[57] Often taking physical form in the shape of maps, plans, diagrams, and other designs, representations of space ideally produce abstract space: that blank space that is "devoid of any indications of the social struggles around its production, or traces of the concrete space it replaces."[58] Abstract space appears empty and homogeneous, but this is simply appearance that has been ideologically constructed to make it appear neutral and commonsensical. The erasure of histories that accompany the production of abstract space enables the state, developers, and elite actors to restructure physical space. As a result, developers, with encouragement from the state, buy up properties that have meaningful historical and cultural value to the neighborhood, demolish them, and replace them with structures that contain businesses that attract a wealthier population. In other words, the discursive space informed by cultural tourism programs, revitalization strategies, and state-sponsored histories reflects conceived representations of an idealized, seemingly abstract space that attracts a different population. This process ultimately creates spaces that are homogenous in their distinctiveness—a calculus of cultural diversity that makes cities start to look the same, despite their unique histories.

This chapter reveals the ways in which methods of understanding H Street's past become entangled in the devastating pressures of structural forces, in the service of visible diversity. The production of an official history not only attracts visitors but also justifies the deployment of diversity measures today, since diversity—a construct that might otherwise deter white residents and patrons—now becomes a cherished asset. Productions of spatial histories are intimately tied to the political, economic, and cultural forces shaping historical memory, through objects, individuals, images, and sites. The cooperation of official and commercial histories exposes how neoliberal logics imbue historical knowledge formation. Both work together to spur residential and commercial growth through tourism. Presenting the commercial corridor as a fundamentally socially inclusive space allows for diversity to operate as a benign, sanitized version of racial difference, scoured of its potential antidevelopment, political, and social content. Endorsing a nostalgic brand of diversity is part of the neighborhood's efforts to remake itself as a cultural, tourist, and investment destination and reflects a desire to tell a positive story rather than engage in a critical examination of the past.

4 Consuming Culture

Authenticity, Cuisine, and H Street's
Quality-of-Life Aesthetics

· ·

> Absences are not just what there is not, but rather what was there and
> *now is not* any longer, or what should be there and *yet is not.*
>
> —Elisa Adami

In 2013, anticipating its forthcoming store on H Street, Whole Foods Market's Mid-Atlantic regional president, Scott Allshouse, spoke of the synergies between the Whole Foods brand and the rapidly gentrifying H Street corridor. He specifically highlighted H Street's demographics as representing what Whole Foods values: "That neighborhood reflects a lot of what Whole Foods is about—diversity, passion for food, history. Things like that. That's what we are too. We are so in tune with that. That sense of community and pride."[1] A press release from the same year announcing the new store also references the corridor's diversity as an attribute and implies that diverse communities with diverse, cultural opportunities can benefit both old and new residents, thus establishing diversity as a desirable commodity and aesthetic. The press release states: "The H Street Corridor is a thriving hub of diversity and cultural richness—a perfect match for Whole Foods Market's goal to support each and every community we're in. . . . Whether you're a long-time resident or new to this neighborhood, we are proud to have the opportunity to join you and help write the next page of history. Being among the flourishing food scene, culture offerings of the arts district and the exciting mix of residents will make Whole Foods Market a great partner to those in the community." Whole Foods uses "diversity" as a way to accrue value for both the Whole Foods brand and the H Street corridor's brand.[2] Again, known for many years as a Black-business downtown district that provided numerous retail options and public spaces for Black residents that were central to economic and social life, H Street is now seen and aesthetically valued as a diverse space for corporate interests.

This chapter considers the significance of authenticity and quality-of-life aesthetics as they relate to city life. Authenticity has become an instrument through which people attach meaning to things and experiences rather than people—hence the proliferation of boutiques, craft breweries, and cafés alongside the practice of branding neighborhoods in terms of distinctive cultural identities. While displacement, through a loss of access to affordable goods and services, is certainly taking place on H Street, this chapter argues that it is this exact tension between the polar class/race/lifestyles that attracts young, upper-income white residents and tourists to the area. At the same time, one can be stern or exhibit anger over the changes (as aesthetic, not critique), as long as the fundamental power relations of society, founded on broad appeal to white buyers, remain intact. Therefore, blackness in the marketplace must be that which *sells*, and that which can be easily transacted by proprietors of capital.

Revitalization efforts have led to the introduction of urban amenities and cultural alcoves that attract a different class of customers and tourists; those interested in improvements to lifestyle (bike lanes, farmers' markets) as opposed to equitable social and economic opportunities. This distinction between presumed Black and white interests also highlights struggles over entitlement between the new crop of residents, who have considerable education and access to resources and have invested their time and energy into the remodeling of the area, versus the old guard, who experienced the neighborhood's most challenging periods when they lacked adequate financial support from the government and other entities. I track the contemporary convergence of hipster aesthetics with a Black cultural space that results in the aesthetic recoding of the neighborhood as a diverse commercial corridor.[3] In chapter 2, I invoke Brenda Weber's theorization of certain racialized spaces as bodies in distress that can be healed only through the power of diversity. Now that diversity has found its rightful place, this chapter demonstrates the mechanisms by which it roams. In particular, this chapter examines the ways in which tempered exoticism in restaurants is used as a discourse of cultural diversity on H Street and the ways in which racial aesthetics link culture, race, and authenticity to elements like design and cuisine.

Representing the Real

Over time, "diversity" has developed incredible linguistic power. This is especially relevant within the context of Whole Foods expanding and opening a store on H Street, evoking the language of diversity. The term "diversity," Gabriella Modan points out, "has maintained its veneer of concern for social justice, but picked up new meanings associated with hipness, as it's used in new contexts that have nothing to do with inclusion, power sharing, or social justice."[4] This façade of interest in social justice, and the depoliticization of diversity, has become a popular rallying cry and organizing principle for emerging businesses that cater to customers who are interested in lifestyle amenities like yoga, organic foods, and fair-trade coffee, buttressed by a commodified ethical mode of consumption. These businesses, which appear in some of the most contested spaces, where the poor and marginalized lived for years without access to basic services, purport to support global initiatives that improve the lives of the most vulnerable populations.

Whole Foods Market was founded in 1980 and grew from a small, natural foods store based in Austin, Texas, to the country's largest organic food store and seventh-largest grocery store chain.[5] Colloquially known as "Whole Paycheck" for its high prices and reputation for catering to a young, upper-middle-class population, Whole Foods thrives on being more than just a grocery store: it's a mission-driven, lifestyle chain that emphasizes its "responsibility to co-create a world where each of us, our communities and our planet can flourish."[6] Furthermore, the chain states its purpose is to improve access to healthy food for underserved neighborhoods, despite little evidence demonstrating the success of this claim.

The H Street Whole Foods Market finally opened on May 15, 2017—a brand-new 40,000-square-foot store on the ground floor of a luxury residential building named Apollo.[7] The H Street location was the third Whole Foods Market within Washington, D.C.'s city limits, and sixth in the D.C. metro area. Although Whole Foods is a global brand, each store features aesthetic elements that reflect the neighborhood the store occupies, thus making customers *feel* like they are in a local market. A few months after the store's grand opening, I walked in to look around. It appeared to be like any other Whole Foods Market in terms of its layout, selection, and ambiance. A couple of aisles down from the organic produce section, next to the nondairy milk products, was an immaculately organized, color-coded display of gourmet chocolates. Above the multitiered tower was the phrase "Chocolate City" featured prominently in white block letters foregrounding a dark brown backdrop. Above the sign was a generic city skyline, resembling paper cutouts, dipped in various hues of chocolate brown. As I mentioned earlier, the "Chocolate City" name was adopted by Black Washingtonians as a sense of pride in the face of the horrifying political and economic conditions they faced in the mid-twentieth century. In light of this popular and recognizable history, it became immediately clear that the "Chocolate City" sign at Whole Foods doubly authenticated remnants of the waning Black culture that had been prominent in the neighborhood and aestheticized the meaning of blackness in this first majority-Black metropolis. This display of black aesthetic emplacement also highlighted how social and political histories are casually decontextualized in the service of capital.

Instances of Black aesthetic emplacement oftentimes share the same space with aesthetics of diversity, evoked by markers of "history." The "Chocolate City" tower was physically positioned alongside common aesthetic markers of a gentrifying landscape. At the new store, three colorful posters hang on the interior windows depicting abstract images of H Street, with phrases like "History & Legacy," "Culture & Arts," and "Heritage & Tradition" emblazoned on them. The organization of images on the posters resembles a quilt. Small thumbnail pictures display scissors, presumably representing the many Black-owned barber and beauty shops that historically lined the corridor; a coffee cup; music notes; an admission ticket to the local Apollo Theatre; and other symbols evoke history, community, continuity, and a rich culture. The posters also have pictures of H Street's historic Victorian-style buildings, and in one of the images is the representation of the newly refurbished streetcar. These posters show a combination of the historic and contemporary; subtle and overt references to racialized objects, people, and locations; a seamless blend of the two evoke notions of authenticity as welcoming, accessible, diverse, and cool for white purveyors. The images are positioned so that shoppers will see them as they enter and leave, no matter which route they take (to the parking garage below ground or at street level).

After a few weeks, the management team at the H Street Whole Foods received significant backlash after images of their very own "Chocolate City" went viral on social media. As a result, "Chocolate City" became "Confectioner's Corner," with a brand-new, tan and white color scheme. Even though "Chocolate City" only lasted a couple of weeks, displays like these shed additional light on why the movement of white residents into Black neighborhoods generates tension and feelings of exclusion.[8] The presence of these racial aesthetics disrupts narratives commonly associated with gentrification, namely, displacement. With Black aesthetic emplacement and aesthetic markers of diversity prominently on display, ready for immediate consumption, "revitalization," "renewal," and "redevelopment" enact violence upon those who lived and toiled around the neighborhood in previous years, despite the euphemistic characterizations.[9]

The Whole Foods Market press release and the "Chocolate City" display exemplify how authenticity and diversity are mapped upon the space. They work together to invite attention, shape how the space should be seen, and attract commerce, while at the same time evoking language of community and belonging. At Whole Foods Market, authenticity is a hyperreality, one that reflects not a prior social reality, but a new one constructed from models or ideas about "the real" and "authentic."[10] Blackness is still a large part of this formulation, but it is in examples like these that we see blackness similarly aestheticized and depoliticized.

To think about why there is a push for diversity, I also consider what diversity is actively working against. Historically, various turns to diversity have been brought about in reaction to conservative, nationalist, nativist movements in support of the "white majority." Diversity was touted as a liberal remedy to explicit forms of discrimination. It inherently avoids engagement with structural racism, sexism, and economic inequalities.[11] What makes the push for diversity an integral part of the neoliberal shift is its commodification and emphasis on individualism. Evoking diversity brings about social and economic rewards, primarily for white people. The Whole Foods Market ethos is a perfect reflection of that, as it emphasizes not only diversity but also entrepreneurialism, which is especially espoused by Chief Executive Officer Mackey, whose libertarian views speak to his advocacy of neoliberal principles in the running of the business.

Authentic Abstractions of Race

Questions of authenticity and cultural appropriation have become popular and contentious topics in the academy and in popular media, especially with the rapid growth of new media technologies in the digital age. Debates about the performance of Black style, dance, speech, and fashion call into question the value of blackness when produced for commercial consumption. Similarly, multiple studies provide ethnographic and statistical evidence of predominantly white gentrifiers having the political clout and racial privilege to reallocate resources and repair the infrastructure of ailing cities. Gentrifiers attempt to tidy up urban space by removing its residents and completing the task that urban renewal of the 1950s, 1960s, and 1970s started. Similarly, with the displacement of longtime Black residents, gentrifiers occupy urban spaces to reap the benefits of a constructed urban life that involves selective reflections of nostalgia, cosmetic grit, and lifestyle amenities, all the while overlooking those who were displaced.

So, what does authenticity mean in a post–Chocolate City neighborhood that claims and aspires to be cool and diverse? Where does the blackness go? We saw from the example above that the aesthetics of stylistic diversity and black aesthetic emplacement work together within transitioning spaces to make them more approachable, appealing, and consumable. On H Street, the form of authenticity that is enacted through consumption does not necessarily follow the pattern of ethnic enclaves or districts, like your typical urban American Chinatowns, Greektowns, or Koreatowns. Instead, it is a place that is distinctly multicultural; not privileging one race, culture, or ethnicity over another. Authenticity here is abstract; it is a representation of a desired social reality. The cosmetic grittiness and danger that Derek Hyra argues are vital to neighborhoods that have adopted Black branding strategies only operate at a surface level; residents and visitors do want to feel safe.[12] The desire for authenticity is about the look but not the feel of a particular neighborhood. Urban should not *look* suburban but can feel suburban in its visual representation of safety (i.e., being walkable, having adequate lighting and welcoming consumer spaces, and having other examples of new urbanism).[13]

Authenticity shows up in various ways on H Street—specifically, through a diversity aesthetic that has been mapped upon the neighborhood and the city's blackness. Drawing on the history and revival of the Apollo building on H Street speaks to a desire for authenticity and purposeful iconographic drift. For example, the Apollo Theatre on H Street was simply a movie house from the early twentieth century that was pulled out of history and drifted to the contemporary imaginations of developers represented by words and images. This purposeful adoption, or drift, of mundane historical structures becomes a significant part of the work developers use to attract attention and investment. It also reflects the interest of "social homesteaders," gentrifiers who want to maintain a piece of the past as representing the social or cultural heyday of the neighborhood, which usually involves negotiation over what spaces, structures, and people have value.[14] Taking control of the narrative of this place privileges a certain history and erases others. Producing these kinds of nostalgic memories and histories gets represented in different ways. From the naming of the building after the Apollo Theatre to the iconic and recognizable images on posters in Whole Foods Market, these are ways not only to "honor" history and tradition but also make people feel like they are connected to the space and its history. But the adoption of certain histories is selective. No one wanted to name the building after the car dealership it became after the Apollo was demolished, or the storage facility that inhabited the space before the residential building was erected. Instead, authenticity ends up being a performance and a chosen lifestyle, as well as an instrument of displacement.[15]

Authenticity might be tied to history, but whose history? We saw a bit of this in the previous chapter, where certain narratives of H Street's history were privileged over others. The quest for authenticity reflects a nostalgic longing for a constructed history that serves the present by presenting a particular version of the past. Ultimately, while some scholars argue that it is the desire for an authentic postindustrial aesthetic that draws in residents and tourists, and helps shape the development of gentrifying neighborhoods, I am also saying that contestations over the meaning of authenticity in urban spaces both complement and supplement black aesthetic emplacement and cultural diversity by emphasizing origins as style.

Claims on the authentic also expose and empower whiteness to determine what and who fits. Cities are able to evoke authentic narratives of place if they effectively "create the *experience* of origins. This is done by preserving historic buildings and districts, encouraging the development of small-scale boutiques and cafés, and branding neighborhoods in terms of distinctive cultural identities."[16] This occurs with the preservation of historic structures and districts that lead to the proliferation of new or revised places and spaces (like the Apollo building and the Atlas District) and the adoption of certain narratives of layered history. One of the ultimate ways to claim space and organize narratives is through (re)naming. For example, a December 2017 story from the local National Public Radio station discussed the naming of new greenspace, organized by the area's growing number of dog owners, in the NoMA neighborhood (North of Massachusetts Avenue), adjacent to the H Street, NE corridor. In order to name the park, the NoMa Parks Foundation encouraged public comment and then a vote. According to the president of the foundation, the name Swampoodle "won by a landslide" (see figure 8).[17] Swampoodle was the name of the neighborhood surrounding H Street mostly inhabited by immigrant Irish families who settled in Washington, D.C., following the famine of the 1840s and 1850s, and who also helped erect the Capitol. The neighborhood was later destroyed with the construction of Union Station in 1907.

Local interest in recognizing a neighborhood's *true* Irish origins effectively reconfigures the space to be devoid of the blackness that characterized the area in recent memory. Focusing on the neighborhood being

FIGURE 8 Swampoodle dog park and kids playground on Third and L Streets, three blocks from the H Street corridor. Photograph by author.

previously inhabited by Irish immigrants who sought refuge after the potato famine of the mid-nineteenth century, and who built the Capitol, makes invisible the slaves and freedmen who also toiled alongside them. Saying that the Irish workers built the Capitol ties them to the land. It justifies their lingering presence. This form of past-making re-centers whiteness by marking territory. By engaging in an active erasure of the space's more recent history, going back to a time before Black people "destroyed" the neighborhood during the "riots," the park can take on a nostalgic meaning and drive decisions about how the space can be developed moving forward. Introducing blackness to the area brings up far too many memories of violence, oppression, and practices of inequality.

The whiteness of Swampoodle's Irish immigrants tells a different and more pleasing story. Whiteness not only represents the norm but also is unthreatening, despite characterizations of the neighborhood being "rough." Therefore, as the landscape shifts, not only is it important to recognize the production and presence of blackness in these urban spaces; it is instructive to notice the ways that whiteness (as ethnicity) appears aesthetically, in this case through naming, to encourage (or substantiate) the presence of more white people, for authenticity is an instrument of power.[18] The naming of Swampoodle Park should be considered within the context of the changes occurring in and around the area. There's nothing alarming about the naming of public space after an ethnic group that inhabited the area in the nineteenth century, but again, the context under which NoMA and H Street are changing adds a different meaning. The naming dictates how the space *should* be remembered in case its history is overshadowed by contested events and populations.

Hipster Economics and the Aesthetic Politics of Belonging

In a May 2014 piece on the *Al Jazeera* website, Sarah Kendzior lamented the encroachment of "hipster economics" on America's urban landscapes. She defines hipster economics by the practice of urban decay becoming "a set piece to be remodeled or romanticized."[19] Kendzior argues that gentrifying hipsters view poverty through the lens of aesthetics and therefore concentrate on aesthetics rather than people, since "people, to them, are aesthetics." If people are aestheticized, so are class relations, which are systematically "depoliticized and reduced to questions of lifestyle choices, consumption patterns, visual pleasures and 'good taste.'"[20] The process of gentrification exposes how public spaces become privatized by white, middle-class interests, and the transformation of urban space demarcates the boundaries of who belongs and who does not.

John Jackson invokes Lefebvre's concept of qualified spaces that are unclaimed by market forces in his discussion of the privatization of public space. He says that privatization "is not solely about how spaces symbolize (as Black or white, rich or poor); it is also a rehearsal of social belonging tethered to people's everyday practices and senses of self. To look out onto one's public sphere and see what was another abandoned storefront (open space for all, especially the least successful) alchemized into a gourmet bakery for a growing middle class, is a different order of displacement entirely, a kind of psychological and semiotic displacement from the sites of one's own, formerly less-fettered, everyday pedestrianism."[21] With the introduction of yoga studios, bicycle shops, hookah bars, tiny art galleries, and vintage and antique furniture stores on H Street, fewer and fewer shops speak to, serve, and reflect the everyday needs of the poor and working class. Although Sharon Zukin and colleagues suggest that boutique businesses arrive in gentrifying urban space as part of an emerging market that institutionalizes the consumption practices of more affluent and educated individuals, Jackson makes a much more nuanced argument about the privatization of public space and how public spaces obtain private, personal,

FIGURE 9 The H Street streetcar construction project along the twelve-block stretch of H Street, NE hurt some businesses as they saw their customer numbers precipitously fall. George's Place was one such store. It was replaced by Ben's Chili Bowl. Photograph taken at the 1000 block of H Street, NE, Washington, D.C. © Joseph Young.

and political meaning for residents, especially long-term residents who are gradually leaving the neighborhood.[22] Not only is physical displacement taking place as small businesses that were patronized by poor and working-class residents leave the corridor, but the affective dimensions of gentrification and displacement structure who belongs in the space and who does not (figure 9). Nevertheless, it is in these spaces that market-driven consumption is depoliticized in favor of the aesthetics of "cool"—and where the streets become "little more than [a] public playground for the authenticities monopolized by middle-class consumerism."[23]

Around the same time Kendzior published her piece, Destination DC, the official tourism and destination marketing organization for D.C., unveiled its newest marketing campaign: "DC Cool." The "cool" brand that Destination DC adopted purposefully reflected how recognizably "cool" D.C. has become, and it gave the organization an opportunity to "promote and expose [tourists] to things out of the three M's: monuments, memorials, and museums, because that does not always resonate as a sexy reason why people want to travel."[24] Destination DC is an economic development organization that focuses solely on the $7 billion hospitality industry. Its primary role is to attract visitors to the District and promote the city as a primary convention destination. The DC Cool campaign reflects the organization and the city's desire to advertise not only D.C.'s "cool people" and cultural diversity but also its "sports, theatre, nightlife, retail, arts, restaurant scene, and outdoor activities."[25]

What the campaign does not highlight are those changes to the cultural makeup and commercial landscape of "declining" districts that have undergone significant transformation in order to make way for the gentrifying hipsters Kendzior bemoans.[26] What commercial districts like H Street are experiencing are a disappearing mode of social and cultural life in favor of an emerging retail ecology, or commercial gentrification, that features "new establishments with particular goods and services—such as clothing boutiques, art galleries, cafes, restaurants, and bars—that open to satisfy the needs of middle-class gentrifiers" and displace longtime, established businesses and people (figure 10).[27] One example is the April 2017 off-market sale of Smokey's Barbershop to the 11th Property Group.[28] The barbershop had been on Thirteenth and H Streets since 1999. The building was sold to the 11th Property group to make way for a mixed-use development, thereby reflecting an ongoing trend on H Street where small, Black-owned businesses are being replaced by developer-driven, mixed-use projects. On the same block, at the former site of the R. L. Christian Library, the Insight Property Group (which also developed the Apollo project discussed above) plans to construct a mixed-use development that is a "100% affordable project" with all thirty-three units being "a combination of 50% [area median income] and 30% units."[29] Although the units will be "affordable," Insight plans to bring retail options to the location similar to those that it brought to the Apollo building.

The changing landscape of the corridor is reflected when projects like these become the norm. That the new buildings are being constructed on the site of a Black-owned barbershop and a public library speaks volumes: the end of local public services and a transition to a new economy that privileges exclusive commerce, gentrified culture, and consumption. These changes impact not only the commercial makeup of the space but also its aesthetic geography.

FIGURE 10 Disinvestment on H Street. Photograph taken at the 1300 block of H Street, NE, Washington, D.C. © Joseph Young.

"Quality-of-Life" Aesthetics

The transitioning landscape of the corridor is reflected by the emerging presence of large national and international businesses: Whole Foods Market, Nando's Peri-Peri, Starbucks, and several others. These establishments sit next to high-end boutiques and niche businesses that in many neighborhoods around the country have gone out of business because major conglomerates like Wal-Mart, Barnes and Noble, and other giants join the commercial landscape. So, independent bookstores, coffee houses, bakeries, and similar service-related businesses become sites of commercial gentrification. There is an element of nostalgia that attaches to these spaces as part of the "good ole days" discussed in chapter 3. These businesses do not help support the poor and working class. Instead, these groups must shop at places like Wal-Mart because they are the only affordable businesses in the area. Ironically, hipsters nostalgically long for a time before big box stores existed, yet the marketing used to draw them in as consumers pushes poor and working-class residents to those very same big box stores.

H Street is not alone. All around D.C. there are examples of race, culture, and class clashes over the usage and aesthetics of space. In another "riot corridor" neighborhood, the Shaw District, new and old residents battled over the development of a multimillion-dollar, mixed-use affordable housing project. The chair of the local ANC and other residents spoke out against the building's "unattractive" appearance, claiming that it resembled affordable housing built during the 1970s and 1980s—when the neighborhood was overwhelmingly Black. In fact, all of the complaints directed at the development were concerned with "design aesthetics, building amenities and the threat that a 100 percent affordable housing unit posed to the community."[30] Others saw the project as an opportunity for poorer residents to achieve middle-class status and "to ensure racial and social equity as the city prospers."[31] One anonymous city official who supported construction of the building and who grew up in Washington, D.C., lamented the local government policies that have decimated so much of the Black history and culture that previously thrived in the District. He says: "White liberals in D.C. don't give a shit about social services because they're not of that element. White liberals in D.C. are more about quality-of-life issues as it relates to the lifestyle they want to have. It is bike lanes. It is dog parks. It is about the state-of-the-art swimming facilities. It is about recreation centers. Capital Bikeshare. Car2Go. Streetcars. It's about a way of life. Black folks want this stuff, they're just not as passionate about it."[32] The official describes the difference between "white liberalism" and "Black liberalism," where Black liberalism involves an investment in strategies that help the poor move toward the middle class and ensure racial and economic parity. "White liberalism" involves lifestyle choices and economic growth for individuals. White liberalism, as implied above, represents the ideological position of new middle-class professionals with "a vocation to enhance the quality of life in pursuits that are not simply economistic."[33] Furthermore, efforts to preserve their consumption practices are bolstered through organizational means like neighborhood associations and "the aesthetic ideology—historic preservation, codified in law."[34]

To emphasize quality-of-life aesthetics signals that white gentrifiers are more interested in "improvements" to lifestyle via upper-middle-class accoutrements, reflecting an investment in the white spatial imaginary, while Black residents evoke a Black spatial imaginary by focusing on equitable social and economic opportunities. Even though displacement, through a loss of access, is certainly taking place on H Street, it is this exact tension between the polar class, race, and lifestyles that spurs attraction to the area.

H Street used to be a destination where the mostly Black shoppers could find basic everyday items and services. Now, vacant storefronts that once held these retail and service shops are replaced by more expensive, boutique shops and (inter)national chains that ultimately exclude "ethnic" shoppers. Revitalization efforts have led to the introduction of urban amenities and cultural alcoves that attract a different class of customers and tourists with alternative consumption practices. This distinction between presumed Black and white interests also highlights struggles over entitlement between the new crop of residents, who have considerable education and access to resources and have invested their time and energy into the remodeling of the area, versus the old guard, who experienced the neighborhood's most challenging periods when they lacked adequate financial support from the government and other entities. Accordingly, lower-income Black residents, who desire better-quality services, identify upscale retail landscapes with "white interests." These residents "resent the implication that white newcomers are responsible for the improvements."[35]

Similarly, in 2006, the tense class and race dynamics of H Street were played out publicly over the opening of a Cluck-U Chicken franchise restaurant. The Cluck-U Chicken's owner, Bernard Gibson, dreamed of opening the restaurant on H Street because his grandparents lived nearby for several years.[36] After receiving a permit for a sit-down restaurant, he opened Cluck-U on the 1100 block of H Street, NE. Challenges to Cluck-U came primarily from the neighborhood ANC, whose commissioners argued that the restaurant was simply another fast-food establishment and was unwelcome along a corridor that was making great strides to raise its standards and transition from "a strip trying to shed its bedraggled past" to becoming "a gleaming urban paradise."[37] The ANC justified its challenge by suggesting their stance against Cluck-U was supported by zoning code. In this case, the ANC claimed that a fast-food restaurant does not qualify as a sit-down restaurant, and therefore does not belong on the corridor.

In *Go-Go Live*, Natalie Hopkinson writes about her experience at Cluck-U Chicken and her dismay at the ANC's challenge to a business "so immaculately kept and [one that] offered chinaware and table service for patrons."[38] While most of the ANC commissioners saw Cluck-U as a blemish to the redevelopment efforts on H Street, according to the *Washington Post*, one commissioner seemed discouraged that the efforts to close Cluck-U would further alienate longtime residents, since the corridor needed to maintain its economic diversity by preserving establishments that were "welcoming and cheap for those who don't have a lot of money."[39] Some residents, business owners, and activists, including H Street Main Street executive director Anwar Saleem, saw the challenge as further evidence of H Street becoming an unwelcome place for Black patrons and Black-owned businesses. Efforts by the ANC to challenge the presence of Cluck-U furthers a neoliberal logic in its attempt to improve quality of life along the corridor by admonishing fast-food franchises in favor of unique, "appropriate" entrepreneurial ventures. In other words, the ANC presents a clear anticorporate, anti–chain restaurant stance, and praise for the healthy, local, organic food businesses offering an upscale environment that came to populate the corridor over the next several years.

Fast-food restaurants in urban environments are most prevalent in predominantly Black and poor neighborhoods where "it is easier to get fried chicken than a fresh apple."[40] In the 1980s and 1990s, the corridor was littered with inexpensive fast-food restaurants because of its declining business climate, high crime rate, and inferior public services. The success of local and national fast-food chains along the corridor was in part because "chicken and fish fast food operations usually capture high sales in Black neighborhoods, especially if the units are located in proximity to a major health service, drug store, supermarket, or liquor store."[41] Therefore, the visible presence of fast-food restaurants along the corridor indicated that the area was poor and Black, since such neighborhood features align with race and class. Although Cluck-U provided the accouterments of a family-friendly, clean, and neat dining experience, that the establishment was hailed as a fast-food restaurant enabled the ANC to justify its objections using government regulations, thus exposing class-specific markings of space that define the boundaries of belonging on H Street.

Race and Architectural Aesthetics

In 2012, the *Washington Post* published an article discussing the presence of roll-down steel security gates on the H Street, NE corridor as a relic of the neighborhood's past in the face of a rapidly gentrifying space. Most of the current businesses along H Street reside in conjoined Victorian-era buildings that were formerly residences. In the early twentieth century, several homes were remodeled to look less residential in order to accommodate small stores (adding new façades and shop front windows). The standard red brick of the older buildings was replaced with a sampling of textured brick in hues from deep red to tan at the turn of the nineteenth century and have, since then, been amended with various colors like blue, black, green, and lavender. Decorative details were simplified and usually borrowed from the classical architectural norms. Contemporary shop fronts featured large plate-glass windows that more effectively display items within.

Local government officials and residents speak of their desire to maintain consistency with the historical character and design of the neighborhood, like the efforts of one local ANC to have development companies like Insight Property Group (who oversaw the destruction of Murry's grocery store and the H Street Storage facility) adhere to the corridor's "historic building fabric." On the other hand, several of the retail businesses that previously served longtime residents before the new development, like check-cashing facilities, carryout eateries, discount stores, and liquor stores, are primarily secured by both steel security gates on the exterior and bulletproof glass on the interior, creating a discordant image of the corridor's revised aesthetic vision.

The corridor is also littered with vacant storefronts that are protected by steel security gates. Anwar Saleem wants to rid the corridor of the menacing gates and bulletproof glass that, for him, are aesthetic symbols of H Street's violent past and in direct contrast to the area's transformation and prosperous future.[42] Nevertheless, some business owners, many of whom are African and Asian immigrants, are afraid to remove the doors, also known in the security industry as "riot architecture," for fear of robberies and/or violent break-ins. Both security measures make the shopkeepers "feel safe" regardless of whether a violent encounter has occurred in the space. For these business owners, the gates operate as a symbol of security. They must be taught to undo race and the racial implications of the gates. The new shopkeepers have not arrived with the same baggage or experience of requiring these symbols of security, since their customers have disposable income. The gates are visual and auditory markers that connect to the meaning of the space.

Saleem shared that he believes businesses applying for local government retail grants should be prohibited from utilizing the steel security gates. The local government's primary role is to enhance the entrepreneurial aspects of H Street's transition. Saleem's suggestion that the local government agency provide grants to entrepreneurs along the corridor revises the role of the state as a caregiver to a body of management in which the state dictates the aesthetic boundaries of urban space. In other words, the local government decides which individuals to reward and which to punish based on the role aesthetics play in organizing and assigning value, designating worthiness, and packaging forms of enterprise.

The trouble with this logic of barring businesses with steel gates from receiving government funds is not about the legitimacy of the business owners' fears. Original need for the gates arose in inner-city neighborhoods during periods of social turmoil, economic decline, and disinvestment. Especially after the 1960s, cities implemented architectural changes in neighborhoods all over the country. Defensive, disciplinary architecture like those steel security gates, large concrete walls, barrel-shaped "bum-proof" benches, and barbed-wire fences effectively produced and policed social boundaries through architecture.[43] Soon after, city officials, business owners, policy makers, and developers began to address these conditions by using "urban revitalization" as a strategy—precipitating gentrification—rather than fostering equitable development.[44] Both crime and fear came to be explicitly linked to Black bodies where the process of criminalizing Black people (as the primary offenders, not victims of crime) produced a fear of blackness. The result was the implementation of riot architecture in primarily lower-income Black communities. For some cities, ridding the buildings of riot architecture is part of a strategy to dictate what information the architecture of these urban spaces conveys and transform how the neighborhoods are experienced. Nevertheless, repealing the riot architecture does not delink blackness from fear or criminality, but it does absolve the state from taking responsibility for perpetuating systemic racial inequalities by disengaging racial inequality from history and social relations of power. What remains is the labeling of objects and spaces as Black even when Black bodies are not present, underscoring the ways in which urban decay and ruin are often attributed to blackness. Despite his support of Black businesses and residents and his desire to maintain a culturally diverse neighborhood, in his promotion of neoliberal strategies to create an equivalent playing field, Saleem only reinforced the state's absolution in responsibility for maintaining social and economic inequities.

Consuming Diversity

Culture and race in the age of neoliberalism affectively shape how we see, feel, and taste diversity, blackness, and authenticity. The aesthetic elements of neoliberalism make diversity a perfect rejoinder, especially in terms of the goods we can consume directly. Sociologists, geographers, and other social scientists have written at length about the role of consumerism, consumption, capital, and changing political economies of cities.[45] What undergirds much of these changes is the way that gentrification represents a phase in urban development in which consumption, aesthetics, and taste have led to an "imagineering of an alternative urbanism to suburbanization" in global cities.[46]

Richard Florida describes approaches for remaking urban spaces as U.S. and Canadian cities introduced urban planning practices that targeted the addition of a "creative workforce."[47] His theory about the "rise of the creative class" posits that a "new" upwardly mobile class will work and reside in places that have strong creative and arts industries, as well as racial and ethnic diversity, café culture, art districts, unique architecture, and a strong and vibrant nightlife. While Florida has been hired to consult with U.S. and Canadian city planners in their rebranding efforts, his neoliberal approach to urban design and planning focuses on the creativity of individual "entrepreneurs" and absolves the government of responsibilities to support wage earners in an economic environment "that increasingly privileges self-employed freelance labor."[48]

In D.C., former mayor Adrian Fenty's vision to buttress the city's growing creative economy resulted in the development of the "Creative DC Action Agenda," which his administration introduced in order to "support creative employment and business opportunities, to promote revitalization and enlivening of underserved areas through arts and creative uses."[49] The discourse of "creativity" works in alignment with "diversity" and provides a charming backdrop for cultural consumption. Some narratives reinforce local discourses on shopping and dining that frame the consumer as an independent and active agent. These discourses, Arlene Dávila argues, "further a romanticized view of consumption and consumption sites as democratic spaces that are open to everyone, whether one comes to shop, browse, or hang out."[50] Adopting this view only hampers an investigation of the "existing social inequalities that are actively reproduced in these spaces."[51]

H Street, like many postindustrial, urban commercial corridors, operates as a "space of consumption."[52] The role of commercial entrepreneurs is tied to the development of H Street privileging consumption in three meaningful ways. First, store owners represent the interests of a *cultural community* that operates in direct contrast with longtime residents. We see this with the explosion and expansion of boutique businesses that cater to an upper-class clientele, actively displacing stores that offer retail and services to long-term, lower-class residents. Second, retailers (as well as developers and investors) enter the consumption space in search of *economic opportunity*.

In the public imagination, everyday people are thought to be the agents of change. However, within revitalizing spaces that are considered ripe for economic opportunity, developers and investors work alongside business owners to enact change. Larger-scale development projects whose ground floors are occupied by custom coffee houses, craft-based retail, and high-priced restaurants dictate the changing landscape, leading to the final way H Street privileges consumption: retailers act as *social entrepreneurs* as they establish social spaces that invite new residents and tourists, while alienating longtime residents and visitors.[53] In this way, spaces of consumption also draw on representations of authenticity in order to fulfill the needs of new residents, thereby enabling them "not so innocently—to stake their own claim to the neighborhood."[54] On H Street, this was a gradual process. As discussed in chapter 2, disinvestment, urban renewal, and construction of the streetcar tracks all contributed to the downfall of the corridor's commercial infrastructure that had supported the needs of its working-class, predominantly Black population.

Within this commercial space, consumption, authenticity, and aesthetics work together. Contemporary discourses of "healthy, clean, and sustainable living" help drive consumption of food products and patronage of certain stores, like Whole Foods, and places, like farmers' markets. These discourses are reinforced by an ethical mode of consumption that is commodified and marketed as responsible. How do these tastes become indoctrinated? The tastes become part of the culture,[55] a structural phenomenon that has temporal and geographical consequences. The aesthetic itself may change across time and space, but the benefactors do not change much, especially along racial lines. That said, blackness is rarely something that reflects high culture or taste. In a modernized space, blackness can accompany or be used as a side dish, but not usually the main course. Consumption is important, but what exactly is being consumed in these spaces? Quite obviously we can look at food as one element that is being consumed, but it is not just the food; it is also the experience. Even restaurants that feature cuisine from various parts of the world have adopted a diverse and eclectic way to incorporate various cultures onto one menu.

Within these neoliberal spaces of consumption, no longer are we interested in contained cultural spaces that have businesses that either cater to or represent a particular ethnic group. Instead, we seek diversity within one location, alongside the increasingly common, seemingly universal establishments that sell raw juice blends, cupcakes, coffee, and pet-grooming services. As a space of diversity, the neighborhood brings to life ideal diverse and creative public spaces to produce individuality, creativity, difference, and social interaction.[56] But Black people fear improvements to Black spaces because the shift will invite others to take over. The conundrum of making the space more desirable is that others will discover it and want to take over, like in other neighborhoods and cities.

Haute Culture and Cuisine

The H Street corridor is organized into three sections—residential, retail, and arts and entertainment[57]—but these categories cannot be contained in such a discrete manner. The force of capital makes the boundaries porous; therefore, the most lucrative elements expand beyond their designated edges, and hence the introduction of more and more restaurants and bars. Strategically, city planners and local government actors attempt to transform blighted urban spaces through art and culture as part of the city's symbolic economy.[58] In particular, the deployment of ethnic cuisine as a form of aestheticized difference relies on "the exotic pleasures of 'visible' and 'edible' ethnicity" and emerges as "more or less neoliberal schemes engineered to 'sell diversity.'"[59] Related to this is a conversation about cultural food appropriation. One argument suggests that white people are stealing ideas from people of color and profiting off of their labor and ideas. Others argue that white people aren't the only ones stealing, but people of color steal ideas from other marginalized groups. So, the logic is, everyone is doing it, not just pioneering, racist white people. On the surface, both are correct. White purveyors, who typically have more capital to start and grow a business, do profit from the ideas generated from other cultures. At the same time, ethnic and racial minorities do borrow or take recipe ideas from others in their culture in order to build a successful business.

Food culture is a contentious area and is tied in many ways to history, region, class, and race. When we think about Indian street food or Vietnamese pho, these items were deemed low class. Today, fine dining menu items include some of these dishes. What matters here is meaning. For example, when pho is sold at a fine dining restaurant that is owned by white people, one can argue that it has a different meaning (and often price point) than pho sold at a small storefront run by Vietnamese immigrants. This argument is significant as we think about the relationship between food fusion and gentrification. The other argument, suggesting that people of color take from each other all the time, does not account for structure and the power of whiteness. That said, my focus on ethnic and exotic food along the H Street corridor has to do with questions of authenticity and diversity. Diversity in food culture is what adds to H Street's being a desirable destination.

The H Street, NE corridor is sprinkled with restaurants selling the trappings of a global village: Belgian mussels, Taiwanese ramen noodles, Lebanese falafels, German ales, Ethiopian injera—plus countless hipster bars, coffee shops, and bakeries. Unlike commercially constructed forms of ethnicity that represent diversity through ethnic-themed neighborhoods and their accompanying cuisines (e.g., "Little Italy," "Little Ethiopia," "Greektown," or "Chinatown"), the H Street, NE corridor produces diversity and authenticity through "creative-food" establishments that provide variations of local, organic, seasonal, ethnic, and/or fusion cuisine. The H Street Northeast Strategic Development Plan specifically incentivizes local entrepreneurs, including restauranteurs, to open businesses along the corridor. These restaurants are tied to the quality of life cities offer to middle-class residents, tourists, and corporate executives. Some scholars have argued that ethnic cuisine has been used to both construct and blur the "boundaries between categories of people"[60] through the current discourses of diversity and multiculturalism.[61] Along with the popularity of farmers' markets, ethnic cuisine acts as a metonym of difference and authenticity.

While many of the restaurants specialize in high-end ethnic cuisine, others, like Little Miss Whiskey's Golden Dollar, The Pug, and Palace of Wonders/Red and Black, structure their menus and décor around whimsical themes. In March 2012, I joined a walking tour of the H Street corridor that included seventeen concierges from Washington, D.C.–area hotels. The concierges organized the visit in order to learn more about the area so they could be knowledgeable about where to send hotel guests. Anwar Saleem acted as our tour guide. We visited restaurants like the now-defunct TruOrleans, which was started by three friends who wanted to provide "authentic" New Orleans Cajun cuisine. The chef and recipes originated from New Orleans and the interior décor included Mardi Gras beads and masks—reinforcing a popular narrative of New Orleans as a fun place to visit and party. We also stopped by Boundary Road, also now-defunct, which looked similar to many of the trendy, new eateries that provide their customers with a casual and upscale dining experience. Like other hipster establishments, Boundary Road's décor was minimal, rustic, and decidedly "urban" with exposed brick and communal tables, while the restaurant featured local, organic food with an extensive wine and beer selection. The physical elements of the space—relationship between inner and outside décor and spatial practice—all have social meaning: sparse furniture, unvarnished wood tables, exposed brick walls, murals, and vintage lighting. While Lefebvre notes that these objects and surfaces are reflexively governed by our social imaginaries, they also constitute the spatial practices that take place in and around these establishments, on the street, where they spend most of their time, their habits, and comfort in multiple spaces.[62]

Smith Commons, a three-story restaurant-lounge that specializes in craft beers, provides a similar casual-upscale décor with exposed brick, chalkboard menus, wood paneling, a fireplace, and dim lighting. The name "Smith Commons" refers to the owner's, Bailey Real Estate Holdings, cheeky idea to use a common surname—Smith—that would be easy to remember. "Commons" references the commoner who comes to dine in their restaurant. Adorning the only exposed side of the building that houses the restaurant is a mural called *Dusk of H Street* (figure 11). The graphic, commissioned by Smith Commons owners, is of a man with a rooster's head, who is opening his red cape to reveal a pastoral image of Yosemite. According to the mural's artist, Gaia, the image of Yosemite is a nod to an Albert Bierstadt landscape painting "referencing American manifest destiny and western expansion." Gaia speaks about the significance of this image being displayed so prominently on H Street and explains that in the image "virgin terrain is contrasted with an old vacant building on H Street which is a historically divested neighborhood currently undergoing a massive transition."[63] The realist imagery of Yosemite National Park painted on the wall of a Washington, D.C., establishment connects to the "frontier" notion of urban space being open to change, as if nothing was there before.[64] H Street can also be conceived as a spatial frontier—the border of the Hopscotch Bridge adds a barrier to those who are east of the train tracks, visually impairing those who are on H Street from looking westward to downtown. As Neil Smith argues, mapping the frontier line allows us to map the spread of gentrification.[65]

Gaia acknowledges that the neighborhood was divested, but presumes that it was uninhabited, "virgin" territory. *Dusk of H Street* evokes the popular narrative of the frontier, but in this contemporary story, the empty landscape isn't eradicated, but buffed into something desirable for consumption. That the primary owner of Smith Commons, Jerome Bailey, is African American contributes to a postracial future that relies on a race-neutral outlook, despite the inherently racialized rhetoric and imagery of "manifest destiny" and "western expansion."

FIGURE 11 *Dusk of H Street* mural that sits on the western wall of Smith Commons. Photograph by author.

Cuisine along the H Street, NE corridor operates as one of the discourses of ethnic cultural diversity. Establishments like Biergarten Haus, a German-themed beer house, invite a young crowd for an authentic German experience. They provide real Oktoberfest beers made in Munich and open at off-peak hours during popular European sporting events like the World Cup. Here, an ethnic German identity is folded into the ever-expanding multicultural story of H Street. Restaurants like Toki Underground and Ethiopic, while wildly different in terms of interior décor and style, provide "authentic" ethnic cuisine (Taiwanese and Ethiopian, respectively) that underscores the ways in which culture is deployed to increase capital. Toki Underground, which is ironically located on the top floor of a two-story building, above

The Pug bar, is a particularly popular destination for residents, tourists, and celebrity chefs. The concept of Toki Underground, as described by its chef-owner Erik Bruner-Yang, is "everything I love about being Taiwanese. Everything I love about Asian culture, food, art, and fashion."[66]

Like traditional ramen restaurants in Taiwan, the only other menu option besides ramen noodle bowls (and dessert) is a selection of Chinese dumplings prepared in a variety of ways. Within the first few years of its location on H, it was not uncommon to experience a two-hour wait time for two seats on a weekday evening. Toki Underground has very limited seating options (twenty-five seats), and like most of the newer restaurants along the corridor, the host uses new technology (iPad) to make reservations, organize seating, and store customers' mobile phone numbers so the host can text them when a seat is available. Diners are made to sit on wooden stools and eat on an elevated glass and wooden bar while gazing at the decorative walls covered in colorful graffiti, mounted skateboards, and Taiwanese toy figurines encased in glass. The tiny kitchen is fully exposed, and diners can watch the chefs prepare each meal.

Similar to sidewalk seating options, which John Jackson describes as the deliberate performance of middle-classness in Harlem, several of H Street's newer restaurants, coffee shops, and cafés feature rooftop patios and second-floor dining where customers can look down to those passing by on the sidewalk below. The configuration of the sidewalks in front of urban restaurants "is a rendition of public space with recognizable middle-class implications—and it signals, from afar, just who belongs and who does not."[67] Establishments like Toki Underground provide "presentational alternatives" and act as a "deliberate rejoinder"[68] to the Chinese carryouts and convenience stores along H Street that personify the space prior to its transition. Where Toki Underground and other newer restaurants offer an open but intimate private space to its customers away from the bustle of the street, the older carryouts offer sterile environments where shopkeepers and their employees serve customers from behind bulletproof glass.

Race and Whit(en)ing

While many of the restaurants, bars, and coffee shops along the H Street, NE corridor represent a distinctive culturally diverse collection, culinary signifiers of blackness remain. One notable example is Horace and Dickie's carryout, an eatery positioned along the H Street, NE corridor on Twelfth Street (figure 12). The restaurant is housed in a tiny, one-story, white con-

FIGURE 12 Good Friday at Horace & Dickie's carryout. Photograph taken at the 1200 block of H Street, NE, Washington, D.C., where there were few sit-down restaurants. © Joseph Young.

crete structure with bright blue trim and a small, blue, removable sign with the name of the business, identification of its culinary specialties (seafood and chicken), and its telephone number. The design of the building complies with most of the unpopular structures built in the 1980s and 1990s along H Street, in clear aesthetic contrast with the two- and three-story Victorian brick row house–style buildings that populate the corridor.[69] The carryout has one front window that is covered by steel security bars painted blue to match the blue trim surrounding the building. Inside, an illuminated menu sits on the wall behind the cashier and lists no more than fifteen items, while the space could probably accommodate as many as fifteen people at one time.

In February 2013, the *Washington Post* Food section featured an article about fried whiting fish fillets, a popular Washingtonian comfort food that is most notably prepared at Horace and Dickie's. The article highlighted the historical importance of fish and fishing—specifically, fried whiting fish— to Black communities across the country. Whiting, the inexpensive, bland fish (also known as "lake trout" in Baltimore) had particular significance in the mid-1970s when Elijah Muhammad's Nation of Islam opened popular fish houses in Harlem and Washington, D.C.[70] While most mainstream and upscale restaurant chefs are unfamiliar with whiting, the fish remains popular among Black Washingtonians, and Horace and Dickie's, which was featured on the popular Travel Channel program *Man vs. Food*, continues to be a favorite neighborhood jaunt for longtime residents, new residents, and visitors to the H Street, NE corridor.

The popularity and present-day success of Horace and Dickie's, recognized immediately by the long lines that spill out onto the street during the lunch and dinner rushes, demonstrate the ways in which food remains a crucial part of the remaking and reimagining of H Street—yet the carryout's prominence in this space is now different than in the past. In the article, Black Washingtonians share stories about their love of Horace and Dickie's and how the food evoked positive recollections of family and community in the 1990s. Fried whiting sandwiches from the carryout conjure positive memories, as one couple notes, "It reminds us of past times."[71] The narrative provided by the *Washington Post* adds context to the history of Horace and Dickie's and ties its notable links to Black Americans and fishing during slavery. The story also creates a palpable narrative that adds cultural value to the presence of eateries along the historic corridor, as it offers legitimacy to an establishment that could be otherwise recognized as a symbol of H Street's unpleasant, recent past.

Horace & Dickie's opened in 1990, at a time when the culinary signifiers of blackness gestured toward segregation and urban blight. Fried fish and other traditional comfort or "soul" food entrees were historically essential to members of the Black American community as they migrated from the South. The preparation and consumption of soul food were symbolically linked to the impropriety of blackness, accentuated by the heaviness, greasiness, and unrefined nature of the food, and as a result, the eating habits of Black southerners were "naturalized as a matter of racial difference," and in contrast to white southern food choices, were "used as explanation and justification for segregation."[72] As cultural historian Camille Bégin writes, the restoration of southern-style cuisine after the Great Migration "took place in the northern and midwestern Black metropolis, itself a crucial site of cultural and sensory identity building for the modern and urban African-American community."[73] Fried whiting, particularly in Washington, D.C., has operated as "a symbol of the racial divide that has defined the city for decades."[74] Now, culinary signifiers of blackness are indicative of diversity and multiculturalism where blackness is not located in terms of the social arrangements of race and practices of blackness but is transformed into a normative multicultural idea.

Horace and Dickie's, which opened the same year that Mega Foods shut its doors, prevailed in the shadows of those restaurants and food stores that catered mostly to Black patrons, with Black owners who were engaged in enterprises that supported the community, like Mega Foods and later De Place: Institute of Healing and Happiness, a Black-owned, vegan restaurant in the 400 block of H Street, which closed in 2005. Some of the Black food establishments that offered a wider selection of foods were not patronized as regularly as Horace and Dickie's. Some blamed Black people for not supporting these businesses (as William Raspberry did in a 1992 article in the *Washington Post*), without taking into consideration the structural conditions that undergirded their failure.

Black Diversity

The transition of blackness into a multicultural ideal is similar to what John Jackson identifies as a "racioscape," which he says "marks the color/culture compressions that pull far-flung corners of the African diaspora into greater and greater everyday contact" and speaks to "the inescapably non-*flow*like constancy of racial inequality as an effective analytical template for understanding globality, diasporic relations, and transnational interconnections in the past, present, and foreseeable future."[75] The success of popular establishments like Sidamo Coffee and Tea (2006), Ethiopic (2010), and Addis Ethiopian Restaurant (2014) by Ethiopian immigrants are offered as ideal examples of "freedom and opportunity" bestowed upon entrepreneurs along the corridor as they "came here in search of the American dream to become an entrepreneur." The presence of these businesses signals a link between culture and diversity, fairness, and representation.[76]

Sidamo Coffee and Tea is a small, quaint shop on the western edge of H Street, owned by husband-and-wife team Kenfe Bellay and Yalemzwed Desta. The shop, named after an Ethiopian province known for coffee, features coffee blends not only from Ethiopia but from several other countries in Africa as well. The casual space has five small round tables along the wall and one high-top table in front of the large bay windows with a perfect view of H Street, NE and Fifth Street, NE. Sidamo treats its customers with a slice of Ethiopian culture each Sunday at 2:00 P.M., when the shop owners perform a thirty-minute traditional Ethiopian coffee ceremony. Yalemzwed Desta, or her sister, Yenu Desta, dresses in traditional garb and lays a green carpet on the sidewalk in front of the shop. Desta then roasts coffee beans over a propane flame while burning incense. Once the roasting process is complete, Desta walks around the shop for customers to smell the aroma. The beans are then ground and added to boiling water to make a particularly strong brew. Small cups of the fresh coffee are passed out to customers, along with a small batch of popcorn.

Ethiopic was opened in 2010 by another Ethiopian husband-and-wife team who were dissatisfied with the choices of Ethiopian cuisine in the District. The building where the restaurant resides was a former drug rehabilitation center. The space is beautifully decorated with Ethiopian paintings and sculptures, and columns adorned with letters of the Ethiopian alphabet. It is the marketability of diversity as multiculturalism that encourages particular expressions of culture in spaces like restaurants and coffee shops. In her discussion about neoliberalism's capacity to deploy multiculturalism, Jodi Melamed writes that neoliberal policy "engenders new racial subjects, as it creates and distinguishes between newly privileged and stigmatized collectivities," like Ethiopians, who have had a long and distinct history in Washington, D.C.[77] Under these conditions, we see how Black difference is expanded and no longer tethered to Black Americanness.

The H Street Organic Market, which opened in 2014, was located in a 3,000-square-foot facility on the northwest side of H Street, NE at Eighth Street, NE. The market was originally named Chez Hareg Organic Market after Hareg Messert, an Ethiopian native and former Ritz-Carlton pastry chef who distributes her vegan baked goods to regional Whole Foods Markets and who recently inked a deal with Costco Wholesale to distribute her vegan cookies.[78] Her cousin, George Ayele, owner of the H Street space, decided to change the store's name because Messert is not yet prepared to carry her popular cookies and pastries at the new location. Replacing the former Z-Mart dollar store, the market received an $85,000 Great Streets Initiative program grant from the office of the Deputy Mayor for Planning and Economic Development (DMPED) to reconstruct the building.[79] The store featured products from local farmers who participate in H Street NE's weekly farmers' market.[80] While the organic store was a stark visual contrast to the surrounding Chinese carryout, liquor stores, and check-cashing facilities, it catered to new (overwhelmingly white and upper-middle-class) residents. The excitement around the opening of the H Street Organic Market[81] demonstrates the marketability of diversity and authenticity in contrast to the Disneyification and Walmartization of America, where both are deployed as a way to encourage "real estate developers to reinvest and

[make] urban living marketable."[82] The H Street Organic Market operated as both a farmers' market and an ethnic food store, therefore fulfilling the need for "nostalgia for 'authentic' neighborhoods," which Sharon Zukin calls "traditional social spaces outside the standardized realm of mass consumption."[83] Even with plans to introduce the Whole Foods Market that arrived to the corridor in 2017, the H Street Organic Market's firm identity as a small, local, organic market owned by Ethiopian immigrants works synergistically with the organic superstore, despite their direct competition for customers because, as Zukin argues, "it is this synergy that creates the meaning of space as a whole as a site of authentic cultural consumption."[84]

The owners of Sidamo, Ethiopic, and the H Street Organic Market are all examples of what Herman Gray calls "self-crafting entrepreneurial subjects," those "whose racial difference is the source of brand value celebrated and marketed as diversity; [subjects] whose very visibility and recognition at the level of representation affirms a freedom realized by applying a market calculus to social relations."[85] H Street's Ethiopian restaurants and stores conform to a preferred aesthetic that places recognizable Ethiopian cultural symbols on display for the enjoyment of their customers. Their presence and activities add to the "authentic" diversity of the corridor while working in concert with recognizably Black American establishments like Horace and Dickie's to convey an interest in and acceptance of certain forms and amounts of blackness.

· · · · · ·

Each year in mid-September, H Street hosts its annual, one-day street festival. The street is closed to automobile traffic from the beginning of the corridor at Fourth Street through Fourteenth Street. Held for nearly fifteen years, the festival is one of the largest events in the city and is a huge tourist draw. Over 250 booths line the corridor, filled with regional food vendors, local and regional artisans, nonprofit organizations, and business merchants. The street is always crowded. Lines wind around the food trucks and food stands as local restaurants display their most popular fare. Crowds spill outside of the designated borders of pop-up cocktail and beer gardens. Tents are erected to advertise the campaigns of local politicians. Vintage cars act as artistic canvases, intricately designed and painted. Dozens of photographers wander the streets. Impromptu dance parties break out as local go-go bands perform covers of both classic and new hip-hop and pop songs. Culture and cuisine are on display as thousands of people pack the streets (figure 13). The festival is an apt representation of a "cosmopolitan

FIGURE 13 Festival and revelry on H Street. Onlookers watch street performers at the H Street Festival. Photograph by author.

canopy" that Elijah Anderson describes as a self-contained, social, exceptional space where people interact easily and "appreciate" diversity. The festival reflects a moment in time when a diverse collection of people of different races, cultures, and classes exist in the same social space.[86] Festivals like these are supposed to represent the best of the neighborhood or city. That is why they are *exceptional*, not a true reflection of the everyday or quotidian. People are often enthralled by these displays of diversity and camaraderie. The scene makes people feel good and safe. There is something desirable and inviting about diversity in this way.

Festivals have become an increasingly relevant component of the tourism industry. They encourage growth in economic activity, even during economic downturns. They are not only helpful in increasing economic growth but also helpful in establishing neighborhood identity and growing local tourism. They are part of the cultural economy, which is based on the production and consumption of cultural symbols like food, tourism, and art and on the spaces in which they are consumed (restaurants, galleries, offices, and the street). The annual festival on H Street firmly establishes the street as an ideal consumption space, one that focuses on producing gentrified spaces for residents and visitors to socialize and hang out but one that also caters to a particular lifestyle that actively reinvents the space.

H Street Festival was originally conceived of as a form of social preservation. Over time, the meaning and intentions shifted to accommodate interests in economic growth opportunities. In the 1980s, when the H Street Festival first appeared, residents and local business owners hoped to focus on the neighborhood's cultural heritage and economic independence in the face of state efforts to disinvest (various forms of political mobilization, racial and cultural awareness, and demands for social justice and fair/equal conditions in the face of urban decline). Organizing a celebratory event became increasingly important in the aftermath of the uprisings that precipitated a downward spiral of H Street's physical and economic conditions. At the time, the corridor was overwhelmingly Black and full of Black and Asian small business owners.

Today, H Street Festival is a visual smorgasbord of color, culture, art, and cuisine. It displays whimsy, joy, celebration, and diversity. According to the festival website, the event has successfully helped commercial building vacancy precipitously drop from 75 percent to 5 percent by using "arts as an engine for the growth for the historic neighborhood."[87] The festival is an opportunity to show off what is new along the corridor but also a way to attract more residents and customers. Anwar Saleem shared that he gets more applications for leases and interest in residences after the festival, hence the popularity of buildings like the Apollo. In this way, the festival puts culture on display in order to generate capital along the corridor. Nevertheless, while the festival helps draw in large, culturally and economically diverse crowds, the group of people who get to stay and live is much less diverse. For example, thirty-five of Apollo's residential units are designated as affordable. This means that tenants may only earn up to 50 percent of the Area's Median Income (AMI). For this building, the figure the D.C. Department of Housing and Community Development (DHCD) used is $108,600 for a family of four. As of 2017, studio apartments started at $1,800, while the affordable units can be rented for $808 only if the tenant makes less than $38,010 per year.[88]

The festival allows various actors and stakeholders to organize ways for the space to be seen, thereby establishing a clear relationship between economics and culture as being constitutive in developing urban spaces. Their desired view of the space combines history, celebration, growth, and diversity. What is significant about how we think and talk about diversity today is that while most people experience diversity in terms of race, they talk about it in terms of difference in exhaustive ways. As a discursive project, diversity is unable to address inequality, privilege, and power, especially when framed in terms of cultural consumption.[89]

With each passing year, H Street Festival becomes more and more popular, with crowds packing onto the streets awaiting musical performances, tasting gourmet and carnival foods, and buying trinkets and clothing from the eclectic collection of street vendors. The festival represents a culmination of the diversity elements that draw traffic into the neighborhood. It is this constructed multicultural urbanity that relies on a depoliticized ethnic cool that decontextualizes the history of the space.

As I have shown in this chapter, the role of diversity on H Street, and in other areas the push for diversity, is ironically supposed to be a postracial (race neutral) project, but it is saturated with and structured by race. To produce H Street as a space of diversity requires an elaborate collection of bodies, social forces, and processes that rationalize the presentation of issues within particular contexts. Within this space, blackness, as distinct and a central component of diversity, becomes an aesthetic tool that can be reflected in and extracted from architecture, food, and text.

5 The Corner

Spatial Aesthetics and Black Bodies in Place

. . . .

Blacks inhabit the street in an intimate manner, public space is transformed by private acts and this is "unnatural." The normative street is enforced as the linear or "straight" path—to stray from it is to enter black space. . . . . The street is public, private[,] and communal space. The street is a site of crime, paranoia, and titillation.

—J. Yolande Daniels, "Black Bodies, Black Space: A-Waiting Spectacle"

If you're on [Eighth and] H Street, at least when the strip mall is there, those who are around there, it sounded like U Street twenty years ago. People cussing somebody on the phone, the hollering, crazy people; it was like generally U Street back in the day. It was very familiar. It was their place. It was their home. It's interesting how that changes. It's not all good, but it's life, it's real, it's city, and it's D.C.

—Nizam Ali, co-owner of Ben's Chili Bowl

In an interview with *Biznow Washington, D.C.,* on August 28, 2017, Henry Fonvielle, president of Virginia-based developer Rappaport, spoke about one of the company's newest development projects on H Street: *Avec,* a $201 million, mixed-use building scheduled to open in 2019. *Avec* will replace the now-demolished H Street Connection strip mall that was built over thirty years earlier by the same developer. Sitting adjacent to the Eighth and H intersection, H Street Connection spanned two blocks in the center of the corridor where Black city dwellers wait for buses. When it opened in 1987, H Street Connection was heralded as the centerpiece of redevelopment efforts on H Street, as the neighborhood was still struggling to gain its footing following the 1968 uprisings and subsequent disinvestment and abandonment by the state and federal government. Its grand opening celebration featured Mayor Marion Barry, city council members, and two marching bands to commemorate the arrival of a Dart Drug Store built on the site where Catherine Fuller was brutally murdered in 1984 (figure 14).[1]

Northeast Redevelopment Is Hailed As H Street Shopping Center Opens

By Ruth Marcus
Washington Post Staff Writer

Mayor Marion Barry, D.C. Council members, two junior high school marching bands and hundreds of community residents turned out yesterday to celebrate the grand opening of the H Street Connection shopping center, the centerpiece of redevelopment efforts for H Street NE.

Once one of the city's most important shopping districts, H Street has been scarred by the 1968 riots that destroyed dozens of buildings and businesses, plagued by drug trafficking and street crime, and tarnished by the brutal 1984 murder of neighborhood resident Catherine Fuller by teen-agers who called themselves the Eighth and H Crew.

Yesterday's ceremonies heralded the arrival of a Dart Drug store on the site of the park where the gang set out to rob and kill Fuller, whose death helped spark an effort to revive the neighborhood. The beige brick suburban-style shopping plaza between Eighth and Ninth streets also houses a dry cleaner, a clothing store, a sandwich shop, a food market and a police substation. A new bank branch is to open next door in August.

"Out of her death, out of her crucifixion, came resurrection," Barry

BY ELIZABETH RICHTER FOR THE WASHINGTON POST

Barry cuts a ribbon for the opening of a shopping center on H Street, which, before the 1968 riots, was one of the city's most important shopping districts.

FIGURE 14 Marion Barry attends the 1984 opening of the H Street Connection strip mall.

While the opening of the H Street Connection in 1987 marked an important moment in the development of the corridor, the construction of *Avec* signals a brand-new era. Most of the H Street Connection stores provided basic services for Black people in the area that had previously been destroyed or relocated during the 1968 uprisings. Coupled with nearby public and private agencies that provided a social safety net, the center of the corridor supported the needs of its overwhelmingly Black and working-class inhabitants. The Chocolate City of the H Street Connection era was a city of services for its residents. The post–Chocolate City of the *Avec* era is a city of amenities. The corner of Eighth and H is the last relic from the past, and the changes are closing in on those who socialize and stake a claim there. This corner is also a site that exposes how and where the past and present-day meet. Once *Avec* is completed, the character and composition of the Corner will certainly change.

Where the previous chapter focused on claims of authenticity through various lifestyle amenities and practices, this chapter discusses the excess of blackness and how this excess works alongside diversity. Specifically, it asks, how does a Black corner interact with a diverse corridor in ways that aesthetically impact the transformation of space? I explore the spatial production of blackness through design, architecture, planning, and other means, and how blackness concurrently produces space. This chapter also highlights how blackness is spatialized on H Street, thereby imagining the role of geography in the production of blackness and the concurrent structuring of space through the aesthetic emplacement of blackness. I am informed by the work of Rashad Shabazz, who defines *spatialized blackness* as the ways in which "mechanisms of constraint [are] built into architecture, urban planning, and systems of control that functioned through policing and the establishment of borders [that] literally and figuratively created a prison-like environment."[2] In other words, spatialized blackness accounts for the ways in which the landscape impacts Black people's literal (im)mobility as well as their sense of (im)mobility through geographies of confinement and surveillance. The built environment shapes the movement of racialized bodies in the same way that these bodies shape the built environment. This chapter explores the processes and practices through which this space becomes racialized. The intersection of Eighth and H Streets, NE, or what I am calling "the Corner," metaphorically speaks to the transition of the H Street corridor and how Black people move within and through the space and is an illustration of how blackness has been mobilized into an aesthetic.

The Corner has had a particularly sordid history. As described in chapter 1, attempts to relieve this intersection of its reputation as the gathering place for the "Eighth and H Crew" came in the form of several plans for commercial redevelopment. Despite the physical changes and redevelopment efforts taking place at the center of the H Street corridor, the intersection of Eighth and H Streets was and continues to be a center of activity, and a meeting place along the corridor. This intersection resembles what John Jackson describes as a reconfiguration of public space that evolved after the introduction of the welfare state.[3] In comparison to the diversity of races and classes found at the eastern and western ends of the H Street, NE corridor, the intersection of Eighth and H Streets, NE is noticeably less heterogeneous, providing clear markers of working-classness and poverty. Or for some, like Trent Smith, a partner at D.C.-based development company Insight Partner Group, the space between Eighth and Tenth Streets "has been a dead zone, where you walk faster to get between the eastern and western ends."[4]

Prior to the closing of the D.C. Economic Security Administration and Family Services Administration offices in 2013, the space that stretched between Sixth and Eighth Streets, NE was often inhabited by scores of Black people, both young and old, perched outside the building, most likely waiting to be seen by agency representatives who provided family care and financial aid for poor D.C. residents. Although Sharon Zukin argues that race and ethnicity survive "on the politics of fear by requiring people to keep their distance from certain aesthetic markers" like baggy jeans and shaggy or shaved heads,[5] it is the aesthetic markers themselves, not fear, that produce blackness as style. In this way, the presence of these Black bodies reflects a different narrative from how a "Black" space would be identified in the past. Their presence is now valued as visible evidence of diversity—even by those who describe the area as sketchy or "a dead zone."

Although the Corner operates as a vital transfer point for public transportation, the sidewalk is used as a form of counter-privatization, in addition to a place for meaningful social exchange and congregation. In *Real Black*, Jackson offers a useful discussion about public and private life in Harlem. Private spaces previously existed within the home, but with the introduction of the welfare state, private became synonymous with the street, since the state's management and surveillance of the poor turned "what was once intimate seclusion into a matter of public record."[6] The street became the location where previously private activities, like wearing hair rollers or pajamas outside, and transactions took place. As a result, "access to privacy becomes a solely bourgeois privilege, and when this publicness is all one is allowed, privatization of public space may be the most obvious riposte."[7] Like those in Harlem, gentrifiers who have begun to move into the neighborhood surrounding H Street deem such behavior inappropriate. Longtime residents are no longer able to use the space of the neighborhood for their own needs. In particular, noise complaints have become a common touch point in the debate over gentrification throughout the country, highlighting disputes related to race, class, and culture.[8] For example, one longtime Black resident, George David Butler, spoke to the *Washington Informer* about his dismay at changes to the corridor. Butler spoke of an afternoon in 2011 when police arrived at the Sherwood Recreation Center "because the new members of the community complained the annual Father's Day celebration at Sherwood was too noisy." While the event served as an important celebration for longtime residents in their quest to build (or perhaps maintain) social cohesion, the fête, put on by H Street merchants, "has taken place over the past 30 years without incident."[9]

In order for the narrative of diversity and inclusion on H Street to survive and thrive (for developers, planners, and local government agencies to attract more attention to the corridor), blackness—as a representation of difference—should be explicitly visible. The containment of Black presence at the Corner makes blackness less intimidating, since the representation of blackness is intimately reduced to the body. The spatial arrangement of the Corner allows us, as Lauren Cramer notes, to visualize "a racial event that is typically impossible to see—the process of rendering a body as black."[10] Furthermore, the architecture of the space constitutes this event. It is through the design of gentrifying spaces like these that Black bodies become Black. Nevertheless, because blackness is everywhere visible, it becomes unremarkable, pervasive, and perhaps even pedestrian.

· · · · · ·

The original H Street Connection resulted from a public-private partnership organized to spur revitalization along the corridor. *Avec* is a privately funded building that will feature 419 apartments (forty units will be set aside for affordable rental),[11] a swimming pool, a community garden, and a rooftop dog park. On the ground floor, there will be 44,000 square feet of retail and space for sidewalk café seating, as well as three floors of underground parking for residents and shoppers.[12] In the *Biznow* interview mentioned above, Fonvielle shared his vision of H Street exuding a "hip quirkiness" that makes its landscape different from other neighborhoods in the city. Despite being touted as a distinctive space, the destruction taking place there joins a familiar narrative. In 2012, restaurateur Joe Englert made similar claims about H Street and described his hope that H Street would never look like Georgetown and would instead maintain its quirkiness.[13] For Englert, this meant H Street should be populated by local establishments rather than large, international retail brands. When asked what he believed precipitated the rapid changes taking place on H Street, Fonvielle credited Englert, the introduction of "unique" establishments like the German alehouse, Biergarten Haus, which accompanied the refurbished Atlas Theater, and the introduction of the long-awaited streetcar. But as demonstrated in previous chapters, the transition of H Street began several years before Englert opened his quirky bars and restaurants despite the fact that Fonvielle and media outlets claim it was his ingenuity alone that brought change to the struggling corridor.

Fonvielle explained that transforming the strip mall into a mixed-use development made sense in order to keep up with "today's urban taste."[14] He continued by articulating that the changing demographics of those moving into the District increases the need to enhance the quality of life for those "highly educated professionals both young and old [who] have been moving into the city seeking out an authentic urban lifestyle." Fonvielle's emphasis on and designation of "urban taste," "character," and "authentic urban lifestyle" combined with his expressed desire to fulfill the "needs" of the growing class of elite new residents creates an even larger division between the incoming white gentry class and the poorer Black residents and city dwellers who have started to leave the neighborhood. Incorporating higher price points and limited retail options reflects clear signs of exclusion as new restaurants, bars, and boutiques have replaced medical service providers, salons, and pharmacies. Fonvielle explicitly articulates these changes in the physical built environment, yet the relationship between urbanity and blackness is undergoing a transition just as stark and entrenched. "Urban" is slowly becoming disassociated with blackness and is instead a commodity for young, highly educated residents and visitors who want a "hip" and "quirky" experience. Fonvielle's comments reflect the notion that lifestyle amenities are understood as "needs" in this era, signaling authenticity's tie to design aesthetics that privilege the desires and tastes of the upper class.[15]

Today, the Corner exemplifies where the white spatial imaginary and the Black spatial imaginary meet.[16] Designated as the central retail and transportation hub of the corridor, the Corner and its impending transition reflect the inherent tensions between both spatial imaginaries: one, a homogenous space that is used for the benefit of investors, tourists, elite consumers, and residents, and the other a devalued space exposing how poor and working-class Black people use the city. There are three different themes or ideas in this chapter that I consider as I conceive of this spatialization of race (particularly in urban spaces). First, I focus on the significance of transit to the development of the corridor—specifically, what transit-oriented development means to the movement and containment of blackness and Black bodies in urban spaces. Then, I examine the relationship between Black containment and (im)mobility. Finally, I focus on the concept of the *unseen* (as distinct from invisibility), which I identify as an active and explicit practice that enables different groups of people to exist within the same space without meaningful interaction.

Transit-Oriented Development and the
Movement of Black Bodies

The H Street, NE corridor is a major transit site that links local trains, commuter trains, bus lines, the Metro, and now, streetcar services. Newer residents and visitors lament the corridor's limited transportation options (the closest Metro line stop, Union Station, is nearly one mile away from the center of the corridor), despite the fact that Eighth and H is the busiest transportation hub in the city.[17] After conducting a transportation and streetscape study, the D.C. Department of Transportation (DDOT) proposed short- and long-term improvements to transportation along the corridor by making it more bicycle- and pedestrian-friendly, hoping to reduce the prevalence of vehicle traffic on the street. DDOT proposed a $229 million streetcar system in 2005 to alleviate these concerns.

Streetcars were immensely popular among Washington-area residents in the late nineteenth and early twentieth centuries. It was not until the 1910s that buses began to replace streetcars as a modern, luxurious form of public transportation. In 1962, the last streetcar ran in Washington, D.C., in the face of the increasing popularity of personal vehicles (influenced by generous public subsidies for automobiles).[18] The resurgence of the streetcar in the twenty-first century emerged within an economic climate in which several cities and metropolitan regions looked for sustainable development solutions in primarily lower-income, historically disinvested neighborhoods. Rather than emphasizing equitable development plans for families and individuals who have increasingly been displaced from transitioning neighborhoods, cities have coupled development solutions with designs for people to become more "environmentally friendly." For D.C., the streetcar became part of the District's plan to "improve transit services available to residents and create walkable, vibrant communities."[19] In 2008, D.C. began the long and disruptive process of laying streetcar tracks along H Street at a time when the neighborhood and the city were undergoing a demographic transition. As discussed in chapter 2, the process wreaked havoc on several local businesses, especially Black-owned service businesses, which lost clients as a result of inadequate parking.[20] After years of planning and construction, the new streetcars arrived on H Street on February 27, 2016. The D.C. streetcar, run by the French company RATP Group, costs the city $8.8 million annually.

Efforts to revive the streetcar system are about providing a public transportation alternative but are primarily a strategy to draw visitors to H

Street—thereby producing development that is both transit and tourism oriented. With a small fleet of six vehicles, the streetcar line spans just 2.2 miles and takes less than twenty minutes to travel from one end of the line to the other. While the route begins on the corridor, the streetcar is proposed to become part of a thirty-seven-mile expanded system expected to reach all eight wards in D.C. At first, the city planned to charge riders the low price of $1 for those with a SmarTrip card and $2 cash, which would be significantly less expensive than most rides on the Metro and a single ride on the bus. Instead, rides on the streetcar are free, and as of March 2017, the city announced plans to keep the rides free indefinitely. With over 3,000 daily passengers, the streetcar's popularity exceeded initial expectations of 1,300 daily riders. However, because of its limited route, most detractors see the streetcar line as a misguided marketing tool that provides a train to nowhere. Given the neighborhood's infusion of massive mixed-use buildings over a short period, it is no wonder initial expectations of streetcar ridership were surpassed. According to the Washington, D.C. Economic Partnership, since 2015, thirteen residential developments either have been completed or are under construction within two blocks of the H Street, NE corridor. Nearly 200,000 square feet of additional retail space are slated to be incorporated into the street's landscape, mostly beneath the residential units.

Since the early 2000s, there has been increasing interest by planners and policy makers in Washington, D.C., to promote transit-oriented projects and policies.[21] Implementation of the D.C. streetcar system is part of the city's plan to "ensure promotion of mixed-use, transit-oriented development where it has not historically occurred."[22] Transit-oriented development (TOD) encourages the development of high-density, pedestrian-friendly areas that are in close proximity to environmentally friendly public transit.[23] TOD practitioners integrate "smart growth" and new urbanism strategies into their projects, which encourage easy access to a blend of residential and commercial real estate, while enabling residents to live close to public transportation options. TOD is a key feature for transit projects, like the D.C. streetcar. TOD has become increasingly popular in cities around the country, as it is shown to promote economic development by increasing property values and tax revenues, thereby justifying the high costs associated with building transit systems.[24] Furthermore, TOD projects are expected to stimulate economic growth and improve the environment by limiting harmful emissions that pollute the air, thereby developing environmentally sustainable and economically thriving communities.[25] TOD works alongside other neoliberal measures that attempt to increase the value of the land and attract foot traffic. Nevertheless, scholars have expressed concerns over the impact of TOD investment on the transition of lower-income neighborhoods into high-income areas, thereby facilitating "transit-oriented gentrification."[26]

From cities like New Orleans and Portland, where streetcars currently exist, to Detroit and Los Angeles, where they are under construction, the streetcar is a major component of local strategies to attract residents, businesses, and tourists. Like these cities, in D.C., what underlies these plans for economic development and "sustainable" transportation are "assumptions about the need to establish a 'creative city' through amenity growth," which results in TOD measures targeting young, "creative," white, upper-income professionals.[27]

Historically, transit systems have been integral to the lives of Black people as they have had to contend with issues stemming from unequal, segregated public transportation facilities to diminished funding for essential bus lines, evidence of how racialized spaces develop in D.C. and beyond. In 1956, while Black leaders were attempting to integrate schools via *Brown v. Board of Education*, the Eisenhower administration passed legislation that funded the interstate highway system, which dissected and destroyed Black neighborhoods and provided vast subsidies for white suburban homeownership. This multibillion-dollar investment by the federal government facilitated deindustrialization as well as the spatial and economic containment of Black people in urban cores with few economic resources and government investment. As Patrick Sharkey notes, the United States is exceptional in its lack of investment in public transportation for city dwellers, since "the policy choices that have been made over the past century frequently have torn urban neighborhoods apart while providing incentives for urban residents and businesses to depart the city."[28] The irony, of course, is that transit is increasingly an important component of redevelopment in major U.S. cities, especially within neighborhoods that are (were) predominantly Black and poor. Today, buses and other forms of public transit "are not more segregated than neighborhoods, jobs, or schools, but in a society where race is coterminous with space, transit vehicles are sites where segregated worlds collide."[29]

The District continues to focus on transit-oriented development on H Street despite the presence of popular bus routes that already exist on the corridor, which is an indicator that such development is about more than providing transportation. Several of the bus lines that run along the H Street corridor have been popular among Black residents and continue to be invaluable for their movement through the city. Anchored at the Eighth and H Street intersection, the X2, which gets 20,000 passengers per day, rides from the Minnesota Avenue Metro station, east of the Anacostia River, along H Street to the White House.[30] The current streetcar route duplicates a portion of the existing course of the X2 bus line. The bus lines that drive through the corridor have been especially useful for transit-dependent Black residents who were transferring to lines that ride east but also for those who needed to stop at some of the service agencies that were on the corridor. In the 1980s, when Mayor Barry established H Street as a prime location for various local social service agencies, having uncomplicated access to the corridor, especially the Eighth and H intersection, was key. The Corner was where people also hung out as they waited for their appointments or rested before having to travel back to their homes in other parts of the city. This was the case until 2013, when two of the last of these agencies, the D.C. Economic Security Administration and Family Services Administration offices, were removed from the corridor during the Gray administration. Where previously the buses that traveled along H Street provided a means to reach important services, with their removal, the Corner operates as a space of transition. Since the social service offices were removed from the corridor, lower- and working-class Black people did not need to stay on the corridor. Also, with very few spaces for seating outside of the benches at the Eighth and H intersection, dwellers are not invited to sit for a while. The design in conjunction with the closing of these offices ensure that Black people move through, not stay along, the corridor.

The relationship between the new streetcar system and the long-standing bus lines highlights the distinctive operation of race, spatial mobility, and transit in this transitioning space. The D.C. streetcar represents "carefree travel" for white, upper-income, mobile tourists, residents, and consumers, while the bus represents *travel as labor* for the largely transit-dependent, poor and working-class Black District residents.[31] Specifically on H Street, the X2 bus is a micro-geography that passes through a gentrifying space where these residents are seemingly more and more out of place, and therefore immediately marked as other.

Establishing the Corner as an integral transit location and transportation hub means that Black bodies are ephemeral, tied to the space but only temporarily. Implementation of the streetcar system on H Street signals permanence, given the cost and labor it would take to remove the tracks, and changes how the street is used. Maintaining the visibility of Black people at the transit corner fosters spatial containment and regulation, while also providing opportunities for surveillance. The Corner has effectively transitioned from a space where Black people could gather to wait for their service appointments and socialize, to a space that intensifies their visibility. The Corner is an important site for Black dwellers to fulfill their transportation needs as they traverse the city. At the same time, the organization of the intersection maintains the city's commitment to achieving a diverse population along the corridor through black aesthetic emplacement. Nevertheless, preserving the bus transit transfer point in its current location is not a strategy to help poor and working-class Black people maintain viable, affordable options for transportation. Instead, it is recognized as part of a wider system of transportation that serves as a universal necessity so that *all* city residents benefit from the walkability of the neighborhood.

Black Containment and (Im)mobility

Movement, as migration, is a central component of African American tradition. Yet, Black Americans have historically been spatially and economically confined to particular areas and conditions, and thereby limitedly mobile. As George Lipsitz writes, the "desire to move freely across space formed an important part of the Black spatial imaginary, but it has rarely been easy to translate hopes of moving freely into the ability actually to do so for African Americans."[32] Historically, there have been several ways that the state has limited movement since slavery, like through convict leasing, Black Codes, loitering laws, redlining, restrictive covenants, racial zoning, redistricting (legal and illegal), increased incarceration and proliferation of prisons, and increased surveillance. Furthermore, mechanisms of surveillance and constraint have been built into the geography through architecture, urban planning, and other systems of control, thereby imposing certain limits on Black mobility.[33] In other words, blackness represents (and reflects) a particular unfreedom under capitalism. Shabazz argues that the significance of carceral power (and policing) impacted how Black subjects moved through both public and private spaces.[34] Whether they were in prison or not, these spaces were made to feel like prison. In terms of the Corner, planning materials show that the space was to be designed to allow for open visibility, which allows for (racialized) surveillance of "appropriate" behavior in public space. I agree that blackness is spatialized and also managed in particular ways that tether Black bodies to a space (via transportation and commerce); however, I am also arguing that they operate as a particular commodity for the commercial corridor. The presence of Black bodies signifies something in particular, something that speaks to the duality of blackness in the modern era—evoking both desire and disgust.

Gentrification poses a different set of conditions that impact the movement of Black bodies in transitioning spaces. As a result of the social and physical transformation, and neoliberal restructuring of previously undesirable neighborhoods (and cities), the built environment has been conceived and ordered, via design and architecture, to privilege white freedom and mobility while controlling and containing blackness. Therefore, it is important to acknowledge the significance of the street itself as it relates to gentrification and race. Neil Smith argues that gentrification is explicitly designed to reduce diversity on the street, and instead render and (re)claim urban space as a safe investment for the wealthy.[35] Gentrification is supposed to tame the unruly streets. Nevertheless, practices of gentrification that operate on H Street are contradictory: diversity is encouraged on the street but at the same time represses it. Gentrification promotes the freedom of movement (for white residents and tourists) while at the same time it establishes control and surveillance (of Black bodies) on the street. Black spatial containment occurs in conjunction with the changing demographic composition and look of the corridor. On both sides, with the increasing presence of high-end residential spaces and entertainment venues, the changes taking place on H Street are squeezing the center of the corridor.

The ways in which Black bodies (and blackness) continue to exist in the neighborhood have much to do with the layout of the corridor and its commercial landscape. Again, Black people can flow through the corridor, as transit riders, exposing an inherent duality to movement and containment, which both function as a means of surveillance. The racialization of space is built into the architecture and planning activities of the state—for example, through the organization of benches, corresponding riot architecture, traffic lights, and the design of transportation hubs. Furthermore, this racializing process plays out via several surveillance measures, like the implementation of security cameras and police patrolling. The curtailing of Black mobility is about both where Black bodies can be located and how Black people are monitored; therefore, (im)mobility is intimately connected to surveillance.

The Corner is perfectly situated and configured for surveillance—watching Black people. Monitoring and spatially restricting Black bodies are elements of what Simone Browne identifies as racialized surveillance.

Surveillance is practiced, narrated, and enacted through blackness, and surveillance is similarly structured by racism and antiblackness.[36] By recognizing racialized surveillance as a form of social control, one that reifies the boundaries of race, we can better imagine the spatial strictures that keep Black bodies in place and/or in transition. The intersection is a repository for all that remains from H Street's past—there is more of a police presence, prostitution zoning laws, and surveillance near that corner than any other area along the corridor. The optics at the Corner are in stark contrast to those at the other ends of the corridor. The intersection is one of two locations that has CCTV cameras installed by the Metropolitan Police Department (MPD), an explicit form of surveillance and monitoring.[37] The Corner has a particularly negative reputation for being an unsafe space, especially as police and news reports continue to pour in about incidences of criminal activity, mainly armed robberies, taking place at businesses that surround the intersection or on the corner itself.[38] Despite the intersection having a particularly negative reputation for criminal activity in comparison to the rest of the corridor, reported data show that few incidences actually take place at the Corner.

Between March 2008 and March 2018, there were 685 reported incidences of violent crimes within a 1,500-foot radius of the 800 block of H Street NE, and 4,034 reports of property crime. In contrast, the number of violent crime and property crime incidences within a 100-foot radius of the Eighth and H Streets intersection during the same period was thirteen and sixty-three, respectively (table 1).

Perception of criminal activities in and around the space have generated numerous reports and calls for the policing, management, and transformation of the intersection. The Corner is just one place that is illustrative of the conflicts over the city's public spaces and outdoor culture, where fear of Black bodies and spaces occupied by them have led to a variety of management efforts. Racializing surveillance operates as an important component of social and spatial control in gentrifying spaces. It enacts power to define what, or who, is in or out of place.[39] Surveillance of the Corner illustrates a clear effort by District agencies to assuage the fear of the space by upper-middle-class and white residents, at the expense of low-income and Black bus riders whose public behavior is often illegible to whites and therefore indistinguishable from illegal behavior.[40] As George Lipsitz writes, "because whiteness rarely speaks its name or admits to its advantages, it requires the construction of devalued and even demonized Blackness to be credible and

TABLE 1 List of reported crimes surrounding Eighth and H Street intersection, March 2008–March 2018.

Crime Type	Number of Crimes (within 100 ft)	Number of Crimes (within 1,500 ft)
Homicide	1	7
Sex Abuse	0	14
Robbery Excluding Gun	7	280
Robbery with Gun	1	187
Assault Dangerous Weapon (ADW) Excluding Gun	4	151
Assault Dangerous Weapon (ADW) with Gun	0	46
Total Violent Crime	13	685
Burglary	0	532
Theft	57	1,931
Auto Theft	5	1,252
Stolen Auto	1	317
Arson	0	2
Total Property Crime	63	4,034
Total Crime	76	4,719

Source: Metropolitan Police Department.

legitimate. Although the white spatial imaginary originates mainly in appeals to the financial interests of whites rather than to simple fears of otherness, over time it produces a fearful relationship to the specter of Blackness."[41] Thus, the blurring—or erasure—of the line between uncomfortable and unsafe is reinforced through the Corner's design and surveillance.

Police containment as a tactic, especially used as a way to keep "undesirable" people in place and out of view from middle-class residents and tourists, is an expressly racializing process. Theories of spatial containment have often focused on larger, segregated, ghettoized spaces that are inhabited by poor and working-class Black and brown people.[42] Containment takes the form of surveillance, as John Logan and Deirdre Oakley point out, notably the surveillance of those who have not yet been displaced by "revitalization" efforts in gentrifying neighborhoods like the H Street, NE corridor.[43] As I consider the significance of discrete spaces designated for poor and working-class Black residents, containment, surveillance, and spatial management, in conjunction with displacement, are central to questions about gentrification generally.

Michel Foucault's extensive work on space and surveillance indicates that space plays a critical role in the exercise of power.[44] There is a shared relationship between space and power. Not only do spatial forms matter, but we must also consider the social processes connected to spatial production. The visible presence of police provides a certain exercise power: to reduce crime, keep public spaces safe, and limit deviance and disorder. Cook and Whowell link (in)visibility as an important component of policing public spaces (specifically, parks, plazas, streets, and other spaces of sociability).[45] Furthermore, it is through visibility of certain bodies that undesirable behaviors and activities can be "policed" by the public.[46] Policing is "about making 'troubling' populations selectively invisible and visible in public space."[47]

In some cases, fear is produced and managed as it relates to economic development—security is framed as fundamental to a district's renewal and revitalization. Crime reduction and prevention, in particular, are not geared toward improving the lives of urban, poor, residents of color. In cities and neighborhoods that have had notoriously high rates of violent crime, sophisticated policing and surveillance strategies and technology are implemented to challenge these reputations and encourage community buy-in.[48] Christopher Mele shows that participation and acceptance by the community "legitimizes not only social control but also the neoliberal state's call for the urban poor to take responsibility for social problems and their own governance in place of an interventionist welfare state."[49] Various reader comments on local blogs that discuss the Corner and redevelopment of the H Street Connection site include those from self-described area residents who still avoid walking past Eighth Street "due to the large numbers of people who hang out on the corners" and others who avoid taking the bus altogether because the intersection is "just too sketchy, especially at night."[50] Though unsaid, race, in this way, operates as a cultural scheme for the production of difference (and danger), of which blackness is the chief signifier. At the Eighth and H intersection, the fear of looming, "sketchy" Black men and women on a busy street corner surrounded by commercial establishments produces blackness, like fear, as an aesthetic category.[51]

Consumption Junction

Adjacent to the Corner are several businesses that typically support a ghettoized economy—a convenience store, a Chinese carryout, a liquor store, an athletic apparel store, a nail shop, and a check-cashing facility, all of which

FIGURE 15 H Street's "ghetto economy." Photograph by author.

are adorned with riot architecture (metal, roll-down gates), as discussed in chapter 4 (figure 15). As much as boutique businesses have come to H Street in order to attract and serve an elite class of shoppers and amenities-seekers, the businesses that represent a ghetto economy serve the poorer class of people, catering not necessarily to their needs but to their economic condition, thereby creating a cycle in which they are exploited while trying to meet their needs.[52] For example, carryout restaurants provide fast, typically inexpensive food and were primary staples in neighborhoods that did not have open access to fresh food. Within the realm of urban redevelopment, and specifically "revitalized" commercial spaces, these Black subjects are meant to shop, consume products, and obtain services. As Christopher Mele argues, poor, Black residents "are rendered invisible in the narrative of development. Alternatively, they are made legible only as individual consumers who participate in development, or as individual deviants or criminals who pose a hindrance to the city's renewal."[53]

The types of businesses that surround the Corner help keep Black people in place. Since the corridor in general and the Eighth and H intersection in particular are being prepared for the continued arrival of "highly educated professionals," as developer Henry Fonvielle remarked, there is little space for the poor and working class to continue using H Street as a viable location. There are designated spaces for the Black and poor to remain so they don't "bother" shopkeepers, residents, and tourists along the corridor, as one local official admitted to me. One of the places is the Corner, at Eighth and H Streets.

This discursive and literal tethering of blackness to the corner of Eighth and H is also exemplified by critiques of those moments when blackness spills out beyond the Corner's designated borders. On a chilly winter morning in December 2012, dozens of young men and women gathered outside the Down Town Locker Room (DTLR) clothing store at the intersection of Ninth and H Streets. The crowd, who mostly hailed from D.C. and neighboring counties in Maryland and Virginia, gathered anticipating the release of the new retro Nike Air Jordan sneakers. Around 7 A.M., three men approached the line and one of them opened fire. According to police accounts, the suspects were attempting to rob people for their new shoes. The shooting was reported on several local websites and blogs as well as in the *Washington City Paper*. Photographs accompanying the story showed a large crowd of Black youth queuing up as police officers erected tape along the perimeter of the building.

The incident brought about dozens of implicit and explicit online comments about blackness on H Street. On the website dcist.com, several of the comments posted by viewers expressed their dismay that such an event could take place in 2012 and is instead reminiscent of H Street in the 1980s and 1990s. One commenter, "cardozomite," said: "I bet someone was playing Go-Go Music, too." Others questioned and analyzed Black "culture" and asked why Black people are so fixated with basketball shoes and "do they spend as much on business shoes or clothing?" This practice of indexing or coding race of this sort "rearranges the importance of racism and pitches its reality toward some group dysfunction."[54] Critiques of the "culture" of blackness are an irrational and irresponsible attempt to explain why Black people "choose" to purchase needless accessories rather than adorn themselves with apparel that enables them to take on the appearance of productive, laboring citizens. This critique also assumes that desire for Air Jordan athletic shoes cannot share space with the requirements of being a "productive" citizen. Indeed, this view of the limits of Black culture illustrates the myth of American exceptionalism under capitalism as it highlights the idea that any individual can choose to shed culture and cultural practices that limit their access to the American Dream. Instead, "phenotypically black people or youth sporting urban styles are always already interpellated as 'ghetto' or culturally and morally deficient."[55] This perspective also reflects an investment in the white spatial imaginary that Lipsitz argues leads people to think "that people with problems *are* problems [and] that the conditions inside the ghetto are created by ghetto residents themselves."[56] Rather than interrogating the social and economic conditions that encourage multibillion-dollar global brands like Nike and the National Basketball Association (NBA) to target young, working-class, and poor people of color to purchase their goods by idealizing (proximity to) basketball as a way to transcend poverty and achieve wealth and fame, this logic invites spectators to harp on the outdated ills of Black culture. At the same time, whiteness requires the devaluation and demonization of blackness in order to maintain power over space. So, as blackness spills beyond the borders of its designated space on the Corner, people conclude that "civic problems should be solved by displacing Black people and creating new homogeneous, pure, and prosperous spaces for white [people]."[57]

The incident at DTLR and the comments posted in response by area residents speak to the hypervisibility of Black bodies in particular locations along the corridor. As Neil Smith argues, gentrification is explicitly designed to reduce diversity on the street, and instead render and (re)claim urban space as a safe investment for the wealthy.[58] Gentrification is supposed to tame the unruly streets, thereby underscoring the significance of the street itself. Gentrification ultimately invites implicit contradiction. It celebrates diversity on the street and at the same time represses it. Gentrification promotes the freedom of movement while it establishes control and surveillance of the street. The negative feedback from the incident at DTLR reflects the boundaries of what Henri Lefebvre calls a spatial economy, one that celebrates certain behaviors and relationships between people in public places, thereby giving way to discursive conventions that determine which places should be "trouble-free, a quiet area where people go peacefully to have a good time, and so forth."[59] The comments especially bring to bear the notion that Black bodies need to be watched and controlled in order to prevent violence and unsavory activities. Individual personhood is rarely applied to Black people when crimes are committed, and instead the actions of one or a few represent the whole.

Unsightly and Unseen

Despite the hypervisibility of Black bodies on the Corner and in other locations along the corridor, there are several ways in which Black people—specifically, poor and working-class Black people—are not seen. In particular, as Simone Browne points out, there is a tension between Black, hypervisible legibility (under surveillance) and Black illegibility.[60] Racialized surveillance impacts Black bodies by making them more visible in some contexts but unseen in other contexts because modern technologies are calibrated to "see" and find whiteness. China Miéville's science fantasy novel *The City and the City* provides a useful metaphor articulating practices of "unseeing" within the urban spatial terrain. In the book, the post-Soviet, eastern European city-states of Beszel and Ul Qoma exist in the same geographic space, but citizens of each must learn to "unsee" the other, and social, political, and economic life operate seamlessly as separate. The cities are separated not by physical barrier but instead by customs and laws. Two buildings could stand alongside each other, one in Beszel and the other in Ul Qoma, but the inhabitants of each will not interact; they will not meet, speak, or glance at each other, no matter how close in proximity their bodies are to one another. Even as they walk side by side, Ul Qoma's citizens and tourists "see" a separate set of individuals, businesses, and public spaces, while "unseeing" similar objects, bodies, and spaces in Beszel. If citizens from one city are caught "seeing" citizens from the other city, they face severe penalties from the faceless, Orwellian authority, "Breach." Ultimately, this independent, surveillance, law enforcement body ensures that a cultural divide is built into the social and political architecture of the city as policy.

Elijah Anderson offers a similar observation when he discusses how urban pedestrians often "see but don't see" each other on the street, while they "look past" and "look through" the diverse sampling of strangers they pass daily.[61] For Anderson, skin color is the barrier that separates individuals in their daily interaction. The metaphor of "unseeing" has a much more significant and specific meaning and application as we think about spaces of inequality, especially those in American cities and neighborhoods where inequalities are racially inflected. To unsee is more than a refusal to recognize different political perspectives, but the act of unseeing, as a technology, structures how people operate in gentrifying spaces. By technology, I mean that unseeing operates as an external, rather than intrinsic, device that helps us navigate the geography upon which we live.[62]

In *The City and the City*, Beszel is the old, decaying city, dependent on investment from the United States, while Ul Qoma is a technologically, architecturally, and culturally progressive city with trendy, gentrified spaces of art and cultural consumption. The fictive city Beszel is just like the

Corner, existing as its own world. It represents the H Street of the past that was deemed deviant. Ul Qoma is like the new, bustling H Street corridor that flanks the Corner, with its new commercial establishments, trendy entertainment locations, and "diverse," elite clientele. Both the Corner and the surrounding corridor exist together, map onto one another, and produce their own subjects.[63] To unsee is a rejection of what lies beneath—namely, institutional racism and making connections between inequality and structural problems and policy.

Unseeing on H Street operates alongside the mechanics of surveillance, as some people are being watched but are not seen. Like the "Breach," surveillance at the Corner keeps bodies in place and maintains the order of things on the street. Surveillance structures how and whether people are seen. Unseeing also effectively secures the spatial privileges of whiteness and reflects the white spatial imaginary, which encourages the Rappaport developers to focus their efforts on the growing number of affluent, educated people "returning" to D.C. rather than those poor and working-class residents who are still in place or have been displaced from the area. The unseen are constitutively excluded from planning and development processes—even though they are ever-present, felt, and especially unaccounted for. While the Corner operates as a space of the unseen, those who congregate on the Corner are not invisible. People on the Corner are certainly visible to those who drive, walk, or ride by the intersection. In fact, as discussed above, they are necessary urban fixtures that signal the thriving diversity of the area. Visible but unseen forms of Black working-classness and poverty around the Corner organize how public space is managed on H Street, how diversity structures the neighborhood development, and specifically how Black subjects are produced through this process.

Unseeing is similar to "colorblindness," which encourages an individual to expressly disavow any ability (not desire) to recognize racial inequality, and in some cases, racial difference. The idea of "not seeing color," or really, unseeing color, signifies a willful self-fulfilling prophecy that allows white people to neither "see" nor acknowledge their own bias and the systemic privilege that benefits them. Colorblindness was enacted as a discursive tool that involved the monitoring of race so that institutions "can be sure they are making 'truly color-blind' choices." It signifies a condition, a racial logic that sets the terms for how we (should) live.[64] It asks the state to "not see" color. The logic behind colorblindness posits that the state's practice of recognizing and categorizing racial identities is a racist and discriminatory practice. The impact of this political framework was, as Keeanga-Yamatta

Taylor points out, that parts of the political establishment actively separated "Black hardship from the material conditions that activists worked so hard to expose."[65] Furthermore, colorblindness connects historic and contemporary discrimination to the baseless notion that "neighborhood configurations were shaped by 'freedom,' 'choice,' and cultural considerations, as opposed to redlining and racism."[66] Unlike colorblindness, through which people maintain that they "don't see color, but people,"[67] to unsee means that the agent does not actively see color, or in some cases, people. It is in the best interest of people who unsee Black people not to see them, especially those who are poor. To *see* them, to envision their lives and conditions, disrupts the narrative of urban progress.

Within the context of urban spaces, unseeing is executed by those in power, who benefit most from it. Unseeing makes space for investors, developers, city officials, tourists, and new residents to ignore the needs of those who existed in the space previously and to address these needs. To unsee is an active process accompanied by explicit practices that enable different types of people to exist in the same space without meaningful interaction. Where invisibility speaks to a vanished presence, being unseen is akin to being ignored, an overlooking that is structurally embedded, in favor of more aesthetic elements. For example, a few blocks down from the Corner between Eleventh and Twelfth is a light post tagged with a highly political and charged statement about H Street's rapid change: "A Gentrified DC" and the hashtag #IWILLNOTBEMOVEDDC. The statement is spray-painted in red in the form of DC's iconic "stars and bars" flag, with the image of a cassette tape hovering above (figure 16). When I walked by, the light post was flanked by a homeless Black man and Black woman. As I struck up a conversation with the pair, the woman shared her desire to move back to Virginia Beach, where she was from, because D.C. had become "unlivable." The woman carried, but had put down, a reusable bag from the popular and tony athletic apparel store Lululemon, which typically has store locations in posh neighborhoods like Georgetown and Logan Circle. On this warm Thursday evening in July, young, white passersby strolled down the corridor, in intimate proximity to the street dwellers without any regard, even as the homeless couple gazed in their direction. The scene was startling and uncomfortable to witness.

This experience led me to wonder whether it is possible to design a streetscape that is welcoming to the poor and homeless as well as "hipster" tourists and residents. Given the ways in which the state and private developers organize the space to privilege more affluent visitors, leading them

FIGURE 16
Antigentrification
public art on H Street.
Photograph by author.

to unsee others, the design and organization of the street demonstrate that this is not possible. Public spaces, especially in urban locales, are specifically designed and structured to minimize unpleasant encounters and "maintain a rigid power relation between Whites and people of color when such encounters do take place, while at the same time maintaining a veneer of unity and homogeneity."[68] While it is true that the poor and homeless are not explicitly ushered off the street, they are not made to feel welcome, as reflected by the design of the street and order of the built environment. There are few places for them to sit and be. None of the new development projects that have been recently constructed or are slated to be built provide space for those on the street to sit. The retooling of blackness as a part of the diversity strategy makes it seem as though differently raced, classed, and gendered bodies give way to the appearance that meaningful interaction is happening even when it is not.

To be clear, within the context of urban development and spatial reorganization, it is Black people, Black humanity, and the needs of Black poor and working-class residents that go unseen and ignored. Nevertheless, *Black bodies* are ever-present and hypervisible. "Unseeing" in this space is not as simple as claiming "I don't see them"; rather, it is an appraisal of what aspects of blackness the state, private developers, business owners, tourists, and residents want to keep, use, and fold into the narrative of H Street as a destination. Therefore, what is "seen" are exceptional, iconic representations of Black life—nostalgic, "more authentic, successful expression[s] of blackness,"[69] but not mundane Black life. Around the city, one can witness representations of Black people being gradually incorporated into stock images for new building advertisements and strategic planning materials, but with very little regard for the experiences of those who are already present. Along H Street, we see additional examples in the posters at Whole Foods celebrating the diverse culture (including African American culture), and images from Cultural Tourism DC's markers that identify the presence of Black people. More prominently, at the end of the corridor, a mural sits in the Starburst Plaza featuring images of two prominent national figures, Rosa Parks and Martin Luther King Jr., as well as two local celebrities who receive national and international attention, Duke Ellington and Marian Anderson. In these ways, blackness continues to exist in the space, helping to underscore H Street's "successful" transition into a diverse space. Therefore, while the structural inequalities are unseen, what is seen and recognized are these expressions of "authentic" blackness that fill the void.

· · · · · ·

Spatial practices of everyday life at Eighth and H, or any other part of the neighborhood, are ordered by the representations that urban planners, local officials, and developers construct. Planning maps, zoning restrictions, and other means order the spaces of cities by keeping land uses and people in their place through their ability to secure abstract space through the distinction of difference. As Sharon Zukin notes, social diversity is managed through the explicit visual representation of different racial and ethnic groups. This acknowledgment can reflect on a visual recognition of "past" oppression, since "establishing a visual order of cultural hegemony seems to equalize by identifying and making formerly 'invisible' social groups visible."[70] The presence of Black people congregating around Eighth and H does not necessarily point to the social and economic disparities between the longtime Black residents and newer white residents who inhabit the neighborhood, but instead shows evidence of H Street as a welcoming, inviting space for all—while maintaining a bit of edginess and perceived danger.

The Corner is the afterlife of the old H Street. The Corner is one of the only places left that reflects this former place. The Corner is a liminal space, temporary, since the terrain is rapidly changing. Within these newly developed spaces, there is no place to hang out anymore. You can go to a restaurant that has a sidewalk café, or you can shop in a store with a large, plate-glass window and gaze at the people on the street, but there is no place to be on the street anymore. Public spaces are transformed into consumption spaces. I use the location of the Corner to illustrate how the built environment is ordered to contain blackness in particular ways—specifically, the blackness that poor, Black bodies register. This chapter is about how Black people exist and move within the gentrifying space. The corridor as a whole is organized for transportation and commerce—specifically, in the tradition of new urbanism and smart growth. Transit-oriented development projects support this kind of development, which has been shown to displace lower-class and disproportionately Black residents. Instead of creating strategies that help Black residents have better access to the services they need, this kind of development ultimately moves them through the space. It does, however, keep them there for aesthetic purposes, hence my argument about the necessity of Black bodies on the Corner. They are needed, but their needs are not met. They are unseen, yet hypervisible.

The Corner signals both displacement and marginalization as the remaining Black population has been pushed to this space. Despite all the change, the Corner has been preserved—not for the inhabitants but for others. There is very much a *place* for blackness in a transitioning urban space. We talk often about displacement but less about those who remain. Sometimes Black bodies are not moved out but moved into a controlled space to be monitored. They contribute to the landscape in meaningful ways. They are evidence of aestheticized diversity but also highlight vestiges of the past (as Nizam Ali's comments at the beginning of the chapter demonstrates). Certainly, one might suggest that Hyra's assertion that white suburban residents move to the Atlas District because of their desire to "live the wire," but instead the dissonance is not necessarily desired by incoming residents.[71] While much of the literature might point to the desirability of certain Black bodies—

especially those that are nonthreatening—bodies like those at Eighth and H have particular significance for the blackness they register (i.e., edgy, gritty, authentic). They may not be necessary forever, however, because their location in this space is temporary as the terrain changes. Ultimately, the Corner signals where and how Black people can be in the gentrifying spaces.

In light of H Street's past, the narrative describing its history reinvents itself as multicultural in order to write the violent times away and repurpose the neighborhood for a new market and a new time. The excesses of blackness can be unwieldy if not disciplined, managed, contained, or deployed for proper use. What happens as a result of H Street's remaking is that the area has not been purged of symbols of blackness in favor of diversity; instead, blackness is transformed to become palatable and consumable while some of its edginess remains. Not only does the Corner spatially restrict the movement of the mostly poor and working-class Black people who spend time there, it is also a visual reminder of the H Street of yesteryear: a neglected, abandoned, divested, Black space.

H Street isn't exceptional, especially in light of neighborhoods like Shaw, U Street, Georgetown, and Capitol Hill, which are more readily recognized, researched, and well known. It probably looks like more commercial corridors in cities around the country. This story relates to more places, beyond neighborhoods like Harlem or the Mission District. We typically find these iconic areas where a cultural explosion takes place and we write about them in ways that make it seem as though they are the norm. On H Street that was not the case, despite the fact that developers, planners, boosters, and state actors are trying to hinge on this particular history of diversity and camaraderie—"this is a 'real' place." H Street is one of those regular places that get attention occasionally because of a new Whole Foods Market or other establishment. Because H Street was not exceptional, but mundane, elite actors and institutions are trying to produce something exceptional in their mundanity. H Street is an unfinished space, unfinished not only in terms of its planned development but also as a neoliberal project.

Conclusion

A Chocolate City Is No Dream

....

Black in Place is a story about H Street, about D.C., about chocolate cities, and about the United States. Ultimately, it tells a deeper story that H Street helps me frame: about the patterns and cycles of blackness and the ambivalent processes of how blackness is emptied out and built up again at different points and places. On H Street, what is emptied out is the historical production of the corridor as a space of danger. H Street is treated as an empty vessel, then filled up again with diversity. *Black in Place* invites a critical vocabulary for thinking about how to contest burgeoning inequalities. The problem is more complex than white people driving up costs in the city, or whether "good" gentrifiers exist. The book takes these things into account but moves toward an evaluation of how neighborhoods rebuild and rebrand themselves through contested historical narratives that are particularly salient in a new economy.

One of my goals for *Black in Place* was to examine the relationship between aesthetics and the ways that knowledge about race is organized to reflect a commonsense notion of how blackness is expressed, recognized, and visualized. While race and aesthetics are embedded and tangled together, neoliberalism repurposes and reassembles race. Blackness is something to watch, practice, perform, and duplicate. The persistence of racial inequality remains at issue today as it has historically, regardless of claims that we are beyond racial considerations, or are colorblind. I detailed the production of a narrative about place, and how blackness came to be mobilized to generate a nostalgic narrative about the neighborhood's multicultural past. Despite an interest in (need for) diversity, institutional measures introduced by the D.C. government were in direct challenge to sustaining traditional Black business ventures (like barbershops, beauty salons, etc.) and instead called for Black entrepreneurs to found "creative" and "innovative" businesses. Such policies and programs demonstrate how race operates today—not explicitly in its recognition of difference and the maintenance of inequality. Discourses of diversity make blackness one of many inflections. At the same time, H Street acts as a neoliberal zone that affirms blackness by using it as an entrepreneurial machine of development.

Various actors rely on representations of a neighborhood to direct funds and development. H Street is a place where difference acts as an enhancement. In light of H Street's violent past, the narrative describing its history must reinvent itself in order to write the violent times away and restructure the neighborhood for a new market and a new time. Nevertheless, the trace is present, even in the most aggressive attempts to eschew the past. It is through statements about diversity (as introduced by Whole Foods Market, local restauranteurs, the D.C. Office of Planning, Main Streets programs, etc.) that the political economy of the H Street, NE corridor is organized.

Despite neoliberalism's success in obscuring the origins and effects of inequality, it nevertheless operates collaboratively with the postmodern turn in which dissent is strategically enveloped, or perhaps, co-opted in the service of capitalism.[1] We learn from efforts led by Anwar Saleem to support the growth of Black businesses along the H Street corridor, that articulating one's disapproval of inequities sheds light on the issue, but despite valiant efforts to impart change, these efforts often reinscribe the stylization of blackness by simply calling for visible representation, often in the form of black aesthetic emplacement. These efforts highlight the challenges involved in building resistance against neoliberal logics, which tends to embolden postrace and colorblindness as commonsense and superficially celebrate diversity.

As I show, racism and other forms of inequality that take place on H Street, and in D.C. generally, are not overt, but subtle, where euphemisms like "creativity," "diversity," and "cultural vibrancy" are used to disinvite. I provide discursive sites—ethnic-themed restaurants and cuisine, crime, security, design, and architecture—to analyze the work of diversity as rooted in cultural and structural economy, which led to the resignification of public space. In the redevelopment of the H Street, NE commercial corridor, "diversity" is used to attract capital, customers, and tourists to the area. It is through the work of diversity that H Street emerges as a hip, yet edgy, district. Nevertheless, while diversity evokes difference, it does not provide commitment to redistributive justice.

Chocolate 'Burbs and the Suburbanization of Black Poverty

In spite of the tremendous economic growth Washington, D.C., continues to experience, the most pervasive poverty in the District has been among

Black Washingtonians. The increased cost of living—due to the policies city governments enacted to attract investment back to the city, bringing back wealthier residents, increasing taxable income and sales tax revenue through renewed retail activity—have left longtime Black residents living under precarious conditions. For example, in Ward 8 (one of D.C.'s two wards with Black populations reaching well over 90 percent), 38 percent of the residents are poor, compared with 26 percent citywide.[2] This phenomenon is, of course, the result of historical drivers like systemic racism, concentrated public housing, and zoning laws that keep the poor Black people out of wealthier neighborhoods. High rates of poverty among D.C.'s Black residents are taking place in conjunction with a national trend: the geographic shift of urban poverty to the suburbs. According to a 2010 Brookings Institute report, the suburban communities of some of the country's largest metropolitan areas "are now home to the fastest-growing and largest poor population in the country."[3] In the Washington, D.C.–metro region, poverty levels have increased significantly in the suburbs, as they have decreased in D.C. In 2008, 120,669 people in D.C. lived below the poverty level ($21,834 for a family of four), compared with 251,096 poor in the surrounding suburbs.[4]

Swelling property values, exorbitant rents, and increasingly higher taxes have led to the large-scale displacement of lower-income Black residents from D.C. Most of these residents have moved to neighboring suburban communities in Northern Virginia and Maryland, like Prince George's County. With the passage of historic legislation from Johnson's Great Society, African Americans who had been largely relegated to the crumbling central cities relocated to the suburbs, but primarily to neighborhoods inside the Capital Beltway because they were prevented or discouraged from purchasing homes in other areas. Prince George's County, in particular, went from being a massive, rural, majority-white, segregated area to the wealthiest majority-Black county in the nation, and income there continues to outpace the national average income. Since the 1970s, the Black population in Prince George's County grew from nearly 15 percent to 65 percent.[5] Black migration to the region put additional strain on the county's infrastructure, leading to ill-equipped public safety services, schools, and social safety nets.[6] Compared with D.C., Prince George's County, also colloquially known as D.C.'s Ninth Ward, has higher crime and poverty rates, and lower home values and student test scores. Despite its sizable well-educated, prestigious Black population, Prince George's County remains largely segregated and is the region's least prosperous county.

Narratives about the conditions and population of Prince George's County today are remarkably similar to stories about D.C., especially in the aftermath of the 1968 uprisings through the end of the twentieth century. With its purportedly greedy and corrupt political leaders, high poverty, and high crime, Prince George's County is perceived, especially by the media, as another region that has been "ruined" by the insurgence of Black residents who "devastated the sanctity of the space," especially in comparison to its affluent neighboring counties, Montgomery and Fairfax. As longtime *Washington Post* reporter Robert McCartney writes, "Prince George's as a whole is regularly viewed as a high-crime community, when in fact most of the shootings and property crimes are concentrated in a fraction of the county inside the Beltway."[7] The 2010 conviction of County Executive Jack Johnson and his wife, city council member Leslie Johnson, on charges of bribery brought about implicit (and explicit) comparisons to Mayor Barry's arrest in 1990 on federal drug charges. During Johnson's tenure, like Barry's, local media regularly raised concerns about the "pay-to-play" business culture nurtured by Johnson and his cronies.[8]

In many ways, the afterlife of H Street, like that of Shaw and the U Street corridors, is reflected in the sprawling D.C. metro's Black diaspora. Vestiges of D.C.'s Chocolate City persist in suburbs like Prince George's County. What is often missing, however, from the clandestine narratives about the region is that Black residents who fled D.C., and other areas of the country, took advantage of remarkable opportunities to (re)build thriving Black communities outside the city limits. Evidenced by the county's nearly 40,000 Black-owned businesses, massive single-family homes, and sizable and concentrated Black middle- and upper-class population (the largest in the country), Prince George's County became an ideal Black space for many who possessed a strong desire to live among other Black people and build stable communities. In fact, scholars have found that Black professionals enjoy living in communities that are predominantly or exclusively Black.[9] As sociologist Karen Lacy explains, scholars devote so much attention to "the burden of blackness that they have devoted scant attention to the possibility that there is something enjoyable about being black and participating in a community of blacks."[10]

A Tale of Two "Cool" Cities

On a sunny Wednesday afternoon, April 29, 1992, a Ventura County, California, jury acquitted four LAPD officers of mercilessly beating Rodney King.

At my Oakland high school, dozens of Black students walked out of our classrooms in solidarity to gather in the quad and discuss the devastating impact of the jury's decision, especially what this meant for us as young Black men and women in the United States. We all saw the video. It was an insult to our intelligence and humanity to imagine the brutal beating of Mr. King's motionless body as anything but another example of exceptional violence and an overreach of police power. King's battered body and the officers' acquittal were the final straws. King became a symbol for racial injustice and civil rights for communities of color with a historical mistrust of law enforcement agencies. Feelings of social isolation, economic abandonment, and scrutiny had reached their climax.

Over the next couple of days, I saw dozens of businesses in popular retail districts of Oakland tarnished, and in some cases, set ablaze, as protestors expressed their anger and disillusionment at both the verdict and the enduring conditions of economic inequality that plagued my hometown. The market-driven system of capitalism that resulted in global economic restructuring, corporate flight, and a shrinking government provided modest economic opportunities for a growing Black middle class, but at the same time left Oakland's largely poor and working-class Black population with fewer employment and housing options. The businesses that received the most damage were the ones in which we most often felt unwelcome. They were the small retail outlets where you could see closed circuit television cameras mounted on the walls, ceilings, and counters, capturing our every move. They were the same stores in which store managers and security guards would follow us around and ask what we intended to buy as we casually browsed the merchandise. These were the same spaces where we were constantly watched, our movement tracked. Even at that young age, I thought about what I had learned about Oakland's history, as I tried to understand what was happening and why.

Beginning in the 1960s, Oakland transitioned from a medium-sized city with a majority white population to a preeminent Black Mecca, a Chocolate City, a hotbed for Black Power, Black aesthetics, and the Black Panther Party. In the era of afros and Black consciousness, Oakland was the epicenter of radical Black cool. Like other metropolitan cities, Oakland experienced economic decline and neglect exacerbated by white flight and a disappearing manufacturing industry that left Black residents in an economically perilous position from the 1980s through the 1990s, when the protests occurred. Growing up in Oakland, I certainly saw the ways in which the local and national media and Bay Area residents contrasted the racialized landscape of Oakland as impoverished, hazardous, and corrupt with the pristine, tony, upscale white neighborhoods of San Francisco and Marin County. Oakland was cast aside as another "Murder Capital." For me, Oakland's reputation never matched the experience of living in the city. In Oakland, I saw Black people constantly negotiating their existence and movement through the city. Even while Oakland remained culturally and spatially segregated through the 1990s, from the Festival at the Lake to Eastmont Mall, Oakland was a place where Black people developed a robust and diverse culture, economy, and social life. But something eventually changed.

Amid its considerable racial and economic restructuring over the past twenty years, Oakland has become a certified hipster paradise. Most recently, Oakland's revised and revitalized reputation as a must-see location, and its proximity to Silicon Valley, has helped its population grow as young, educated white and Asian entrepreneurs seek "affordable" housing as they enter the explosive technology market that has taken over the Bay Area since the early 2000s. Of course, with gentrification abounding, Oakland's formerly prominent Black population has dwindled precipitously. Cultural institutions that once served its vast working-class Black population were replaced by trendy shops and hipster outlets. Oakland exemplifies how racialization and racism are indispensable to the durability of capitalism.[11]

With its countless farmers' markets, community gardens, clean and green energy production, "vibrant" communities, trendy ethnic enclaves, and cultural diversity, Oakland is globally recognized as an ideal tourist destination. Two articles from the British newspapers, the *Telegraph* and the *Independent*, revived age-old comparisons between Oakland and San Francisco, its "cousin across the water," but cast Oakland as "the cool alternative to San Francisco."[12] But with this designation as a "cool" city has come a revised narrative of Oakland's rich history, a narration that involves selectively reviving certain memories and suppressing others. Through these accounts, Oakland's cultural shift can be described as a movement from hippie to hipster, and not much before or in between. The city is characterized as historically radical, violent, and countercultural, but certainly not Black. Despite its "darker" yet starkly white history, in comparison to San Francisco, Oakland was the heart of "biker machismo" in the 1960s and 1970s, not Black Power. This erasure of Oakland's prominent Black history exemplifies how "coolness" is commodified through white consumer aesthetics of hipsterism. This retelling detaches from roots of resistance, or Black cool aesthetics.[13]

Three thousand miles away, D.C. has undergone a renaissance similar to that of Oakland as it has attracted a growing population of young, white, educated professionals who are contributing to the shifting cultural landscape of the nation's capital. D.C.'s transition to "cool," both celebrated and bemoaned in a tone-deaf *Washington Post* article in 2018, seamlessly connects with the city's latest "DC Cool" marketing strategy. The author, a George Washington University law professor, identified several neighborhoods, including H Street, NE, that have inevitably become "cooler" over the past few years, elevating D.C. to the same status as that of some of the country's coolest, hippest locales—namely, Williamsburg, Brooklyn, and the Mission District of San Francisco. The article references slavery and the birth of American democracy as contrasting rather than complementary elements of D.C. history, since according to the author, David Fontana, "Washington was also the product of honorable and not just horrifying motivations." Fontana's piece echoes conclusions offered by the tourism pieces from the *Independent* and the *Telegraph*, as he sidesteps D.C.'s notable Black cultural and political history. For, as Fontana claims, the District spent 200 years "transitioning from backwater to merely boring."[14] The article focuses on D.C. being a federal city, America's city, where "govsters" (not hipsters) effortlessly roam, thereby erasing the majority of the population who are Black and Latinx or not federal employees. Fontana's D.C. is an imagined city that can exist in the minds of the elite and disconnected. Rather than offering up D.C.'s history as unique, Fontana portrays the nation's capital as being like every other gentrified city in the United States.

It is both startling and fascinating to see what it takes to disassociate both Oakland and D.C. from their Black pasts to reimagine the birth of a postracial "cool." These examples demonstrate how the historical transformation of "cool" highlights a shift from social difference as antagonistic to social difference as aesthetic and marketable.[15] Reflecting back to the scene from the introductory chapter involving the white owner of the holistic and wellness center, it remains perplexing to witness the tactics required to extract "cool" from blackness and disassociate blackness from two chocolate cities. Both examples show us how malleable, transformable, and transportable Black space is in the context of capitalist accumulation that is largely driven by white and middle-class interests. This is not unique to D.C., but something we can see across both space and time. Despite the dispossession and displacement of Black people in these cities, blackness leaves an indelible mark on the space, even after the Black people leave.

Chocolate Futures

What do Black life and Black space look like in the wake of a post–Chocolate City, and how does resistance signal the possibilities for the future that Black activists are distinctly shaping? Since the advent of modernity, capitalism has placed an undue burden on Black bodies. An important aspect of this burden lies in the surveillance that capitalism imposes on them. This has become even more evident over the past couple of years as the country has endured tremendous social tension and political upheaval. Cities like Ferguson, Baltimore, Milwaukee, and Oakland, where Black people and Black communities are under constant surveillance, are also experiencing renewed federal assault as they continue to be sites of abysmal economic conditions. Black residents continually experience disproportionately high unemployment, inadequate public transportation, and residential and commercial segregation. Rebellions that occur in these communities, while often instigated by state-sanctioned violence, take place amid habitual feelings of oppression and neglect.

Recent national uprisings in response to publicized incidences of police brutality are part of a national discontent felt by Black people in various cities over the stagnant "progress" following the civil rights movement and organized fights against racial injustice (much like the vexation felt by Black people in the mid-1960s). Poor communities of color are disproportionately on the receiving end of state-enacted brutality and surveillance, which clearly highlights an explicit contradiction of the American tenets of our liberal democracy: that freedom and equality in this country coexist with structural inequality, violence, and contempt. The uprisings bring into focus the lived experiences of Black people despite the proliferation of race-neutral policies advocated by the neoliberal state. They disrupt the racial discourses of postrace and race neutrality to expose the hypervisibility and expendability of Black bodies.

These instances cannot be thought apart from the violence of gentrification and its impact on Black communities, and the ways in which neoliberal capital provides both logic and alibi for gentrification while framing "urban renewal" in the form of gentrification as natural.[16] As urban designer and architect Craig Wilkins argues, urban planners often imagine the urban environment as spaces to clear (urban renewal), places to fear (racial and spatial profiling), and places to manage (redlining) until they are constructed as desirable spaces again (gentrification).[17] Sometimes it is hard to see potential when reality is so sobering. And yet, even when this reality seems daunting, these rebellions are the seeds of what futurity could look like. Black urban spaces are "sites of attachment and struggle."[18] I look to Katherine McKittrick, who ruminates on Black geographies as spaces "of survival, resistance, creativity, and the struggle against death."[19] She proposes a notion of Black city space as "imbued with a narrative of Black history that is neither celebratory nor dissident but rooted in an articulation of city life that accepts that relations of violence and domination have made our existence and presence in the Americas possible as it recasts this knowledge to envision an alternative future."[20] McKittrick's provocation leads me to ask: What world do these uprisings and movements allow us to imagine? Activists are not only looking to eradicate the racialized and gendered violence enacted by the state; they are imagining a different way of relating to each other and to the space in which they inhabit. The traces of a Chocolate City remain temporally and spatially significant as resistant, radical, and imaginative in the face of oppression. I posit the new post–Chocolate City as a terrain upon which we engage new struggles and uncover new possibilities.

Notes

Preface

1. Hall, "Introduction," 5.
2. Asch and Musgrove, *Chocolate City*, 447.
3. Gilbert, *Ten Blocks*.
4. Carroll, "Meaning of Funk."
5. M. Jackson, "Employment, Population & Housing," 5.
6. District of Columbia Chamber of Commerce, *2018 State of the Business Report*, 4.
7. Richardson, Mitchell, and Franco, "Shifting Neighborhoods."

Introduction

1. Kitsock, "Beer."
2. Barry was also popularly known as "Mayor for Life," who served four terms as mayor between 1979 and 1991, and between 1995 and 1999. The promotional video that accompanied Chocolate City Beer's "Mister Mayor" brew included the tagline "Beer for Life" while funk music played in the background.
3. Kitsock, "Beer."
4. Kitsock.
5. Hall, "Introduction."
6. To read more on blackness as experiential and an identity with shared, contested, and contingent histories and specific geographies, see Du Bois, *Souls of Black Folk*; Gilroy, *Black Atlantic*; Hall, "What Is This 'Black'"; Hall, *Representation*; McKittrick, *Demonic Grounds*; McKittrick and Woods, *Black Geographies*.
7. A critical understanding of blackness positions it as a challenge to antiblackness structured by hegemonic formulations that define Black people as criminal, barbaric, intellectually inferior, and subhuman (Fanon, *Black Skin, White Masks*). At the same time, I am interested in not only these articulations of blackness as identity but also those that involve the consumption of blackness as both desired and disposable.
8. Elam, "Change Clothes and Go."
9. Some scholars recognize neoliberalism as an economic ideology that deploys market logic as a way to protect and promote social equality and individual liberties—while relying on the market to meet the desires and needs of individuals. In this way, neoliberal ideology promotes the state as inefficient and advances the notion that the intrusion of a powerful state constrains personal freedom (Duggan,

Twilight of Equality; Ong, *Neoliberalism as Exception*; Rose, *Politics of Life Itself*; Melamed, "Spirit of Neoliberalism"). I draw on Wendy Brown ("Neoliberalism's Frankenstein"), who alternatively extends Michel Foucault's lectures in the *Birth of Biopolitics* to theorize neoliberalism not as an *ideology* but as a "productive" and "world-making" rationality that "economizes every sphere and human endeavor, and it replaces a model of society based on the justice-producing social contract with society and conceived and organized as markets and with states oriented by market requirements" (W. Brown, 62).

10. B. Williams, *Upscaling Downtown*; Modan, *Turf Wars Discourse*; Ruble, *Washington's U Street*; Hyra, *Race, Class*.

11. Saito, "From 'Blighted' to 'Historic,'" 169.

12. Boulder, "Young, Middle-Income Blacks."

13. Meyer, "Washington Retail District."

14. Brenner and Theodore, "Cities and the Geographies"; D. Wilson, *Cities and Race*.

15. Florida, *Rise of the Creative Class*.

16. District of Columbia Deputy Mayor for Planning and Economic Development (DMPED), *H Street N.E. Retail*, 2.

17. Wingfield, *Doing Business*.

18. Gill, *Beauty Shop Politics*.

19. Wilson, "Capital's Need," 968.

20. Dávila, *Culture Works*, 11.

21. Montgomery, "Reappearance," 777.

22. McKittrick, "Plantation Futures," 7.

23. Lipsitz, "Racialization of Space," 12.

24. Low, *Spatializing Culture*, 7.

25. Kobayashi and Peake, "Racism," 393.

26. Low, *Spatializing Culture*, 8.

27. McKittrick and Woods, in *Black Geographies*, also speak to the ways in which race and space are both essentialized, where race (as nonwhiteness) is tied to the body and signifies difference, while space "just is." "The dilemmas that arise when we think about space and race often take three very separate approaches (bodily, economic/historical materialist, metaphoric) that result in reducing Black geographies to either geographic determinism (Black bodies inherently occupying Black places), the flesh (the body as the only relevant Black geographic scale), or the imagination (metaphoric/creative spaces, which are not represented as concrete, everyday, or lived). Consequently race, or blackness, is not understood as socially produced and shifting but is instead conceptualized as transhistorical, essentially corporeal, or allegorical or symbolic. In this process, which might be called bio-geographic determinism, Black geographies disappear—to the margins or to the realm of the unknowable. In short, a Black sense of place and Black geographic knowledges are both undermined by hegemonic spatial practices (of, say, segregation and neglect) and seemingly unavailable as a worldview" (7).

28. McKittrick, *Demonic Grounds*, xiii.

29. McKittrick, "On Plantations, Prisons," 949.

30. I recognize the important work of theorists who centralize the Black body and tie blackness to the flesh as connected to the afterlife of slavery (Spillers, "Mama's Baby"; Hartman, *Scenes of Subjection*; Hartman and Wilderson, "Position of Unthought"); however, I am informed by McKittrick and Woods in *Black Geographies*, who maintain that "Black bodies (rather than a Black sense of place) are integrated into many discussions of 'difference' in order to briefly point to race and racism, thus reiterating, rather than critically engaging with, the Fanonian predicament of Manichean space" (6). This formulation helps me think about the traces of blackness that linger in urban spaces even after the Black people have left. To imagine a formulation of blackness in this way inherently indicates, as media studies theorist Lauren Cramer claims, "the de-corporealization of blackness" ("Race at the Interface," 2). I do not limit my analysis to that of the Black body, but instead identify the ways in which white ideas of Black symbolism structure the state and elite actors' reduction of Black people into Black bodies—as reflexive judgments on people who are considered Black—in their attempt to accrue capital.

31. Lipsitz, *How Racism Takes Place*, 50, 56–57.

32. McKittrick, *Demonic Grounds*; McKittrick, "On Plantations."

33. Tyner, "Urban Revolutions."

34. Bledsoe, Eaves, and Williams, "Introduction," 10.

35. Contemporary forms of gentrification accompanied political and economic shifts (namely, neoliberalism) in Europe and North America during the last quarter of the twentieth century. As governments moved from urban renewal to deregulated, market-based revitalization, private actors—namely, bankers and other investors—became increasingly involved in urban development, while local government officials emphasized local tax revenues (Davidson, "Spoiled Mixture"; Slater, "North American Gentrification").

36. My use of the term "revitalization" borrows from Kennedy and Leonard, who define it as "the process of enhancing the physical, commercial and social components of neighborhoods and the future prospects of its residents through private sector and/or public sector efforts. Physical components include upgrading of housing stock and streetscapes. Commercial components include the creation of viable businesses and services in the community. Social components include increasing employment and reductions in crime" (Kennedy and Leonard, "Dealing with Neighborhood Change," 6).

37. Dvorak, "Craft Coffee."

38. Hannigan, *Fantasy City*; Zukin, *Culture of Cities*.

39. Hannigan, *Fantasy City*; Zukin, "Consuming Authenticity."

40. Harvey, *Condition of Postmodernity*; Zukin, *Culture of Cities*; N. Smith, "New Globalism"; Lees, Slater, and Wyly, *Gentrification*; Zukin, *Naked City*.

41. Deutsche and Ryan, "Fine Art of Gentrification," 98.

42. In a 1963 interview with Dr. Kenneth Clark, novelist and activist James Baldwin famously stated that "urban renewal means Negro removal," as he spoke about the devastating impact of federally sanctioned redevelopment on Black families. Interview on WNDT-TV, New York City, May 28, 1963.

43. Cf. N. Smith, *New Urban Frontier*; Brown-Saracino, "Social Preservationists"; Osman, *Invention of Brownstone Brooklyn*; Tissot, *Good Neighbors*; Schlichtman, Patch, and Hill, *Gentrifer*.

44. Hannigan, *Fantasy City*, 73.

45. Derek Hyra (*Race, Class*) discusses "black branding" as a way to identify how the city invests in representations of "authentic" and stereotypical blackness to invite tourists and residents to the Shaw neighborhood in D.C. Like Pattillo and Boyd before him, Hyra uses "black branding" to explain how blackness is consumed by white people in an urban context (Pattillo, *Black on the Block*; Boyd, *Jim Crow Nostalgia*).

46. J. Jackson, *Real Black*; Pattillo, *Black on the Block*; Brown-Saracino, *Neighborhood That Never Changes*; Zukin, "Consuming Authenticity"; Zukin, *Naked City*.

47. In particular, Sharon Zukin offers useful commentary to help think about spaces of authenticity that are constantly being rediscovered by urban gentrifiers. She writes: "We can only see spaces as authentic from outside them. Mobility gives us the distance to see a neighborhood in terms of the way it looks, enables us to hold it to an absolute standard of urbanity or cosmopolitanism, and encourages us to judge its character apart from any personal history or intimate social relationships we have there. The more connected we are to its social life, especially if we grew up there, the less likely we are to call a neighborhood *authentic*." Zukin, "Consuming Authenticity," 728.

48. Brown-Saracino, *Neighborhood That Never Changes*.

49. Sharon Zukin (*Naked City*) speaks to the marginalization of authenticity in urban places as "style" through the process of branding neighborhoods, producing heritage projects, and other commercial enterprises (like coffee shops or specialized furniture stores).

50. Hannigan, *Fantasy City*.

51. At the same time, like Ann Stoler who adopts the "post" of postcolonial as a mark of skepticism, I use "post" to both advocate for the persistence of tangible and intangible forms of blackness, and acknowledge the systemic violence that has pushed Black Washingtonians to the margins. Stoler, *Duress*.

52. Hunter and Robinson, *Chocolate Cities*, xiii.

53. The relationship between aesthetics and urban processes has become increasingly recognized in geography and urban studies research. D. Asher Ghertner similarly engages the significance of aesthetic politics, but in the production of world-class cities and world-class subjects in Delhi, India. This formulation, what he calls a "world-class aesthetic," is "oriented toward producing aesthetic, not ideological, consensus" as it relates to the spatial transformation of global urban centers. Therefore, central to planning in Delhi is how developments "look," where "world-class" is an aesthetic marker. Aesthetics can be used as primary drivers of policy interventions that improve the "look" of the landscape. I add that aesthetics are also embedded within the urbanizing process. These kinds of urban aesthetics draw on race to structure how and what we see in the urban landscape. Abdou-Maliq Simone theorizes a "generic blackness," like the color black, signaling practices of opacity through which the making of the urban takes place. Jakarta notes that many refer to the city, in his case, as "becoming too black. Black becomes a catchall

term for all that is wrong, non-modern, and inexplicable; all that must be clarified and straightened out." Ghertner, *Rule by Aesthetics*, 22; Simone, "Generic Blackness," 185.

54. Cramer, "Race at the Interface," 2.

55. Hooks, *Yearning*, 104.

56. Simone, "The Black City."

57. I want to be clear about the distinction I am making between Black aesthetics and my theorization of blackness as an aesthetic that is deployed through black aesthetic emplacement. Black aesthetics are part of a radical tradition, emphasizing cultural production for and by Black people—one that appeals to racial blackness without essentializing it. Philosopher Paul Taylor (*Black Is Beautiful*) describes Black aesthetics as aesthetic of self-fashioning; he says that Black aesthetics insist "on agency, beauty, and meaning in the face of oppression, despair, and death" (2). He defines Black aesthetics as "the practice of using art, criticism, or analysis to explore the role that expressive objects and practices play in creating and maintaining black life-worlds" (12). I am curious about the processes that have caused blackness to be of practical significance in everyday life. Rather than making a case for true or authentic representations of blackness, I look to the ways that blackness is aestheticized and deployed to achieve particular social and economic ends. Exploring the aesthetic function of blackness, as distinct from identity, allows for an engagement with otherness and the constitutive outside (as Kobena Mercer has previously written). To think of blackness as an aesthetic speaks to its constructedness and a discursive investment in its presence especially in light of our presumptive movement toward the "postracial."

58. Winnubst, *Way Too Cool*, 3.

59. Ahmed, *On Being Included*; Modan, "Mango Fufu."

60. Ahmed, *On Being Included*, 164.

61. Modan, "Mango Fufu."

62. Walks, "Aestheticization."

63. Berrey, *Enigma of Diversity*, 8.

64. Schwartzman, "Lawsuit."

65. B. Weber, "In Desperate Need."

66. Mele, "Revisiting the Citadel," 357.

Chapter One

1. D. Wilson, *Cities and Race*.

2. Jaffe and Sherwood, *Dream City*.

3. Glazer, *Beyond the Melting Pot*, xxxiv. The "ethnic" groups against which Blacks were compared in the Glazer and Moynihan study included Italians, Jews, Puerto Ricans, Irish, Slovaks, and others within the specific urban contexts (Chicago and New York City).

4. United States and Moynihan, *Negro Family*, 5.

5. A 2010 article in the *New York Times* (Cohen, "Culture of Poverty") suggests the resurgence of scholarship on culture in general and the "culture of poverty"

thesis in particular. In the article, Douglas S. Massey notes that we in the United States "have finally reached the stage where people aren't afraid of being politically correct." Several sociologists and anthropologists, including Massey, continued to research and write about the cultural roots of poverty (Small, Harding, and Lamont, "Reconsidering Culture and Poverty").

6. Lipsitz, *How Racism Takes Place*, 27.

7. Several scholars, including Miriam Greenberg (*Branding New York*), highlight the discourse of "urban crisis" that emerged in the 1960s with the increasing concentration of Blacks and Latinos in America's inner cities.

8. Gilbert, *Ten Blocks*.

9. National Advisory Commission on Civil Disorders, *Civil Disorders*, 275.

10. National Advisory Commission on Civil Disorders, 276.

11. Hannerz, *Soulside*.

12. Hannerz not only lays out economic practices that often put the Black poor in a financial bind, he also outlines the "unfair business practices" Black ghetto dwellers experience when they attempt to follow regulations. He gives examples of when Black consumers provide a down payment for goods and receive neither the item nor the deposit if they are unable to complete the purchase (Hannerz, *Soulside*).

13. Gilbert, *Ten Blocks*, 79–80.

14. I use the terms "rebellions" and "uprisings" in lieu of "riots" to recognize the systemic, sociospatial nature of the events of the 1960s. Characterizing the D.C. rebellions as such connects them to others taking place in cities like Newark, Detroit, Watts, Chicago, and other places. As Kerner Commission research director Robert Shellow and his colleagues concluded, the "riots" were direct responses to systemic and institutional white domination; therefore, "the riots were rebellions" (Hopkind, "White on Black," 2).

15. Tyner, "Urban Revolutions," 221.

16. Abu-Lughod, *Race, Space*.

17. Jaffe and Sherwood, *Dream City*.

18. Schaffer, "1968 Washington Riots," 7.

19. Raspberry, "Washington Lays Antiriot Plans"; Jaffe and Sherwood, *Dream City*; Gilbert, *Ten Blocks*.

20. Raspberry, "Washington Lays AntiRiot Plans."

21. Gilbert, *Ten Blocks*, 5.

22. Schaffer, "1968 Washington Riots."

23. Gilbert, *Ten Blocks*, 5.

24. Gilbert, 7.

25. Gilbert, 11.

26. Gilbert, 71.

27. Schaffer, "1968 Washington Riots."

28. S. Smith, *Captive Capital*, 126.

29. Gilbert, *Ten Blocks*, 80.

30. On April 5, Marlowe walked into the building and never walked out. First responders never searched for his body, despite pleas from his family. Marlowe's

remains were discovered two decades later when the building was finally destroyed to make room for a government building. Mohammed, "After '68 Unrest."

31. Sarro, "Panel to Begin Probe."

32. "$24 Million Insured Loss"; Roeber, "Fires of April." This reported value of physical damage has been contested. A *Washington Daily News* article, "Coverage Was Lacking: Merchants Stand More Riot Loss," of March 12, 1969, claims that the National Capital Planning Commission's estimates were much higher by early 1969. Ronald Sarro's article "Panel to Begin D.C. Riot Probe" echoes this increase, contending that a "new Washington Civil Disturbance Survey report disclosed that the rioting here April 4–15, [1968,] reached $57 million, about double the previous estimates." Other articles in the *Washington Post* that appeared several years later still reflect the $24 million damage estimate.

33. National Capital Planning Commission, *Report on Civil Disturbances.*

34. National Capital Planning Commission, *Alternative Approaches.*

35. Raspberry, "City's Fury."

36. Gillette, *Between Justice and Beauty*, 170.

37. Wright, "D.C. Renewal."

38. Schaffer, "1968 Washington Riots," 20–21.

39. Ulf Hannerz describes the actions of the looters as being based in anger and resentment toward years of mistreatment: "They were affirming an emergent community morality. It was as if goods hoarded by somebody who had no right to it were suddenly released for general consumption. Although profits were derived from looting, it could be easily understood as a political act against white oppression and exploitation. At the very least, there was little question of 'theft' on the part of any individual participant, as previous ownership became simply irrelevant when the stores came temporarily under generous community control. Furthermore, the burning which often followed on looting was obviously to be seen within the framework of Black-white conflict; nobody could profit directly from throwing Molotov cocktails. Even more important, the participants abided quite strictly by their definition of the ghetto moral community and generally did not harm businesses with 'soul brother' or 'soul sister' signs" (Hannerz, *Soulside*, 174).

40. Gilbert, *Ten Blocks*, 141–42, 149.

41. Lipsitz, *How Racism Takes Place*, 145.

42. Lipsitz, 145.

43. One article from the DC Public Library's 1968 Riots vertical file describes the strategy: "Despite the frenzy in the streets over the past 72 hours, looters have been using an often sophisticated selection process about what stores they attacked, officials and inspections by newsmen have found" ("Looting Was Often Selective," *Washington Informer*).

44. S. Smith, *Captive Capital*, 127.

45. S. Smith, 25.

46. In a 2007 event hosted by the Washington Historical Society, participants in the Empowerment 1968–2008 Panel Discussion spoke about the 1968 uprisings as a response to legacies of police harassment and brutality. Essentially, like in many other instances, a Black man died and Black people revolted.

47. Hannerz, *Soulside*, 160.

48. Jaffe and Sherwood, *Dream City*, 18–19.

49. McKittrick, "On Plantations," 949.

50. McKittrick; Lipsitz, *How Racism Takes Place*.

51. These causes are outlined in the Kerner Report as reasons for the outbreaks in several U.S. cities.

52. Besides Watts in 1965 and Detroit in 1967, the uprisings of April 1968 in Washington caused the most damage of any large-city disturbances.

53. Gillette, *Between Justice*, 179.

54. Kaiser, "Burned Out."

55. Gillette, *Between Justice*, 180.

56. National Capital Planning Commission, *Alternative Approaches*, 39.

57. Kalb, "Williams Considers."

58. Kalb.

59. Lipsitz, *How Racism Takes Place*, 30.

60. Lipsitz, 41.

61. Kalb, "Williams Considers."

62. Some white merchants agreed and argued that on H Street, "more black people should own and operate their businesses." One white hardware store owner expressed his desire for "a Negro or Negro group to buy his store" (Kaiser, "Burned Out").

63. Lipsitz, *How Racism Takes Place*, 52.

64. "Negro-Run Ghetto."

65. Ethridge, "Black Architects."

66. Nash, "Black Architect," 36, 96.

67. These conversations were taking place at the same time that President Nixon's administration neutralized Black radical resistance by adopting "Black Capitalism" as a strategy to encourage Black self-sufficiency and integration. See Baradaran, *Color of Money*; Weems and Randolph, "National Response"; Hill and Rabig, *Business of Black Power*.

68. Asher and Kaiser, "Broken Promises."

69. Edwards, "Some Insurance."

70. Edwards.

71. Asher and Kaiser, "Broken Promises," B1.

72. Weber, "In Desperate Need."

73. Jacoby, "Battle Rages." For more local coverage on Fauntroy and D.C. City Council's push for H Street to be designated an urban renewal site, see Welsh, "Riot-Area Renewal"; Basham, "Council Cites Intent."

74. Braestrup, "Planning Commission."

75. In response to white flight to the suburbs, federal planners instituted the largest urban renewal plan in the country, hoping to reduce the significant loss of D.C.'s primary sources of revenue: property and income taxes. In 1954, the Supreme Court unanimously agreed that much of Southwest D.C., a "slum," required aggressive "redesigning." This "urban renewal" plan resulted in the overwhelming destruction of land (approximately 600 acres) and displacement of thousands of impoverished

Black residents, since RLA compensated property owners, not renters. In addition, the agency implemented few programs to help displaced residents find new places to live. While the language of "urban renewal" was eventually replaced with "revitalization," the disappointing results remained the same. Plans on H Street following the uprisings marked the beginning of several smaller-scale "revitalization" plans that continued through the 1990s.

76. Braestrup, "Planning Commission."

77. With the passage of the Housing Act of 1949 and the Housing Act of 1954, the federal government granted U.S. cities aid to implement urban renewal projects. To receive funds, they had to provide development plans, organize renewal agencies, and demonstrate how they would acquire devalued real estate. In 1977, the National Capital Planning Commission published *Worthy of the Nation: The History of Planning for the National Capital* (Gutheim, "Worthy of the Nation"), in which the agency traced the history of planning activities in D.C. from its origins in 1790 until the book's publication in 1977. The text, full of maps, diagrams, and photographs from various Washington neighborhoods, generously lauds the efforts of the commission over the years, especially in the aftermath of World War II. What is noticeably absent from the text is any consideration of race and the fact that urban renewal projects in Washington, D.C., disproportionately impacted Black residents, while subsequently strengthening segregation. The book offers a generous view of urban renewal efforts in Southwest D.C., as well as other areas like the three "riot corridors." While they talk about the unlivable conditions of slums and ghettos of D.C. (using the language of obsolescence and blight), what is missing are the people. The book gives sterile details about redevelopment (renewal) plans in neighborhoods like Barry Farms and Marshall Heights, both poor and Black. They seemed most concerned about the conditions of the land and the buildings, and how to properly assess those conditions (again, as obsolete or blighted).

78. J. Williams, "Out of the Ashes."

79. McCombs, "Banker."

80. McCombs, "Bitterness."

81. McCombs, "Merchant."

82. Dash, "Barry in NE."

83. Pyatt, "H Street Merchants."

84. For example, in 1979, the city announced that an $8–9 million shopping mall and residential complex were to be constructed on H Street between Eighth and Tenth Streets. This space, one of two sites purchased by the RLA under the city's urban renewal program, was sold to a Cleveland construction firm, but the project was unable to secure financing for both the commercial and townhouse phases of the development (Hudge, "Recovery").

85. Pyatt, "H Street Merchants"; Dunson, "A Street."

86. Lipsitz, *How Racism Takes Place*, 56.

87. Leland Saito writes that highway projects, ones like the Hopscotch Bridge, between the 1950s and 1970s were inherently racialized "because of their disproportionate impact on racial minorities as compared to Whites and the way that local governments strategically developed and employed images of communities of

color as 'ghettos,' 'blighted,' and 'slums' to justify the eradication of neighborhoods and displacement of residents and businesses" (Saito, "'Blighted' to 'Historic,'" 169). Freeways and other developed roadways (bridges, etc.) isolated impoverished communities, choked them from access to important goods and services, and reinforced segregation even after it was formally eradicated. There were tense conversations and strategic organizing efforts (interracial) that resisted the expansion of freeways—specifically, in Washington, D.C. (see Asch and Musgrove, *Chocolate City*).

88. Lewis, "H Str. Overpass."

89. Schaffer, "1968 Washington Riots," 28.

90. Milloy, "She's in Command."

91. Mele, *Selling*, 182.

92. Elijah Anderson identifies the "iconic ghetto" as a place and as a designation that follows Black people who may not be poor or live in inner-city neighborhoods. The iconic ghetto, according to him, is typified by poverty, violence, and a lack of personal responsibility. Stereotypical inhabitants of the iconic ghetto, he proclaims, are "iconic negroes," who are excessively violent, immoral, physically threatening, street criminals. The "iconic negro woman" is represented by the "welfare queen" stereotype, who is lazy, aggressive, overweight, hypersexual, and hyperfertile. Anderson argues that the iconic ghetto not only exists spatially but exists on the Black body regardless of one's identity, class, or status. The trouble with this formulation is that Anderson does not properly account for the historical and sociospatial dynamics that accompany gentrification. With the increasing levels of poverty in suburbs where Black people live, the ghetto takes on a different meaning. Where he stops short is designating the ghetto as discursively produced and upheld by various institutions. I find the notion of a racialized ghetto more generative, which acknowledges enduring mechanisms of spatial isolation and marginalization: see Anderson, "Iconic Ghetto." See also Woods, "Life after Death"; D. Wilson, *Black-on-Black*.

93. Bowman, "District Rethinking."

94. These were conditions that plagued Black inner-city residents around the United States, as William Julius Wilson demonstrates in *The Truly Disadvantaged*. In his study of the deteriorating conditions of Black life between 1960 and 1980, Wilson attributes these changes primarily to the transformation of the national economy, rather than the behaviors of Black inner-city residents, as many social scientists proclaimed.

95. Bowman, "District Rethinking," B1.

96. Bowman, "Agency Cheers."

97. "15 Years Later."

98. J. Williams, "Out of the Ashes."

99. Bowman, "District Rethinking."

100. Teeley, "NE Corridor's."

101. Teeley.

102. Bowman, "District Rethinking."

103. White, "Safeway."

104. Dávila, *Culture Works*, 11.

105. Liebow, *Tally's Corner*, xxvii.

106. Mansfield, "H Street Rebuilding."

107. Thompson, "Stocking Grocery Shelves."

108. Dunson, "What Riots Did."

109. Hopkinson, *Go-Go Live*, 89.

110. Sargent, "Desolate NE Intersection."

111. I will discuss the transformation and use of space at the Eighth and H intersection in more detail in chapter 5.

112. Sargent, "Desolate NE Intersection."

113. Sargent.

114. Sargent.

115. Wheeler, "Vitality." In 1987, the suburban-style strip mall H Street Connection opened at the center of the corridor, spanning two blocks on H Street. Of the fourteen stores occupying the plaza, nine were owned by Korean immigrants, signaling a clear shift in the commercial makeup of the corridor.

116. Fisher and Pianin, "Riots and D.C.'s Underclass."

117. Escobar, "H Street NE."

118. CNN, "Nation's Capital."

119. CNN.

120. Gaines-Carter, "Closing of Mega Foods."

121. Lipsitz, *How Racism Takes Place*.

122. Massey and Denton, *American Apartheid*; Kelley, *Race Rebels*; McKittrick and Woods, *Black Geographies*; Lipsitz, *How Racism Takes Place*; Connolly, *World More Concrete*.

123. McCombs, "Bitterness and Despair."

124. Schaffer, "1968 Washington Riots."

125. Jaffe and Sherwood, *Dream City*, 81.

Chapter Two

1. Mele, *Race*, 7.

2. Zukin, "Gentrification"; Harvey, *Condition of Postmodernity*; N. Smith, *New Urban Frontier*.

3. N. Smith, *New Urban Frontier*; Lees, Slater, and Wyly, *Gentrification*.

4. Jaffe and Sherwood, *Dream City*.

5. Jaffe and Sherwood, 169. Several scholars have noted multiple inconsistencies surrounding Barry's administration, including his strong advocacy of Black businesses, which ultimately benefited those with strong social and political ties to Barry. Despite his precipitous fall from grace in the 1990s, Barry was incredibly popular among Black poor and working-class residents, from his early days as a community organizer, through his four terms as mayor and Ward 8 city council member, until his death in 2014. Also see Musgrove, *Rumor, Repression*; Asch and Musgrove, *Chocolate City*.

6. Asch and Musgrove, *Chocolate City*.

7. Hackworth and Smith, "Changing State of Gentrification"; N. Smith, "New Globalism."

8. Asch and Musgrove, *Chocolate City*, 423.

9. Asch and Musgrove, 423.

10. Deneer, "Commerce as Structure and Symbol," 294.

11. Modan, "Mango Fufu."

12. McCann, "Cultural Politics," 397.

13. Dávila, *Culture Works*, 11.

14. Schwartzman, "Whose H Street"; Meyer, "Signs of Recovery"; Sullivan, "Gentrification."

15. Young, "D.C. Residents."

16. Schwartzman, "Whose H Street"; Young, "H Street NE Corridor."

17. Zukin, *Culture of Cities*, 7.

18. Zukin, 7.

19. Hackworth and Rekers, "Ethnic Packaging," 232.

20. Weber, "In Desperate Need," 179.

21. In addition to Weber's study, there are similar analyses of urban reinvention in New Orleans (Woods, "Katrina's World"; Thomas, "Roots Run Deep Here") and New York (Greenberg, *Branding New York*).

22. Weber, "In Desperate Need," 179.

23. Saito, "From 'Blighted,'" 168.

24. Jacoby, "Battle Rages."

25. Levy and Downie, "Lights Are Still Out."

26. John W. Hechinger is the same man who later developed a large commercial complex, Hechinger Mall I & II, at the eastern end of the H Street corridor.

27. Hechinger, "Statement," 2–3.

28. Neubauer, "Wells Eyes Money." TIF has been a popular means of financing redevelopment since the 1990s. It demarcates unique taxing jurisdiction around areas designated for redevelopment by the state and assigns revenues from future property taxes to pay for the costs of redevelopment. These areas must be appropriately designated as "blighted" in order to qualify for the funds. Therefore developers, local government agencies, and consultants must document vacancies, land deterioration, decreasing property values, and other shifts in the built environment. As Rachel Weber ("Extracting Value") points out, the criteria for blight under these conditions "resemble some of those used to identify blight during urban renewal, although they have been purged of any reference to race, health, or hygiene" (534).

29. Sutton, "Rethinking Commercial Revitalization," 354.

30. Saito, "From 'Blighted.'"

31. Mele, "Revisiting the Citadel," 368.

32. Wells, Tommy Wells War.

33. Stover and Associates, "Value of H Street."

34. Willett, "Hands across the Table."

35. Mohammed, "Black Businesses."

36. Mohammed.

37. December 7, 2012, interview with Brian Kenner, former chief of staff, Office of the Deputy Mayor for Planning and Economic Development (DMPED), Washington, D.C.

38. Barnes et al., "Community and Nostalgia," 337.

39. ANCs are nonpartisan, neighborhood bodies established as part of the city's Home Rule Charter. The purpose of an ANC is to advise the D.C. government on behalf of its residents on matters that affect their neighborhoods. Each ANC area is subdivided into smaller areas. ANC 6C, the area surrounding the H Street, NE corridor, is divided into six parts. ANC meetings are public gatherings where renters and homeowners can address needs and concerns related to the neighborhood, like zoning, traffic, parking, crime, and policing. The meetings are hosted by a democratically elected commissioner.

40. Alexander, "Fading, Twisting, and Weaving"; Harris-Lacewell, *Barbershops, Bibles, and BET*; E. Wright, "Haircut"; Wood and Brunson, "Geographies."

41. Hart and Bowen, "Feasibility," 270.

42. District of Columbia Office of Planning, "Revival," 32.

43. Ahmed, *On Being Included*, 53.

44. Washington DC Economic Partnership, "DC Neighborhood Profiles."

45. Asch and Musgrove, "Not Gone, Not Forgotten."

46. Young, "H Street NE Corridor."

47. Young, "D.C. Residents."

48. Rowley, "H Street Revitalization."

49. Zukin et al., "New Retail Capital," 58.

50. This emphasis on the preservation of H Street's historic architectural aesthetic is in accordance with the H Street Strategic NE Development Plan of 2003, drafted by the District of Columbia Office of Planning, which implemented a branding plan to H Street that divided the corridor into three distinct parts: between Second and Seventh Streets is urban living; between Seventh and Twelfth Streets is commercial retail; and between Twelfth and Bladensburg is arts and entertainment (District of Columbia Office of Planning, "Revival").

51. Zukin, "Gentrification," 135.

52. Dávila, *Culture Works*.

53. Walks, "Aestheticization."

54. B. Weber, "In Desperate Need."

55. Meyer, "Signs of Recovery."

56. Sabar, "Joe Englert."

57. B. Weber, "In Desperate Need," 182.

58. B. Weber, 182.

59. Sidman, "Whole Foods."

60. Stephen A. Crockett Jr. describes "swagger-jacking" as a form of "cultural vulturism" of African American tradition that has taken place along the U Street corridor with the introduction of popular hipster bars and restaurants that capitalize on Black culture. Spearheaded by well-known local entrepreneurs like Andy Shallal, Eric and Ian Hilton, and Joe Englert, establishments like Busboys and

Poets, Marvin's, Blackbyrd (now closed), Eatonville (now closed), Patty Boom Boom, and Brixton were all named after some individual or experience in Black history (Crockett, "The Brixton"). In response, other journalists wrote about the virtue of Washington, D.C.'s "culturally dexterous" residents and the benefits of encroaching diversity on spaces that were previously recognized as Black (Cashin, "Culturally Dexterous Washington"). One *Washington Post* writer rejected Crockett's vision of "nouveau-Columbusing"—the practice of settling in a neighborhood and operating as if its history began the moment you arrived, like Christopher Columbus—and instead argues that Black Washingtonians have an unrealistic view of the District as historically Black and should recognize its diverse history instead of lamenting the impact of gentrification throughout the city (Yates, "Columbusing Black Washington").

61. Ritter, "Inauguration Fever."
62. Hackworth and Rekers, "Ethnic Packaging."

Chapter Three

1. D. Brown, "U-Turn."
2. The D.C. Home Rule Act allowed the city to elect a mayor and a city council and to designate an annual payment for the District. Nevertheless, final say over the District's budget and legislative power over city matters remained with the House Committee on D.C., which also has the veto right on any city legislation.
3. Ramanathan, "Where the Arts Intersect."
4. Jameson, *Archaeologies of the Future*; Muñoz, "Stages."
5. Mele, "Revisiting the Citadel."
6. M. Davis, *City of Quartz*; Zukin, *Culture of Cities*; Hannigan, *Fantasy City*.
7. Ahmed, *On Being Included*; Berrey, *Enigma of Diversity*; Modan, "Mango Fufu"; Winnubst, *Way Too Cool*.
8. Ahmed, *On Being Included*.
9. Mele, "Neoliberalism," 599.
10. Zukin, *Naked City*.
11. Zukin, 220.
12. See Lynch, "From Vision to Reality."
13. Mitchell, "End of Public Space"; Riddick, "Constructing Difference"; Lees, "Ambivalence of Diversity"; Modan, "Mango Fufu."
14. Zukin, *Culture of Cities*; Mele, *Selling the Lower East Side*; Lees, "Ambivalence of Diversity"; Hackworth and Rekers, "Ethnic Packaging"; Lin, *Power*.
15. Lees, "Ambivalence of Diversity."
16. Maly, Dalmage, and Michaels, "Idyllic World," 757.
17. J. Wilson, *Nostalgia*, 25.
18. Maly, Dalmage, and Michaels, "Idyllic World," 758.
19. Maly, Dalmage, and Michaels, 758.
20. Kasinitz and Hillyard, "Old-Timers' Tale."
21. Thomas, "Roots Run Deep," 750–51.
22. Maly, Dalmage, and Michaels, "Idyllic World."
23. Maly, Dalmage, and Michaels, 758.

24. Milloy, "Success Story."

25. Westwood and Williams, *Imagining Cities*, 1.

26. Zukin, *Naked City*, 3.

27. The study was also funded in part by Federal Historic Preservation Fund, National Park Service, with additional funding provided by the Capitol Hill Restoration Society.

28. Meethan, *Tourism in Global Society*.

29. Deckha, "Beyond the Country House," 403.

30. Schwartz and Layman, *Near Northeast*, 52.

31. Schwartz and Layman, 52.

32. Schwartz and Layman, 52.

33. Schwartz and Layman, 53–54.

34. Schwartz and Layman, 40.

35. Schwartz and Layman, 54.

36. Zukin, *Naked City*, 18.

37. Schwartz and Layman, *Near Northeast*, 57.

38. In some instances, the study offers contradictory characterizations of H Street as both ethnically diverse and "historically" Black. For example, the authors describe the popular entertainment venue the Uline Arena as an incompatible "neighbor" to the corridor because of its segregationist policies. Schwartz and Layman write: "The building's location across from an historically Black street, made its segregated seating policies particularly glaring. Violence after concerts and the street crime attracted by the crowds aroused continued protests from neighbors" ("Near Northeast," 55).

39. Schwartz and Layman, 57.

40. Schwartz and Layman, 64.

41. Thomas, "Roots Run Deep," 753.

42. Main Street America (webpage), https://www.mainstreet.org/.

43. Dane, "Main Street Success Stories."

44. Robertson, "Main Street Approach," 55.

45. Anwar Saleem, author interview, Washington, D.C., December 6, 2011.

46. Zukin, *Naked City*, 220.

47. Meyer, "Washington Retail District's Future."

48. Kinney, *Beautiful Wasteland*.

49. Cultural Tourism DC, *Hub, Home, Heart*.

50. Derek Hyra (*Race, Class, and Politics*) writes about his interview with Kathryn Schneider Smith, founder of the DC Heritage and Tourism Coalition, which later became Cultural Tourism DC. Smith discusses how she had to provide tourists with a vision and version of the Shaw neighborhood's history that emphasized its triumph over its more recent crime-ridden, violent past in order to attract foot traffic.

51. Deckha, "Beyond the Country House," 404.

52. Saito, "From 'Blighted.'"

53. Deckha writes about gentrification in London that historic preservation "can mobilize new histories and uses of older spaces to become a vibrant cultural politics of space that reflects the new urban realities of cosmopolitanism, multiculturalism and diasporic cultures" (418).

54. Mele, "Revisiting the Citadel," 362.

55. Hannigan, *Fantasy City*, 78.

56. Lefebvre, *Production of Space*. Lefebvre is fundamental when thinking about discursive production of space. While his research does not explicitly engage racialized geographies, his work is useful to better understand "urban sociospatial processes" (McCann, "Race, Protest, and Public Space," 164).

57. Lefebvre, *Production of Space*, 39.

58. McCann, "Race, Protest, and Public Space," 169.

Chapter Four

1. O'Connell, "Whole Foods Market."

2. The irony of the Whole Foods claim on diversity, culture, community, and history is its leadership by proclaimed libertarian CEO John Mackey. While the Whole Foods brand is often associated with progressive politics and "socially minded commerce" due to its adoption of spiritual, sustainable, and countercultural practices, Mackey has spoken openly about his commitment to advance individual freedom without regard for social equality. J. C. Davis, *Whole Foods*.

3. My use of the term "hipster" borrows from Bjørn Schiermer, who characterizes hipsters as "young, white and middle class, typically between 20 and 35 years old." They are specifically known for gentrifying "former 'popular,' working-class, ethnic or 'exotic' neighbourhoods [*sic*] in the big Western cities." Schiermer, "Late-Modern Hipsters," 170. Although I recognize that hipsters are not universally white, the use of labels like "blipsters" to signify "Black hipsters" signals a distinction between Black people who perform hipsterism and "authentic" (white) hipsters.

4. Modan, "Mango Fufu," 190.

5. J. C. Davis, *Whole Foods*.

6. Whole Foods Market, "Our Higher Purpose Statement."

7. The building was named after the Apollo Theatre, which originally opened in 1913 and was located in the same area as the new Apollo building. The theater closed in 1955 and the land was later sold to Ourisman Chevrolet. It later became the site of Murry's grocery store and H Street Storage.

8. Boyd, *Jim Crow Nostalgia*; Lees, "Gentrification and Social Mixing"; Lees, Slater, and Wyly, *Gentrification*; Hyra, *Cappuccino City*.

9. N. Smith, *New Urban Frontier*; Kern, "Rhythms of Gentrification."

10. Baudrillard, *Simulacra and Simulation*; Baudrillard, *Consumer Society*.

11. Berrey, *Enigma of Diversity*.

12. Hyra (*Cappuccino City*) echoes much of what Zukin (*Naked City*) argues about the desire for young, white professionals to move into neighborhoods thought to be "authentic"—whether that be authentically Black or unspecified "ethnic" areas. There is an increase in cultural and symbolic capital that invites them to these spaces to consume and grow them.

13. Richard Florida spends the bulk of *The Rise of the Creative Class* discussing the role of the new economy on cities and their shifting populations. New Urbanism is a design approach that started in the 1980s but became popularized in the

1990s, in reaction to the exponential growth and sprawl of the suburbs. The idea was to reimagine urban spaces via shifts to the built environment that privileged greenspace, walkability, sustainability, innovation, and regionally relevant architecture as the economy shifted from an industrial and manufacturing-based system to one that was dominated by service-related businesses. This "new economy," also focused on sustainability and innovation, and increased competition and technology, has been driven by the explosion of high-growth industries specifically in technological fields.

14. Brown-Saracino, "Social Preservationists."

15. Zukin, *Naked City*, 4.

16. Zukin, 3.

17. Schweitzer, "Silly Little Name."

18. Zukin, *Naked City*, 3.

19. Kendzior, "Peril of Hipster Economics."

20. Pow, "Neoliberalism," 373.

21. J. Jackson, *Real Black*, 55.

22. Zukin et al., "New Retail Capital."

23. J. Jackson, *Real Black*, 55.

24. Interview with Elliott Ferguson, president and chief executive officer, Destination DC, August 22, 2017.

25. Interview with Elliott Ferguson.

26. Shannon Winnubst notes that focusing on the depoliticized and deracialized notion of "cool" deepens analyses of how categories like diversity, multiculturalism, and colorblindness are the afterlife of "long-standing, historical cathexis with xenophobia in the times of classic liberalism into an aestheticized, ahistorical cathexis with o so cool forms of fungible difference in the social rationality of neoliberalism" (Winnubst, *Way Too Cool*, 3). The historical transformation of "cool" highlights the shift from social difference as antagonistic to difference as aesthetic, formal, and fungible. Deracialization takes place in the shifting meanings and posture of cool which strips historical and political meaning of cool as a historical form of Black resistance.

27. Ocejo, "Early Gentrifer," 285.

28. According to a press release, distributed by the Feldman Group of Marcus & Millichap, the 11th Property Group "had already closed on the property next door at the time of the sale. The Feldman Group was able to facilitate the acquisition of 1338 H Street NE so that they could increase the size of their project."

29. Bannister, "Developer Q&A."

30. Ross, "Separate and Unequal," 15.

31. Ross, 16.

32. Ross, 16.

33. Ley, *New Middle Class*, 15.

34. Zukin, "Consuming Authenticity," 744.

35. Zukin et al., "New Retail Capital," 48.

36. Schwartzman, "Whose H Street."

37. Schwartzman.

38. Hopkinson, *Go-Go Live*, 95.

39. Schwartzman, "Whose H Street."

40. Brownell and Horgen, *Food Fight*, 37.

41. Melaniphy, *Restaurant*, 83.

42. Wax, "Dreaming of a Streetscape."

43. M. Davis, *City of Quartz*.

44. Equitable development stands in contrast to gentrification, since it involves the development and preservation of "economically and socially diverse communities that are stable over the long term, through means that generate a minimum of transition costs that fall unfairly on lower income residents." Kennedy and Leonard, "Dealing with Neighborhood Change," 4.

45. Zukin, *Culture of Cities*; Baudrillard, *Consumer Society*; Hannigan, *Fantasy City*; Florida, *Creative Class*; Ley, *New Middle Class*; Lees, Slater, and Wyly, *Gentrification*; Brown-Saracino, *Neighborhood That Never Changes*; Zukin, *Naked City*; Hyra, *Cappuccino City*; Low, *Spatializing Culture*.

46. Ley, *New Middle Class*, 15.

47. Florida, *Creative Class*.

48. Banet-Weiser, *Authentic*, 109.

49. DC.gov, Office of Planning, "Creative DC Action Agenda."

50. Dávila, *Culture Works*, 24.

51. Dávila, 24.

52. Zukin, *Naked City*.

53. Zukin, 19–20.

54. Zukin, "Consuming Authenticity," 734.

55. Bourdieu, *Distinction*.

56. This ideal was most notably espoused by Jane Jacobs, who relentlessly advocated for social and cultural preservation in cities in the face of increasing pressure from developers, who she believed destroyed the urban landscape for purely economic interests.

57. In 2004, the D.C. Office of Planning implemented a strategic development plan for H Street NE, which identified three thematic areas along the corridor: The Hub and Urban Living, Central Retail District, and Arts & Entertainment. The plan was used to encourage and organize development efforts within the space according to the designated theme.

58. Zukin, *Culture of Cities*; Florida, *Creative Class*; Banet-Weiser, *Authentic*.

59. Goonewardena and Kipfer, "Spaces of Difference," 672.

60. Douglas, *Implicit Meanings*, 259.

61. Gunew, "Introduction"; Kalcik, "Eating Foodways."

62. Lefebvre, *Production of Space*.

63. Rushmore, "Gaia Mural in DC."

64. N. Smith, *New Urban Frontier*; Brown-Saracino, "Social Preservationists"; Kinney, *Beautiful Wasteland*.

65. N. Smith, *New Urban Frontier*, 190.

66. Kirylo, "Eat Me DC."

67. J. Jackson, *Real Black*, 53.

68. J. Jackson, 54.

69. Current plans to redevelop the H Street corridor include the preservation of H Street's "historic building fabric," as Advisory Neighborhood Commission 6A chairman David Holmes wrote to the secretary of the D.C. Zoning Commission in February 2003. H Street's development as a "vibrant" corridor relies on its "distinctive collection of historic commercial buildings that reflect that history of the people that lived, worked, and shopped there." D.C. Office of Planning, "Revival," 19.

70. Carman, "Fried Whiting."

71. Carman.

72. Bégin, "Southern Style," 128.

73. Bégin, 138.

74. Carman, "Fried Whiting."

75. J. Jackson, *Real Black*, 56.

76. Melamed, "Spirit of Neoliberalism," 19. Asch and Musgrove discuss the tensions between East African and African American residents in D.C. as Ethiopians and Eritreans attempt to make their mark on the space in order to acknowledge their history. Asch and Musgrove, *Chocolate City*, 443. Longtime Black residents and business owners see this desire as a direct threat to the history and identity of the neighborhood. This discord speaks to many of the challenges over space in D.C., especially as longtime Black residents continue to experience the violence of dispossession and displacement. Nevertheless, as McKittrick and Woods note, "Because we live in and through social systems that reward us for consuming, claiming, and owning things—and in terms of geography this means that we are rewarded for wanting and demarcating 'our place' in the same ways that those in power do (often through displacement of others)—we also need to step back and consider how these geographic desires might be bound up in conquest" (McKittrick and Woods, *Black Geographies*, 5).

77. Melamed, "Spirit of Neoliberalism," 1. Shelly Habecker writes about the resistance of some Ethiopian and Eritrean immigrants to racialization and their decision to identify themselves as culturally (and sometimes racially) distinct from Black Americans, "by situating themselves outside of the American racial hierarchy." Habecker, "Not Black," 1216.

78. Cooper, "Chez Hareg."

79. Wiener, "More Upscale." In the press release, Deputy Mayor Victor Hoskins listed H Street Organic Market (Chez Hareg) as "a market that will feature locally grown and sustainable products with weekly opportunities for shoppers to learn about healthier cooking techniques and new ways to use locally grown and seasonal goods." Other grant recipients on H Street NE included Cirque de Rouge, a modern art studio; Creative Hands Massage, a skin care, massage, and physical therapy business; RowHouse Company, an art supply store focusing on green, nontoxic children's art supplies; and Integrity Self MovementArts, a movement arts studio. Awarding these small businesses with lucrative grants follows a pattern of praise for new stores and restaurants by elected officials and community development groups that supports the logic of the establishments as "signs of capital reinvestment,

enabling them to proclaim an urban 'renaissance' or at least to hope for a new period of growth" (Zukin et al., "New Retail Capital," 49).

80. Kaufman, "Progress."

81. Several local blogs and websites like washingtoncitypaper.com, frozentropics .com, and elevationmediadc.com wrote about their enthusiasm for the H Street Organic Market to join the neighborhood, finally offering fresh, local, organic food choices to residents every day of the week so they would not have to wait until the Saturday morning farmers' market.

82. Zukin, "Consuming Authenticity," 725.

83. Zukin, 736.

84. Zukin, 737. Unfortunately, H Street Organic Market did not last a full year and joined a long history of natural foods stores, owned by Black entrepreneurs, that were unsuccessful. With the introduction of larger and more recognizable brands to the corridor that can afford higher property taxes and that provide options for organic and natural food, H Street Organic Market was poised for an uphill challenge to survive. As I will discuss in chapter 5, the store's spatial location in the center of the corridor, across from the city's highest bus transfer point, certainly impacted its ultimate failure.

85. Gray, "Subject(ed) to Recognition," 771.

86. Anderson, *Cosmopolitan Canopy*.

87. H Street Festival (webpage), https://www.hstreetfestival.org/about/.

88. Affordable housing offered at market rate is still expensive to some poor and working-class families as the AMI continues to shift upward.

89. Bell and Hartmann, "Diversity in Everyday Discourse."

Chapter Five

1. Marcus, "Northeast Redevelopment."

2. Shabazz, *Spatializing Blackness*, 2.

3. J. Jackson, *Real Black*.

4. Bannister, "Development Q&A."

5. Zukin, *Culture of Cities*, 41–42.

6. J. Jackson, *Real Black*, 54.

7. J. Jackson, 54.

8. One of the most well-known recent examples is the controversy over the presence of drum circles in Harlem's Marcus Garvey Park. For years, on Saturdays, a group of men and women have gathered to drum for a diverse crowd of residents and tourists. With the changing demographics and landscape of Harlem, "noise" has become a contentious issue between newer, wealthy, white residents moving to the neighborhood and the older, lower-income Black residents.

9. Young, "H Street NE Corridor."

10. Cramer, "Race at the Interface," 3.

11. The city's Inclusionary Zoning Program requires 8 to 10 percent of residential buildings to be set aside for affordable rental and for-sale units (based upon the Median Family Income of the metropolitan area) for projects that have ten or more units.

12. Stein, "D.C. Strip Mall."

13. Sabar, "Joe Englert."

14. Stein, "D.C. Strip Mall."

15. Bourdieu, *Distinction*.

16. Lipsitz, *How Racism Takes Place*.

17. The prominence of this common assessment of the H Street corridor is ironic because transportation is not often cited as a hindrance for young revelers to visit the Georgetown neighborhood, another popular location featuring popular boutiques, bars, and restaurants.

18. America on the Move exhibit, Smithsonian National Museum of American History, "A Streetcar City" (http://amhistory.si.edu/onthemove/exhibition/exhibition _4_6.html).

19. D.C. Office of Planning, "Streetcar Land Use."

20. Mohammed, "Minority-Owned H Street Businesses."

21. WMATA, *Joint Development Policies and Guidelines*.

22. D.C. Office of Planning, "Streetcar Land Use."

23. Cervero, Ferrell, and Murphy, "Transit-Oriented Development and Joint Development," 52; Belzer and Autler, "Transit Oriented Development"; Brock, "Transit-Oriented Development."

24. Smith and Gihring, "Financing Transit Systems"; Zukin et al., "Gentrification."

25. The inherent contradiction of TOD is that while lower-income households should benefit most from increased accessibility to improved transit options, the neighborhoods in which TOD takes place experience gentrification and the displacement of lower-income families, since they are no longer able to afford the neighborhoods because of higher rents and housing costs. Research shows that home prices are 6 to 45 percent higher in neighborhoods with nearby transit stations compared with equivalent sites without them. Cervero et al., "Transit-Oriented Development in the United States."

26. Dawkins and Moeckel, "Transit-Induced Gentrification"; Kahn, "Gentrification Trends"; Talen, Menozzi, and Schaefer, "Great Neighborhood"; Cervero et al., "Transit-Oriented Development in the United States."

27. Brock, "Transit-Oriented Development," 1500.

28. Sharkey, *Stuck in Place*, 68.

29. Lipsitz, *How Racism Takes Place*, 66.

30. O'Connell, "Metro's X2 Bus." The X2 line is one of the most notorious and popular bus routes in the city. The line is known for its "diverse" ridership, large crowds, and occasional incidents of violence. In fact, as recently as 2017, local news reports described multiple assaults against X2 Metrobus drivers, causing service to be temporarily discontinued. See Collins and Barnes, "X2 Metrobus Drivers Victimized."

31. Dwyer and Jones note that the idea of carefree travel "raises the question, for whom is travel play, and for whom is travel better understood by making reference to its shared etymological roots with travail, to toil and labour, to suffer? The latter is the sense that emerges from bell hooks' persuasive rendering of black travel as an encounter with the terror of moving through places that whites have claimed as their own" (Dwyer and Jones, "White Socio-Spatial Epistemology," 216).

32. Lipsitz, *How Racism Takes Place*, 66.

33. Lipsitz; Shabazz, *Spatializing Blackness*.

34. Shabazz, *Spatializing Blackness*.

35. N. Smith, *New Urban Frontier*.

36. Browne, *Dark Matters*, 9.

37. The other location is at the eastern end of the corridor near the Starburst Plaza, another gathering place for Black poor and working-class city dwellers and residents. The intersection where the plaza sits has two CCTV cameras, one installed by the D.C. Department of Transportation (DDOT) and the other by MPD. The plaza is directly across the street from both the Pentacle Group Apartments and Delta Towers, two low-income housing buildings that have long-term contracts.

38. WJLA, "WATCH"; WJLA, "Police."

39. Browne, *Dark Matters*, 16.

40. Mele, "Revisiting the Citadel"; Sandercock, "Negotiating Fear and Desire."

41. Lipsitz, *How Racism Takes Place*, 37.

42. Anderson, "Iconic Ghetto"; Duneier, *Ghetto*.

43. Logan and Oakley, "Black Lives and Policing."

44. Foucault, *Discipline and Punish*; Foucault, *Power/Knowledge*.

45. Cook and Whowell, "Visibility and Policing."

46. Cook and Whowell; Cresswell, *In Place*; Herbert, *Policing Space*.

47. Cook and Whowell, "Visibility and Policing," 613.

48. Mele, "Revisiting the Citadel."

49. Mele, 365.

50. Prince of Petworth, "Foot Locker."

51. Zukin, *Culture of Cities*, 42.

52. Check-cashing facilities are used by people who would not qualify for checking accounts and must pay high transaction fees for cashing their checks.

53. Mele, "Revisiting the Citadel," 366.

54. D. Davis, "Narrating the Mute," 351.

55. Paperson, "Postcolonial Ghetto," 19.

56. Lipsitz, *How Racism Takes Place*, 77.

57. Lipsitz, 77.

58. N. Smith, *New Urban Frontier*.

59. Lefebvre, *Production of Space*, 56.

60. Browne, *Dark Matters*.

61. Anderson, *Cosmopolitan Canopy*, 2.

62. Coleman, "Race as Technology."

63. Some of the sociology literature discusses the gentrification and the convergence of different populations by demonstrating that people live side by side but do not necessarily interact in these spaces (Hyra, *Cappuccino City*; Freeman, *There Goes the 'Hood*). Hyra introduces the phenomenon in terms of "diversity segregation." He also argues that white, upper-class enclaves reproduce segregation as they construct "gilded ghettos," where white, upper-class residents can lead separate lives from those surrounding the area and still experience "edge" and "authenticity."

Freeman finds that people in close spatial proximity do not necessarily have closer "social proximity."

64. Mukherjee, *Racial Order of Things*.

65. K. Taylor, *From #BlackLivesMatter*, 53.

66. K. Taylor, 64.

67. Bonilla-Silva, *Racism without Racists*, 1.

68. McCann, "Race, Protest, and Public Space," 179.

69. Boyd, *Jim Crow Nostalgia*, xiii.

70. Zukin, *Culture of Cities*, 274.

71. Hyra, *Cappuccino City*.

Conclusion

1. Jameson, *Postmodernism*.

2. Morello, "Poverty Rates."

3. Kneebone and Garr, "Suburbanization of Poverty," 14.

4. Brookings Institution analysis of Census 2000 and 2008 ACS data.

5. Fletcher, "Progress, but Not Perfect."

6. Ellison, "Suburban Poverty."

7. McCartney, "'Perception' Problem."

8. McCartney.

9. Landry, *New Black Middle Class*; Lacy, *Blue-Chip Black*; Pattillo, *Black Picket Fences*; Pattillo, *Black on the Block*.

10. Lacy, *Blue-Chip Black*, 17.

11. Robinson, *Black Marxism*.

12. Leadbeater, "Oakland"; Chubb, "Oakland."

13. Winnubst, *Way Too Cool*.

14. Fontana, "Washington a Cool City."

15. Winnubst, *Way Too Cool*, 4.

16. Shukla, "Harlem's Pasts."

17. Wilkins, *Aesthetics of Equity*.

18. Gray and Gómez-Barris, *Toward a Sociology*, 11.

19. McKittrick, "Plantation Futures," 14.

20. McKittrick, 14.

Bibliography

Abu-Lughod, Janet L. *Race, Space, and Riots in Chicago, New York, and Los Angeles.* Oxford: Oxford University Press, 2007.

Ahmed, Sara. "The Nonperformativity of Antiracism." *Meridians: Feminism, Race, Transnationalism* 7, no. 1 (2006): 104–26.

———. *On Being Included: Racism and Diversity in Institutional Life.* Durham, NC: Duke University Press, 2012.

Alexander, Bryant. "Fading, Twisting, and Weaving: An Interpretive Ethnography of the Black Barbershops as Cultural Space." *Qualitative Inquiry* 9, no. 1 (2003): 105–28.

Anderson, Elijah. *The Cosmopolitan Canopy: Race and Civility in Everyday Life.* New York: W. W. Norton, 2012.

———. "The Iconic Ghetto." *ANNALS of the American Academy of Political and Social Science* 642, no. 1 (2012): 8–24.

Asch, Chris Myers, and George Derek Musgrove. "Not Gone, not Forgotten: Struggling over History in a Gentrifying D.C." *Washington Post*, October 19, 2012. Retrieved October 19, 2012. http://www.washingtonpost.com/blogs /therootdc/post/not-gone-not-forgotten-struggling-over-history-in-a -gentrifying-dc/2012/10/18/09ad8c24-1941-11e2-b97b-3ae53cdeaf69_blog.html.

———. *Chocolate City: A History of Race and Democracy in the Nation's Capital.* Chapel Hill: University of North Carolina Press, 2017.

Asher, Robert, and Robert Kaiser. "Broken Promises Line Riot Area Streets." *Washington Post*, December 29, 1968, B1.

Banet-Weiser, Sarah. *Authentic: The Politics of Ambivalence in a Brand Culture.* New York: New York University Press, 2012.

Bannister, Jon. "Developer Q&A: Insight Property Group Partner Trent Smith." *Bisnow*, March 13, 2018. Retrieved March 13, 2018. https://www.bisnow.com /washington-dc/news/neighborhood/developer-qa-insight-property-group -partner-trent-smith-86080.

Baradaran, Mehrsa. *The Color of Money: Black Banks and the Racial Wealth Gap.* Cambridge, MA: The Belknap Press of Harvard University Press, 2017.

Barnes, Kendall, Gordon Waitt, Nicholas Gill, and Chris Gibson. "Community and Nostalgia in Urban Revitalisation: A Critique of Urban Village and Creative Class Strategies as Remedies for Social 'Problems.'" *Australian Geographer* 37, no. 3 (2006): 335–54.

Basham, William. "Council Cites Intent on Riot-Hit Areas." *Evening Star*, March 4, 1969, B1.

Baudrillard, Jean. *Simulacra and Simulation.* Ann Arbor: University of Michigan Press, 1994.

——. *The Consumer Society: Myths and Structures.* New York: SAGE, 1998.

Bégin, Camille. "'Partaking of Choice Poultry Cooked a la Southern Style': Taste and Race in the New Deal Sensory Economy." *Radical History Review* 110, no. 1 (2011): 127–53.

Bell, Joyce, and Douglas Hartmann. "Diversity in Everyday Discourse: The Cultural Ambiguities and Consequences of 'Happy Talk.'" *American Sociological Review* 72, no. 6 (2007): 895–914.

Belzer, Dana, and Gerald Autler. "Transit Oriented Development: Moving from Rhetoric to Reality." Washington, DC: Brookings Institute Center on Urban and Metropolitan Policy, 2002.

Berrey, Ellen. *The Enigma of Diversity: The Language of Race and the Limits of Racial Justice.* Chicago: University of Chicago Press, 2015.

Bledsoe, Adam, Latoya E. Eaves, and Brian Williams. "Introduction: Black Geographies in and of the United States South." *Southeastern Geographer* 57, no. 1 (2017): 6–10.

Bonilla-Silva, Eduardo. *Racism without Racists: Color-Blind Racism and the Persistence of Racial Inequality in America.* 3rd ed. Lanham, MD: Rowman & Littlefield, 2010.

Boulder, Jacqueline. "Young, Middle-Income Blacks Are Moving to the Hill." *Washington Star,* April 5, 1978, A8.

Bourdieu, Pierre. *Distinction: A Social Critique of the Judgement of Taste.* London: Routledge & Kegan Paul, 1986.

Bowman, LaBarbara. "Agency Cheers Plan to Revive H Street NE." *Washington Post,* August 25, 1982, DC1.

——. "District Rethinking Development Plans for H St. Corridor." *Washington Post,* March 8, 1982, B1.

——. "Why H Street Is Still Waiting: Without Yuppies, NE's Commercial Strip Will Never Come Back." *Washington Post,* March 30, 1986, D5.

Boyd, Michelle. "Defensive Development: The Role of Racial Conflict in Gentrification." *Urban Affairs Review* 43, no. 6 (2008a): 751–76.

——. *Jim Crow Nostalgia: Reconstructing Race in Bronzeville.* Minneapolis: University of Minnesota Press, 2008b.

Braestrup, Peter. "Planners, Citizens Fight over H St." *Washington Post,* April 18, 1969a, B2.

——. "Planning Commission Backs Rebuilding Plan for H Street: 'Mayor's Man' Open Meeting Monday Meeting." *Washington Post,* April 19, 1969b, 24.

Brenner, Neil, and Nik Theodore. "Cities and the Geographies of 'Actually Existing Neoliberalism.'" *Antipode* 34, no. 3 (2002): 356–86.

Brock, Timothy J. "Transit-Oriented Development." In *Encyclopedia of Transportation: Social Science and Policy,* edited by M. Garrett, 1500–501. Thousand Oaks, CA: SAGE, 2014. doi: 10.4135/9781483346526.n521.

Brown, DeNeen. "U-Turn on H Street: If You Were Eight Blocks Past Uncertainty, Three Steps from Neglect, Five Houses Down from Hope, and You Just Saw a

White Man with Ear Buds Rollerblading Past a Crack House without Looking Up, Would You Know What Street You Were On in the City?" *Washington Post*, March 18, 2007, D1.

Brown, Wendy. "Neoliberalism's Frankenstein: Authoritarian Freedom in Twenty-First-Century 'Democracies.'" *Critical Times* 1, no. 1 (2017): 60–79.

Brown-Saracino, Japonica. "Social Preservationists and the Quest for Authentic Community." *City & Community* 3, no. 2 (2004): 135–56.

———. *A Neighborhood That Never Changes: Gentrification, Social Preservation, and the Search for Authenticity*. Chicago: University of Chicago Press, 2009.

Browne, Simone. *Dark Matters: On the Surveillance of Blackness*. Durham, NC: Duke University Press, 2015.

Brownell, Kelly D., and Katherine Battle Horgen. *Food Fight: The Inside Story of the Food Industry, America's Obesity Crisis, and What We Can Do about It*. New York: McGraw-Hill, 2003.

Carman, Tim. "Fried Whiting: Washington's Fillet of Soul." *Washington Post*, February 13, 2013. Retrieved February 13, 2013. http://www.washingtonpost .com/lifestyle/food/2013/02/11/a82dcd3c-7076-11e2-8b8d-e0b59a1b8e2a_story .html.

Carroll, Kenneth. "The Meaning of Funk." *Washington Post*, February 1, 1998. Retrieved August 12, 2014. http://www.washingtonpost.com/wp-srv/local /longterm/library/dc/dc6898/funk.htm.

Cashin, Sheryll. "Moving toward a Culturally Dexterous Washington." *Washington Post*, August 3, 2012. Retrieved September 12, 2013. http://www .washingtonpost.com/blogs/therootdc/post/moving-toward-a-culturally -dexterous-washington/2012/08/02/gJQAcQIkSX_blog.html.

Cervero, Robert, Christopher Ferrell, and Stephen Murphy. "Transit-Oriented Development and Joint Development in the United States: A Literature Review." *TCRP Research Results Digest*, no. 52 (2002): 1–144. Washington, DC: Transportation Research Board.

Cervero, Robert, Stephen Murphy, Christopher Ferrell, et al. "Transit-Oriented Development in the United States: Experiences, Challenges, and Prospects." Washington, DC: Transportation Research Board of the National Academies, 2004.

Chubb, Laura. "Oakland: How San Francisco's Cousin across the Water Became the Coolest City in the Bay Area." *Independent*, April 13, 2017. Retrieved May 1, 2018. https://www.independent.co.uk/travel/48-hours-in/oakland-city-guide -best-restaurants-food-bars-drink-sights-shopping-san-francisco-a7647171 .html.

Cohen, Patricia. "'Culture of Poverty,' Long an Academic Slur, Makes a Comeback." *New York Times*, October 18, 2010, A1.

Coleman, Beth. "Race as Technology." *Camera Obscura* 24, no. 1 (2009): 177–207.

Collins, Pat, and Sophia Barnes. "Two More X2 Metrobus Drivers Victimized as Assault Numbers Climb." *NBC Washington*, October 4, 2017. Retrieved October 15, 2017. https://www.nbcwashington.com/news/local/More-X2 -Metrobus-Drivers-Victimized-as-Assault-Numbers-Climb-449488043.html.

Connolly, Nathan D. B. *A World More Concrete: Real Estate and the Remaking of Jim Crow South Florida*. Chicago: University of Chicago Press, 2014.

Cook, Ian, and Mary Whowell. "Visibility and the Policing of Public Space." *Geography Compass* 5, no. 8 (2011): 610–22.

Cooper, Rebecca. "Chez Hareg Moves into Warehouse, New Market on H Street." *Washington Business Journal*, March 25, 2013. Retrieved March 1, 2014. http://www.bizjournals.com/washington/blog/2013/03/chez-hareg-moves -into-warehouse-new.html?page=all.

"Coverage Was Lacking: Merchants Stand More Riot Loss." *Washington Daily News*, March 12, 1969.

Cramer, Lauren M. "Race at the Interface: Rendering Blackness on WorldStarHipHop.com." *Film Criticism* 40, no. 2 (2016): 1–20.

Cresswell, Tim. *In Place/Out of Place: Geography, Ideology, and Transgression*. Minneapolis: University of Minnesota Press, 1996.

Crockett, Stephen A., Jr. "The Brixton: It's New, Happening and Another Example of African-American 'Swagger-Jacking.'" *Washington Post*, August 3, 2012. Retrieved August 3, 2012. http://www.washingtonpost.com/blogs/therootdc /post/the-brixton-its-new-happening-and-another-example-of-african -american-historical-swagger-jacking/2012/08/03/b189b254-dcee-11e1-a894 -af35ab98c616_blog.html.

Cultural Tourism DC. *Hub, Home, Heart: Greater H Street NE Heritage Trail*. Washington, DC: Cultural Tourism DC, 2011.

Dane, Suzanne G. "Main Street Success Stories." Washington, DC: National Main Streets Center, 1997.

Daniels, J. Yolande. "Black Bodies, Black Space: A-Waiting Spectacle." In *White Papers, Black Marks: Architecture, Race, Culture*, edited by L. Lokko, 194–217. Minneapolis: University of Minnesota Press, 2000.

Dash, Leon. "Barry in NE: Barry Takes Campaign to the Streets; Economic Plan Outlined in Sidewalk Statement." *Washington Post*, June 17, 1978, C1.

Davidson, Mark. "Spoiled Mixture: Where Does State-Led 'Positive' Gentrification End?" *Urban Studies* 45, no. 12 (2008): 2385–406.

Dávila, Arlene. *Latinos, Inc.: The Marketing and Making of a People*. Berkeley: University of California Press, 2001.

———. "Empowered Culture?: New York City's Empowerment Zone and the Selling of El Barrio." *ANNALS of the American Academy of Political and Social Science* 594, no. 1 (2004): 49–64.

———. *Culture Works: Space, Value, and Mobility across the Neoliberal Americas*. New York: New York University Press, 2012.

Davis, Dana-Ain. "Narrating the Mute: Racializing and Racism in a Neoliberal Moment." *Souls: A Critical Journal of Black Politics, Culture, and Society* 9, no. 4 (2007): 346–60.

Davis, Joshua Clark. *From Head Shops to Whole Foods: The Rise and Fall of Activist Entrepreneurs*. New York: Columbia University Press, 2017.

Davis, Mike. *City of Quartz: Excavating the Future of Los Angeles*. New York: Vintage Books, 1992.

Dawkins, Casey, and Rolf Moeckel. "Transit-Induced Gentrification: Who Will Stay, and Who Will Go?" *Housing Policy Debate* 26, nos. 4–5 (2016): 801–18.

DC.gov. "Creative DC Action Agenda." Office of Planning, n.d. https://planning.dc .gov/page/creative-dc-action-agenda.

DC.gov. Great Streets, n.d. http://greatstreets.dc.gov/release/mayor-vincent-c -gray-and-deputy-mayor-planning-and-economic-development-victor-l -hoskins.

Deckha, Nityanand. "Beyond the Country House: Historic Conservation as Aesthetic Politics." *European Journal of Cultural Studies* 7, no. 4 (2004): 403–23.

Deener, Andrew. "Commerce as the Structure and Symbol of Neighborhood Life: Reshaping the Meaning of Community in Venice, California." *City & Community* 6, no. 4 (2007): 291–314.

Deutsche, Rosalyn, and Cara Gendel Ryan. "The Fine Art of Gentrification." *October* 31 (1984): 91–111.

District of Columbia Chamber of Commerce. *2018 State of the Business Report: Towards a More Inclusive Economy.* Washington, DC: D.C. Policy Center, 2018.

District of Columbia Department of Transportation (DDOT). "H Street NE Corridor Transportation & Streetscape Study: Recommendations Report." Washington, DC: Michael Baker Corporation, 2004.

District of Columbia Deputy Mayor for Planning and Economic Development (DMPED). *H Street N.E. Retail Priority Grant Request for Applications, RFA#EOM-DMPED-012* (Revised). Washington, DC: Government of the District of Columbia, 2011.

District of Columbia Office of Planning. "Revival: The H Street NE Strategic Development Plan." Washington, DC: Government of the District of Columbia, 2004.

———. "District of Columbia Streetcar Land Use Study: Phase One," January 2012. Retrieved March 13, 2013. https://comp.ddot.dc.gov/Documents/Streetcar%20 Land%20Use%20Study%20Phase%20One.pdf.

District of Columbia Zoning Commission. *Zoning Commission Public Hearing,* July 19, 2010. Washington, DC: D.C. Zoning Commission.

Douglas, Mary. *Implicit Meanings: Essays in Anthropology.* London: Routledge, 1975.

Du Bois, W. E. B. *The Souls of Black Folk.* Oxford: Oxford University Press, 1903.

Duggan, Lisa. *The Twilight of Equality?: Neoliberalism, Cultural Politics, and the Attack on Democracy.* Boston: Beacon Press, 2004.

Duneier, Mitchell. *Ghetto: The Invention of a Place, the History of an Idea.* New York: Farrar, Straus and Giroux, 2016.

Dunson, Lynn. "A Street Scores in Cleanup." *Washington Star,* February 26, 1974, B-3.

———. "What Riots Did to Two Businesses: They Never Doubted They'd Rebuild Store." *Washington Star,* April 3, 1978, A1 and A8.

Dvorak, Petula. "Craft Coffee, Million-Dollar Condos and D.C.'s Relentless Gentrification." *Washington Post,* July 17, 2017. Retrieved July 17, 2017. https://

www.washingtonpost.com/local/craft-coffee-million-dollar-condos-and-dcs
-relentless-gentrification/2017/07/17/c0f44b32-6b14-11e7-b9e2-2056e768a7e5
_story.html?utm_term=.eb877ce0f501.

Dwyer, Owen J., and John Paul Jones III. "White Socio-Spatial Epistemology." *Social & Cultural Geography* 1, no. 2 (2000): 209–22.

Edwards, Paul G. "Some Insurance Costs to Rise in Wake of Riot." *Washington Post*, April 14, 1968.

Elam, Harry J., Jr. "Change Clothes and Go: A Postscript to Postblackness." In *Black Cultural Traffic: Crossroads in Global Performance and Popular Culture*, edited by Harry J. Elam Jr. and K. Jackson, 379–88. Ann Arbor: University of Michigan Press, 2005.

Ellison, Charles. "Is Suburban Poverty Pulling Prince George's Backward?" *Washington Post*, March 3, 2013. Retrieved October 2, 2018. https://www .washingtonpost.com/opinions/is-suburban-poverty-pulling-prince-georges -backward/2013/03/01/6921e98e-8124-11e2-b99e-6baf4ebe42df_story.html ?utm_term=.d6ad91e4b2da.

Escobar, Gabriel. "H Street NE Looks Black to Its Future: Festival Celebrates Promise of Renewal." *Washington Post*, October 4, 1992, B3.

Ethridge, Harrison Mosley. "The Black Architects of Washington, D.C., 1900–Present." PhD diss., Catholic University of America, 1979.

Fanon, Frantz. *Black Skin, White Masks*. New York: Grove, 1967.

Ferguson, Roderick A. *Aberrations in Black: Toward a Queer of Color Critique*. Critical American Studies Series. Minneapolis: University of Minnesota Press, 2004.

"15 Years Later, the Shames Remain." *Washington Post*, April 3, 1983, D6.

Fisher, Marc, and Eric Pianin. "The Riots and D.C.'s Underclass: City's Poor Still Feel Effects of Black, White Exodus after Uprising Series; The Fires of April, 20 Years Later." *Washington Post*, April 4, 1988, A1.

Fletcher, Michael. "Progress, but Not Perfect." *Washington Post*, May 19, 2014, A1 and A16.

Florida, Richard. *Rise of the Creative Class: And How It's Transforming Work, Leisure, Community and Everyday Life*. New York: Basic Books, 2002.

Fontana, David. "Washington Is Now a Cool City. That's Terrible News for American Democracy." *Washington Post*, May 7, 2018. Retrieved May 7, 2018. https://www.washingtonpost.com/lifestyle/magazine/washington-is-now-a -cool-city-thats-terrible-news-for-american-democracy/2018/05/04/380682da -3f40-11e8-974f-aacd97698cef_story.html?utm_term=.b7c37e4ef298.

Foucault, Michel. *Discipline and Punish: The Birth of the Prison*. New York: Pantheon Books, 1977.

———. *Power/Knowledge: Selected Interviews and Other Writings, 1972–1977*. New York: Vintage Books, 1980.

Freeman, Lance. *There Goes the 'Hood: Views of Gentrification from the Ground Up*. Philadelphia: Temple University Press, 2006.

Gaines-Carter, Patrice. "Closing of Mega Foods Slows Bustle along H St." *Washington Post*, July 29, 1990, B1.

Ghertner, D. Asher. *Rule by Aesthetics: World-Class City Making in Delhi*. Oxford: Oxford University Press, 2015.

Gilbert, Ben. *Ten Blocks from the White House: Anatomy of the Washington Riots of 1968*. New York: F. A. Praeger, 1968.

Gill, Tiffany. *Beauty Shop Politics: African American Women's Activism in the Beauty Industry*. Urbana: University of Illinois Press, 2010.

Gillette, Howard, Jr. *Between Justice and Beauty: Race, Planning, and the Failure of Urban Policy in Washington, D.C.* Baltimore: Johns Hopkins University Press, 1995.

Gilroy, Paul. *The Black Atlantic: Modernity and Double Consciousness*. New York: Verso, 1993.

Glazer, Nathan. *Beyond the Melting Pot*. Cambridge, MA: MIT Press, 1970.

Goonewardena, Kanishka, and Stefan Kipfer. "Spaces of Difference: Reflections from Toronto on Multiculturalism, Bourgeois Urbanism and the Possibility of Radical Urban Politics." *International Journal of Urban and Regional Research* 29, no. 3 (2005): 670–78.

Gray, Herman. "Subject(ed) to Recognition." *American Quarterly* 65, no. 4 (2013): 771–98.

Gray, Herman, and Macarena Gómez-Barris, eds. *Toward a Sociology of the Trace*. Minneapolis: University of Minnesota Press, 2010.

Greenberg, Miriam. *Branding New York: How a City in Crisis Was Sold to the World*. New York: Routledge, 2008.

Gunew, Sneja. "Introduction: Multicultural Translations of Food, Bodies, Language." *Journal of Intercultural Studies* 21, no. 3 (2000): 227–37.

Gutheim, Frederick Albert. *Worthy of the Nation: The History of Planning for the National Capital*. National Capital Planning Commission Historical Studies. Washington, DC: Smithsonian Institution Press, 1977.

H Street Festival, n.d. https://www.hstreetfestival.org/about/.

Habecker, Shelly. "Not Black but Habasha: Ethiopian and Eritrean Immigrants in American Society." *Ethnic and Racial Studies* 35, no. 7 (2012): 1200–19.

Hackworth, Jason, and Josephine Rekers. "Ethnic Packaging and Gentrification: The Case of Four Neighborhoods in Toronto." *Urban Affairs Review* 41, no. 2 (2005): 211–36.

Hackworth, Jason, and Neil Smith. "The Changing State of Gentrification." *Tijdschrift Voor Economische En Socioale Geografie* 92, no. 4 (2001): 464–77.

Hall, Stuart. "What Is This 'Black' in Black Popular Culture?" In *Black Popular Culture*, edited by G. Dent, 21–33. Seattle: Bay Press, 1992.

——. "Introduction: Who Needs 'Identity'?" In *Questions of Cultural Identity*, edited by S. Hall and P. du Gay, 1–17. London: SAGE, 1996.

——. *Representation: Cultural Representation and Signifying Practices*. London: SAGE, 1997.

Hannerz, Ulf. *Soulside: Inquiries into Ghetto Culture and Community*. New York: Columbia University Press, 1969.

Hannigan, John. *Fantasy City: Pleasure and Profit in the Postmodern Metropolis*. New York: Routledge, 1998.

Harris-Lacewell, Melissa. *Barbershops, Bibles, and BET: Everyday Talk and Black Political Thought.* Princeton, NJ: Princeton University Press, 2005.

Hart, Alton, Jr., and Deborah Bowen. "The Feasibility of Partnering with African-American Barbershops to Provide Prostate Cancer Education." *Ethnicity & Disease* 14, no. 2 (2004): 269–73.

Hart, Alton, Jr., R. Wally Smith, Raymond H. Tademy, Donna K. McClish, and Micah McCreary. "Health Decision-Making Preferences among African American Men Recruited from Urban Barbershops." *Journal of National Medical Association* 101, no. 7 (2009): 684–89.

Hartman, Saidiya. *Scenes of Subjection: Terror, Slavery, and Self-Making in Nineteenth-Century America.* New York: Oxford University Press, 1997.

Hartman, Saidiya, and Frank Wilderson, III. "The Position of Unthought: An Interview with Saidiya V. Hartman Conducted by Frank Wilderson, III." *Qui Parle* 13, no. 2 (2003): 183–201.

Harvey, David. *The Condition of Postmodernity: An Enquiry into the Origins of Cultural Change.* Oxford, UK: Blackwell, 1989.

Hechinger, John W. "Statement by John W. Hechinger, Chairman of the City Council at a News Conference on Rebuilding and Recovery of the City," Washington, D.C., May 10, 1968.

Herbert, Steve. *Policing Space: Territoriality and the Los Angeles Police Department.* Minneapolis: University of Minnesota Press, 1997.

Hill, Laura Warren, and Julia Rabig. *The Business of Black Power: Community Development, Capitalism, and Corporate Responsibility in Postwar America.* Rochester, NY: University of Rochester Press, 2012.

hooks, bell. *Yearning: Race, Gender, and Cultural Politics.* Boston: South End Press, 1990.

Hopkind, Andrew. "White on Black: The Riot Commission and the Rhetoric of Reform." *Hard Times* 44 (September 1969): 15–22.

Hopkinson, Natalie. *Go-Go Live: The Musical Life and Death of a Chocolate City.* Durham, NC: Duke University Press, 2012.

Hudge, Paul. "Recovery In Sight for H Street NE Corridor." *Washington Post,* April 14, 1982, DC1.

Hunter, Marcus Anthony, and Zandria F. Robinson. *Chocolate Cities: The Black Map of American Life.* Berkeley: University of California Press, 2018.

Hyra, Derek S. *Race, Class, and Politics in the Cappuccino City.* Chicago: University of Chicago Press, 2017.

Jackson, John, Jr. *Real Black: Adventures in Racial Sincerity.* Chicago: University of Chicago Press, 2005.

Jackson, Maurice, ed. "African American Employment, Population & Housing Trends in Washington, D.C." McCourt School of Public Policy. Washington, DC: Georgetown University, 2017.

Jacobs, Jane. *The Death and Life of Great American Cities.* New York: Vintage Books, 1992.

Jacoby, Susan. "Battle Rages for Control of Riot-Area Renewal." *Washington Post,* March 15, 1969, B1.

Jaffe, Harry, and Tom Sherwood. *Dream City: Race, Power, and the Decline of Washington, D.C.* New York: Simon & Schuster, 1994.

Jameson, Fredric. *Postmodernism, or, the Cultural Logic of Late Capitalism.* Durham, NC: Duke University Press, 1990.

———. *Archaeologies of the Future: The Desire Called Utopia and Other Science Fictions.* London: Verso, 2005.

Kahn, Matthew. "Gentrification Trends in New Transit-Oriented Communities: Evidence from 14 Cities That Expanded and Built Rail Transit Systems." *Real Estate Economics* 35, no. 2 (2007): 155–82.

Kaiser, Robert. "Burned Out in Riots, Many Owners Won't Reopen." *Washington Post*, August 1, 1968, H3.

Kalb, Barry. "Williams Considers Handling Businessmen's Suit on Riots." *Sunday Star*, May 12, 1968, B-4.

Kalcik, Susan. "Eating Foodways in America: Symbol and the Performance of Identity." In *Ethnic and Regional Foodways in the United States: The Performance of Group Identity*, edited by L. Brown and K. Mussell, 37–65. Knoxville: University of Tennessee Press, 1984.

Kasinitz, Philip, and David Hillyard. "The Old-Timers' Tale: The Politics of Nostalgia on the Brooklyn Waterfront." *Journal of Contemporary Ethnography* 24, no. 2 (1995): 139–64.

Kaufman, Rachel. "Progress on Long-Awaited H Street Organic Market." *Elevation DC*, May 2, 2014. Retrieved June 2, 2014. http://www.elevationdcmedia.com/devnews/hstreetorganicmarket_050214.aspx.

Kelley, Robin. *Race Rebels: Culture, Politics, and the Black Working Class.* New York: Free Press, 1994.

Kendzior, Sarah. "The Peril of Hipster Economics." *Al Jazeera*, May 28, 2014. Retrieved May 28, 2014. http://m.aljazeera.com/story/201452710552115885.

Kennedy, Maureen, and Paul Leonard. "Dealing with Neighborhood Change: Primer on Gentrification and Policy Choices." Discussion paper prepared for the Brookings Institution Center on Urban and Metropolitan Policy, 2001. Retrieved March 30, 2014. http://www.brookings.edu/~/media/research/files/reports/2001/4/metropolitanpolicy/gentrification.pdf.

Kern, Leslie. "Rhythms of Gentrification: Eventfulness and Slow Violence in a Happening Neighborhood." *Cultural Geographies* 23, no. 3 (2016): 441–57.

Kinney, Rebecca J. *Beautiful Wasteland: The Rise of Detroit as America's Postindustrial Frontier.* Minneapolis: University of Minnesota Press, 2016.

Kirylo, Ariell. "Eat Me DC: An Interview with Toki Underground's Chef, Erik Bruner-Yang." *D*mnGoodTimes*, 2011. Retrieved June 5, 2014. http://www.dmngoodtimes.com/interview-toki-underground-chef-erik-bruner-yang/.

Kitsock, Greg. "Beer: Chocolate City Starts Small, Plans to Stay That Way." *Washington Post*, September 20, 2011. Retrieved September 20, 2011. http://www.washingtonpost.com/lifestyle/food/beer-chocolate-city-starts-small-plans-to-stay-that-way/2011/09/19/gIQAK89piK_story.html.

Kneebone, Elizabeth, and Emily Garr. "The Suburbanization of Poverty: Trends in Metropolitan America, 2000 to 2008." Metropolitan Policy Program. Washington, DC: Brookings Institution, 2010.

Kobayashi, Audrey, and Linda Peake. "Racism Out of Place: Thoughts on Whiteness and an Antiracist Geography in the New Millennium." *Annals of the Association of American Geographers* 90, no. 2 (2000): 392–403.

Lacy, Karen. *Blue-Chip Black: Race, Class, and Status in the New Black Middle Class.* Berkeley: University of California Press, 2007.

Landry, Bart. *The New Black Middle Class.* Berkeley: University of California Press, 1987.

Leadbeater, Chris. "Oakland: The Cool Alternative to San Francisco." *The Telegraph*, March 23, 2017. Retrieved May 1, 2018. https://www.telegraph.co.uk /travel/destinations/north-america/united-states/california/articles/oakland -the-cool-alternative-to-san-francisco/.

Lees, Loretta. "The Ambivalence of Diversity and the Politics of Urban Renaissance: The Case of Youth in Downtown Portland, Maine." *International Journal of Urban and Regional Research* 27, no. 3 (2003): 613–34.

———. "Gentrification and Social Mixing: Toward an Inclusive Urban Renaissance?" *Urban Studies* 45, no. 12 (2008): 2449–70.

Lees, Loretta, Tom Slater, and Elvin Wyly. *Gentrification.* New York: Routledge, 2008.

Lefebvre, Henri. *The Production of Space.* Oxford, UK: Blackwell, 1991.

Levy, Claudia, and Leonard Downie, Jr. "The Lights Are Still Out from Riots: First in a Series." *Washington Post*, April 5, 1970, A1.

Lewis, Robert. "H Str. Overpass Design of Railroads Okayed." *Evening Star*, June 5, 1970, B-4.

Ley, David. 1996. *The New Middle Class and the Making of the Central City.* Oxford: Oxford University Press.

Liebow, Elliot. *Tally's Corner: A Study of Negro Streetcorner Men.* Boston: Little, Brown, 1967.

Lin, Jan. *The Power of Urban Ethnic Places: Cultural Heritage and Community Life.* New York: Routledge, 2011.

Lipsitz, George. "The Racialization of Space and the Spatialization of Race: Theorizing the Hidden Architecture of Landscape." *Landscape Journal* 26, no. 1 (2007): 10–23. doi: 10.3368/lj.26.1.10.

———. *How Racism Takes Place.* Philadelphia: Temple University Press, 2011.

Logan, John, and Deirdre Oakley. "Black Lives and Policing: The Larger Context of Ghettoization." *Journal of Urban Affairs* 39, no. 8 (2017): 1031–46.

"Looting Was Often Selective," *Washington Informer*, April 12, 1968.

Low, Setha. *Spatializing Culture: The Ethnography of Space and Place.* New York: Routledge, 2017.

Lynch, Teresa. "From Vision to Reality: Reviving Two African-American Main Streets." *National Trust Main Street Center—Main Street Story of the Week*, February 25, 2013. Retrieved March 3, 2013. http://www.preservationnation .org/main-street/main-street-news/story-of-the-week/2013 /130225sweetauburn/from-vision-to-reality.html#.U6iEmxZOhfM.

Maly, Michael, Heather Dalmage, and Nancy Michaels. "The End of an Idyllic World: Nostalgic Narratives, Race, and the Construction of White Powerlessness." *Critical Sociology* 39, no. 5 (2012): 757–79.

Mansfield, Virginia. "H Street Rebuilding Sparked City Plans to Locate Offices in Proposed Shopping Complex." *Washington Post*, May 30, 1985, DC1.

Marcus, Ruth. "Northeast Redevelopment Is Hailed as H Street Shopping Center Opens." *Washington Post*, May 10, 1987, D3.

Massey, Douglas S., and Nancy A. Denton. *American Apartheid: Segregation and the Making of the Underclass*. Cambridge, MA: Harvard University Press, 1993.

McCann, Eugene J. "Race, Protest, and Public Space: Contextualizing Lefebvre in the U.S. City." *Antipode* 31, no. 2 (1999): 163–84.

———. "The Cultural Politics of Local Economic Development: Meaning-Making, Place-Making and the Urban Policy Process." *Geoforum* 33, no. 3 (2002): 385–98.

McCartney, Robert. "The 'Perception' Problem in Prince George's." *Washington Post*, November 18, 2010, B1.

McCombs, Phil. "The Banker; 'People Who Come In . . . Don't Understand.'" *Washington Post*, November 27, 1977a, A12.

———. "Bitterness and Despair on H Street NE; Progress Seen in H Street Riot Corridor Redevelopment; Delay in Rebuilding Riot-Torn Area Creates Problems, Tensions." *Washington Post*, November 27, 1977b, A1.

———. "The Merchant: '(Banks) Won't Let an Individual . . . Have a Loan.'" *Washington Post*, November 27, 1977c, A12.

McKittrick, Katherine. *Demonic Grounds: Black Women and the Cartographies of Struggle*. Minneapolis: University of Minnesota Press, 2006.

———. "On Plantations, Prisons, and a Black Sense of Place." *Social & Cultural Geography* 12, no. 8 (2011): 947–63.

———. "Plantation Futures." *Small Axe* 17, no. 3 (2013): 1–15.

McKittrick, Katherine, and Clyde Adrian Woods. *Black Geographies and the Politics of Place*. Cambridge, MA: South End Press, 2007.

Meethan, Kevin. *Tourism in Global Society: Place, Culture, Consumption*. New York: Palgrave, 2001.

Melamed, Jodi. "The Spirit of Neoliberalism: From Racial Liberalism to Neoliberal Multiculturalism." *Social Text* 89, no. 4 (2006): 1–24.

Melaniphy, John. *Restaurant and Fast Food Site Selection*. New York: Wiley Books, 1992.

Mele, Christopher. *Selling the Lower East Side: Culture, Real Estate, and Resistance in New York*. Minneapolis: University of Minnesota Press, 2000.

———. "Neoliberalism, Race and the Redefining of Urban Development." *International Journal of Urban and Regional Research* 37, no. 2 (2013): 598–617.

———. "Revisiting the Citadel and the Ghetto: Legibility, Race, and Contemporary Urban Development." *Sociology of Race and Ethnicity* 2, no. 3 (2016): 354–71.

———. *Race and the Politics of Deception: The Making of an American City*. New York: New York University Press, 2017.

Meyer, Eugene. "MICCO Cutoff Ends Citizen Control of Urban Renewal." *Washington Post*, January 22, 1973, C1.

——. "Signs of Recovery in a 'Riot Corridor.'" *New York Times*, December 2, 2007. Retrieved September 12, 2013. http://www.nytimes.com/2007/12/02/realestate /02nati.html?pagewanted=all&_r=0.

——. "Washington Retail District's Future Rides on Streetcars." *New York Times*, April 15, 2014. Retrieved September 12, 2013. http://www.nytimes.com/2014/04 /16/business/washington-retail-districts-future-rides-on-streetcars.html?_r=0.

Milloy, Courtland. "She's in Command: City's 1st Black Woman Police Captain Commands Precinct on Capitol Hill; Black Woman Police Captain Runs Capitol Hill Precinct." *Washington Post*, August 22, 1978, C1.

——. "Success Story: Safeway Store in the Hechinger Mall Becomes One of the Most Profitable in City." *Washington Post*, July 21, 1984.

Mitchell, Don. "The End of Public Space? People's Par, Definitions of the Public and Democracy." *Annals of the Association of American Geographers* 85, no. 1 (1995): 108–33.

Modan, Gabriella Gahlia. *Turf Wars Discourse, Diversity, and the Politics of Place.* Malden, MA: Blackwell, 2007.

——. "Mango Fufu Kimchi Yucca: The Depoliticization of 'Diversity' in Washington, D.C. Discourse." *City & Society* 20, no. 2 (2008): 188–221.

Mohammed, Valencia. "After '68 Unrest, Other Factors Complicated Recovery." *Afro-American Red Star*, April 5, 2008, A1.

——. "Minority-Owned H Street Businesses Decry Tax Increase." *Afro-American*, April 30, 2011a, A1.

——. "DC Government Bans Black Businesses from H St Grant." *Afro-American*, October 5, 2011b. Retrieved March 13, 2013. http://afro.com/dc-government -bans-black-businesses-from-h-st-grant/.

Montgomery, Alesia. "Reappearance of the Public: Placemaking, Minoritization and Resistance in Detroit." *International Journal of Urban and Regional Research* 40, no. 4 (2016): 776–99.

Morello, Carol. "Poverty Rates Higher for Blacks and Hispanics than Whites and Asians." *Washington Post*, February 21, 2013. Retrieved September 20, 2018. https://search-proquest-com.dclibrary.idm.oclc.org/docview/1289219581 ?accountid=46320.

Mukherjee, Roopali. *The Racial Order of Things: Cultural Imaginaries of the Post-Soul Era.* Minneapolis: University of Minnesota Press, 2006.

Muñoz, José Esteban. "Stages: Queers, Punks, and the Utopian Performative." In *The SAGE Handbook of Performance Studies*, edited by D. S. Madison and J. Hamera, 9–20. London: SAGE, 2005.

Musgrove, George Derek. *Rumor, Repression, and Racial Politics: How the Harassment of Black Elected Officials Shaped Post–Civil Rights America Since 1970.* Athens: University of Georgia Press, 2012.

Nash, Robert J. "A Black Architect Speaks Frankly." *AIA Journal* (October 1968): 36, 96.

"Nation's Capital Still Recovering from the 1968 Riots." *CNN*, April 4, 1998. Retrieved May 19, 2013. http://www.cnn.com/US/9804/04/mlk.dc.riots/.

National Advisory Commission on Civil Disorders. *Report of the National Advisory Commission on Civil Disorders*. New York: Bantam Books, 1968.

National Capital Planning Commission. *Report on Civil Disturbances in Washington, D.C.*, Washington, D.C., April 1968a.

———. *Alternative Approaches to Rebuilding Seventh Street, 14th Street, NW. and H Street, NE*, Washington, D.C., 1968b. Report presented August 28.

National Main Street Center, n.d. http://www.preservationnation.org/main-street /about-main-street/.

"Negro-Run Ghetto Mapped by Pride." *Washington Post*, April 17, 1968, A21.

Neubauer, Michael. "Wells Eyes Money for H Street Business." *Washington Business Journal*, July 12, 2010. Retrieved December 11, 2013. http://www .bizjournals.com/washington/blog/2010/07/wells_eyes_money_for_h_street _business.html?page=all.

Ocejo, Richard E. "The Early Gentrifer: Weaving a Nostalgia Narrative on the Lower East Side." *City & Community* 10, no. 3 (2011): 285–310.

O'Connell, Jonathan. "Whole Foods Market Signs Lease for H Street NE Store and Eyes Another at Walter Reed." *Washington Post*, November 5, 2013. Retrieved November 5, 2013. http://www.washingtonpost.com/business /capitalbusiness/whole-foods-market-signs-lease-for-h-street-ne-store-and -eyes-another-at-walter-reed/2013/11/05/cf22eaa4-4649-11e3-bf0c -cebf37c6f484_story.html.

———. "24 Tweets about Metro's X2 Bus." *Washington Post*, March 10, 2015. Retrieved July 15, 2015. https://www.washingtonpost.com/news/digger/wp /2015/03/10/24-tweets-about-metros-x2-bus/?utm_term=.507144875f17.

Ong, Aiwa. *Neoliberalism as Exception: Mutations in Citizenship and Sovereignty*. Durham, NC: Duke University Press, 2006.

Osman, Suleiman. *The Invention of Brownstone Brooklyn: Gentrification and the Search for Authenticity in Postwar New York*. Oxford: Oxford University Press, 2011.

Paperson, La. "The Postcolonial Ghetto: Seeing Her Shape in His Hand." *Berkeley Review of Education* 1, no. 1 (2010): 5–34.

Pattillo, Mary E. *Black Picket Fences: Privilege and Peril among the Black Middle Class*. Chicago: University of Chicago Press, 1999.

———. *Black on the Block: The Politics of Race and Class in the City*. Chicago: University of Chicago Press, 2007.

"Police: DC Man Arrested and Charged with 15 Burglaries in the District." *WJLA*, February 6, 2018. http://wjla.com/news/crime/police-dc-man-arrested-and -charged-with-15-burglaries-in-the-district.

Pow, Choon-Piew. "Neoliberalism and the Aestheticization of New Middle-Class Landscapes." *Antipode* 41, no. 2 (2009): 371–90.

Prince of Petworth. "Foot Locker Closing in October at 8th and H Street, NE." PoPville.com, 2013. https://www.popville.com/2013/06/foot-locker-closing-in -october-at-8th-and-h-street-ne/.

Puwar, Nirmal. "Multicultural Fashion . . . Stirrings of Another Sense of Aesthetics and Memory." *Feminist Review* 71, no. 1 (2002): 63–87.

Pyatt, Rudolph, Jr. "H Street Merchants Have Own Plan." *Washington Star,* October 27, 1974, B5.

Ramanathan, Lavanya. "Where the Arts Intersect." *Washington Post,* February 19, 2010, WE41.

Raspberry, William. "Washington Lays Antiriot Plans Wisely." *Washington Post,* March 4, 1968.

———. "The Day the City's Fury Was Unleashed: Lessons of the Riot Series; The Fires of April, 20 Years Later." *Washington Post,* April 3, 1988, A1.

———. "Save a Black Business." *Washington Post,* July 15, 1992, A19.

Richardson, Jason, Bruce Mitchell, and Juan Franco. "Shifting Neighborhoods: Gentrification and Cultural Displacement in American Cities." Washington, DC: National Community Reinvestment Coalition, 2019.

Riddick, Susan. "Constructing Difference in Public Spaces: Race, Class and Gender and Interlocking Systems." *Urban Geography* 17, no. 2 (1996): 132–51.

Ritter, Judith. "Inauguration Fever: The Best Places to Party in Washington." *Globe and Mail,* January 8, 2013. Retrieved March 13, 2013. https://www.theglobeandmail.com/life/travel/destinations/inauguration-fever-the-best-places-to-party-in-washington/article7020166/.

Robertson, Kent. "The Main Street Approach to Downtown Development: An Examination of the Four-Point Program." *Journal of Architectural Planning and Development* 21, no. 1 (2004): 55–73.

Robinson, Cedric. *Black Marxism: The Making of the Black Radical Tradition.* London: Zed Press, 1983.

Roeber, Bridget. "The Fires of April: 20 Years Later, 'An Anatomy of the Riots.'" *Washington Post,* April 3, 1988.

Rose, Nikolas. *The Politics of Life Itself: Biomedicine, Power, and Subjectivity in the Twenty-First Century.* Princeton, NJ: Princeton University Press, 2006.

Ross, Dax-Devlon. "Separate and Unequal in D.C.: A Story of Race, Class, and Washington Politics." *Forefront* 52, no. 1 (2013): 1–29.

Rowley, Dorothy. "H Street Revitalization Hits a Snag." *Washington Informer,* March 16, 2011. Retrieved September 12, 2013. http://washingtoninformer.com/news/2011/mar/16/h-street-revitalization-hits-a-snag/.

Ruble, Blair. *Washington's U Street: A Biography.* Washington, DC: Woodrow Wilson Center Press, 2010.

Rushmore, RJ. "Gaia Mural in DC." *Vandalog,* May 27, 2012. Retrieved September 12, 2013. https://blog.vandalog.com/2012/05/gaia-mural-dc/.

Sabar, Ariel. "Joe Englert: The Life of the Party." *Washingtonian,* March 1, 2012. Retrieved March 1, 2012. http://www.washingtonian.com/articles/people/joe-englert-the-life-of-the-party/index.php.

Saito, Leland. "From 'Blighted' to 'Historic': Race, Economic Development, and Historic Preservation in San Diego, California." *Urban Affairs Review* 45, no. 2 (2009): 166–87. doi: 10.1177/1078087408327636.

Sandercock, Leoni. "Negotiating Fear and Desire: The Future of Planning in Multicultural Societies." *Urban Forum* 11, no. 2 (2000): 201–10.

Sargent, Edward. "Desolate NE Intersection Gave Name to the 'Eighth and H Street Crew'; Some Youths See Street Crime as Only Alternative." *Washington Post*, December 13, 1984, A38.

Sarro, Ronald. "Panel to Begin D.C. Riot Probe." *Washington Star*, May 26, 1969.

Schaffer, Dana Lanier. "The 1968 Washington Riots in History and Memory." *Washington History* 15, no. 2 (2004): 4–33.

Schiermer, Bjørn. "Late-Modern Hipsters: New Tendencies in Popular Culture." *Acta Sociologica* 57, no. 2 (2013): 167–81. doi: 10.1177/0001699313498263.

Schlichtman, John Joe, Jason Patch, and Marc Lamont Hill. *Gentrifer.* Toronto: University of Toronto Press, 2017.

Schwartz, Nancy, and Richard Layman. *Near Northeast Historical Study.* DC Historic Preservation Office/Federal Historic Preservation Fund, National Park Service, with additional funding provided by the Capitol Hill Restoration Society, 2002.

Schwartzman, Paul. "Whose H Street Is It, Anyway?" *Washington Post*, April 4, 2006. Retrieved December 7, 2013. http://www.washingtonpost.com/wp-dyn /content/article/2006/04/03/AR2006040301762.html.

———. "Lawsuit: D.C. Policies to Attract Affluent Millennials Discriminated against Blacks." *Washington Post*, May 25, 2018. Retrieved May 25, 2018. https://www.washingtonpost.com/local/dc-politics/lawsuit-dc-policies-to -attract-affluent-millennials-discriminated-against-blacks/2018/05/24/3549f7fe -5a1e-11e8-858f-12becb4d6067_story.html?utm_term=.eoc26d02f681.

Schweitzer, Ally. "Not Just a Silly Little Name: 'Swampoodle' Park Pays Tribute to D.C.'s Irish Past." *WAMU*, December 18, 2017. Retrieved December 20, 2017. https://wamu.org/story/17/12/18/not-just-silly-name-swampoodle-park-pays -tribute-d-c-s-irish-past/.

Shabazz, Rashad. *Spatializing Blackness: Architectures of Confinement and Black Masculinity in Chicago.* Urbana: University of Illinois Press, 2015.

Sharkey, Patrick. *Stuck in Place: Urban Neighborhoods and the End of Progress toward Racial Equality.* Chicago: University of Chicago Press, 2013.

Shukla, Sandhya. "Harlem's Pasts in Its Present." In *Ethnographies of Neoliberalism*, edited by C. Greenhouse, 177–94. Philadelphia: University of Pennsylvania Press, 2010.

Sidman, Jessica. "Joe Englert on Whole Foods Coming to H Street Northeast: 'It's Sad in Some Ways.'" *Washington City Paper*, November 6, 2013. Retrieved November 6, 2013. http://www.washingtoncitypaper.com/blogs/youngand hungry/2013/11/06/joe-englert-on-whole-foods-coming-to-h-street-ne-its-sad -in-some-ways/.

Simone, AbdouMaliq. "Urbanity and Generic Blackness." *Theory, Culture & Society* 33, no. 7–8 (2016): 183–203.

———. "The Black City." *International Journal of Urban and Regional Research*, 2017. Retrieved December 18, 2018. http://www.ijurr.org/spotlight-on/race -justice-and-the-city/the-black-city/.

Slater, Tom. "North American Gentrification? Revanchist and Emancipatory Perspectives Explored." *Environment and Planning A* 36, no. 7 (2004): 1191–213.

Small, Mario Luis, David J. Harding, and Michèle Lamont. "Reconsidering Culture and Poverty." *Annals of the American Academy of Political and Social Science* 629, no. 1 (2010): 6–27. doi: 10.1177/0002716210362077.

Smith, Jeffrey, and Thomas Gihring. "Financing Transit Systems through Value Capture." *American Journal of Economics and Sociology* 65, no. 3 (2006): 751–86.

Smith, Neil. *The New Urban Frontier: Gentrification and the Revanchist City.* New York: Routledge, 1996.

———. "New Globalism, New Urbanism: Gentrification as Global Urban Strategy." *Antipode* 34 (2002): 427–50.

Smith, Sam. *Captive Capital; Colonial Life in Modern Washington.* Bloomington: Indiana University Press, 1974.

Spillers, Hortense J. "Mama's Baby, Papa's Maybe: An American Grammar Book." *Diacritics* 17, no. 2 (1987): 65–81.

Stein, Perry. "This D.C. Strip Mall Was Built to Keep Shoppers Safe. Now It's Getting Demolished." *Washington Post,* July 21, 2017. Retrieved November 16, 2017. https://www.washingtonpost.com/local/after-nearly-30-years-a-strip -mall-on-a-busy-dc-street-is-being-demolished/2016/07/20/97a79292-4e9c-11e6 -aa14-e0c1087f7583_story.html?utm_term=.08de115afcd6.

Stoler, Ann. *Duress: Imperial Durabilities in Our Time.* Durham, NC: Duke University Press, 2016.

Stover, Jon, and Associates. "The Value of H Street Main Street and Barracks Row Main Street: Return on Investment of District of Columbia Funding for Barracks Row Main Street and H Street Main Street." Washington, DC: Jon Stover & Associates, 2014.

Sullivan, Laura. "Gentrification May Actually Be Boon to Longtime Residents." *National Public Radio,* January 22, 2014. Retrieved January 22, 2014. http:// www.npr.org/2014/01/22/264528139/long-a-dirty-word-gentrification-may-be -losing-its-stigma.

Sutton, Stacey. "Rethinking Commercial Revitalization: A Neighborhood Small Business Perspective." *Economic Development Quarterly* 24, no. 4 (2010): 352–71.

Talen, Emily, Sunny Menozzi, and Chloe Schaefer. "What Is a 'Great Neighborhood'? An Analysis of APA's Top-Rated Places." *Journal of the American Planning Association* 81, no. 2 (2015): 121–41.

Taylor, Keeanga-Yamahtta. *From #BlackLivesMatter to Black Liberation.* Chicago: Haymarket Books, 2016.

Taylor, Paul. *Black Is Beautiful: A Philosophy of Black Aesthetics.* Malden, MA: Wiley, 2016.

Teeley, Sandra Evan. "NE Corridor's Newest Renewal Plan Emphasizes Neighborhood." *Washington Post,* June 25, 1983, B3.

Thomas, Lynell. "'Roots Run Deep Here': The Construction of Black New Orleans in Post-Katrina Tourism Narratives." *American Quarterly* 61, no. 3 (2009): 749–68.

Thompson, Vernon. "Stocking Grocery Shelves with Dreams and Smiles." *Washington Post*, March 8, 1979, DC1.

Tissot, Sylvie. *Good Neighbors: Gentrifying Diversity in Boston's South End.* London: Verso Books, 2015.

"$24 Million Insured Loss Caused in D.C. Apr. Riots." *Washington Star*, January 5, 1969.

Tyner, James. "Urban Revolutions and the Spaces of Black Radicalism." In *Black Geographies and the Politics of Place*, edited by Katherine McKittrick and Clyde Woods, 218–32. Cambridge, MA: South End Press, 2007.

United States and Daniel Patrick Moynihan. *The Negro Family: The Case for National Action.* Washington, DC: Office of Policy Planning and Research, United States Department of Labor, 1965.

Walks, R. Alan. "Aestheticization and the Cultural Contradictions of Neoliberal (Sub)urbanism." *Cultural Geographies* 13, no. 3 (2006): 466–75.

Washington, Adrienne T. "Spirit of Partnership Marks Area Revival." *Washington Times*, April 1, 1988.

Washington, D.C., Economic Partnership. "DC Neighborhood Profiles 2014: H Street, NE." Washington, DC: Washington DC Economic Partnership, 2013. http://www.wdcep.com/wp-content/uploads/2010/08/hstreet.pdf.

Washington Metropolitan Area Transit Authority (WMATA). *WMATA Joint Development Policies and Guidelines.* Washington, DC: Office of Property Development & Management, 2008.

"WATCH: T-Mobile Store in D.C. Robbed Twice in Separate Incidents; 4 Wanted by Police." *WJLA*, January 16, 2018. https://wjla.com/news/local/watch-t-mobile-store-in-dc-robbed-twice-in-separate-incidents-4-wanted-by-police.

Wax, Emily. "Heritage Trails Mark the Path to Preserving D.C. History." *Washington Post*, January 30, 2012a. Retrieved February 1, 2012. http://www.washingtonpost.com/lifestyle/style/heritage-trails-mark-the-path-to-preserving-dc-history/2012/01/13/gIQARcRkdQ_story.html.

———. "Dreaming of a Streetscape without Roll-Down Security Gates." *Washington Post*, April 5, 2012b. Retrieved April 5, 2012. http://www.washingtonpost.com/lifestyle/style/dreaming-of-a-streetscape-without-roll-down-security-gates/2012/04/05/gIQAsfWKyS_story.html.

Weber, Brenda. "In Desperate Need (of a Makeover): The Neoliberal Project, the Design Expert, and the Post-Katrina Social Body in Distress." In *Old and New Media after Katrina*, edited by D. Negra, 175–201. New York: Palgrave Macmillan, 2010.

Weber, Rachel. "Extracting Value from the City: Neoliberalism and Urban Redevelopment." *Antipode* 34, no. 3 (2002): 519–40.

Weems, Robert, and Lewis Randolph. "The National Response to Richard M. Nixon's Black Capitalism Initiative." *Journal of Black Studies* 32, no. 1 (2001): 66–83.

Wells, Tommy. Tommy Wells War (website). http://www.tommywellsward6.com.

Welsh, James. "Riot-Area Renewal Control Disputed." *Evening Star*, March 4, 1969, B1.

Westwood, Sallie, and John Williams. *Imagining Cities: Scripts, Signs, Memory.* New York: Routledge, 1997.

Wheeler, Linda. "Vitality, Money Returning to H Street." *Washington Post,* April 12, 1987, B1.

White, Ronald. "Safeway Closes Store on H Street: A Setback to Renewal in Depressed Corridor." *Washington Post,* January 15, 1984, B3.

Whole Foods Market. "Our Higher Purpose Statement," n.d. http://www.wholefoodsmarket.com/mission-values/core-values.

Wiener, Aaron. "More Upscale Groceries for H Street, and Other Winners of Your Tax Dollars." *Washington City Paper,* June 19, 2013. Retrieved April 8, 2019. https://www.washingtoncitypaper.com/news/housing-complex/blog/13123429/more-upscale-groceries-for-h-street-and-other-winners-of-your-tax-dollars.

Wilkins, Craig. *Aesthetics of Equity: Notes on Race, Space, Architecture, and Music.* Minneapolis: University of Minnesota Press, 2007.

Willett, Julie. "Hands across the Table: A Short History of the Manicurist in the Twentieth Century." *Journal of Women's History* 17, no. 3 (2005): 59–80.

Williams, Brett. 1988. *Upscaling Downtown: Stalled Gentrification in Washington.* Ithaca, NY: Cornell University Press.

Williams, Juan. "Out of the Ashes of H Street." *Washington Post,* September 22, 1981, A21.

Wilson, Bobby M. "Capital's Need to Sell and Black Economic Development." *Urban Geography* 33, no. 7 (2012): 961–78.

Wilson, David. *Inventing Black-on-Black Violence: Discourse, Space, and Representation.* Syracuse, NY: Syracuse University Press, 2005.

———. *Cities and Race: America's New Black Ghetto.* London: Routledge, 2007.

Wilson, Janelle L. *Nostalgia: Sanctuary of Meaning.* Lewisburg, PA: Bucknell University Press, 2005.

Wilson, William Julius. *The Truly Disadvantaged.* Chicago: University of Chicago Press, 1987.

Wingfield, Adia Harvey. *Doing Business with Beauty: Black Women, Hair Salons, and the Racial Enclave Economy.* Lanham, MD: Rowman and Littlefield, 2008.

Winnubst, Shannon. *Way Too Cool: Selling out Race and Ethics.* New York: Columbia University Press, 2015.

Wood, Patricia Burke, and Rod Brunson. "Geographies of Resilient Social Networks: The Role of African American Barbershops." *Urban Geography* 32, no. 2 (2011): 228–43.

Woods, Clyde. "Life After Death." *Professional Geographer* 54, no. 1 (2002): 62–66.

———. "Katrina's World: Blues, Bourbon, and the Return to the Source." *American Quarterly* 61, no. 3 (2009): 427–53.

Wright, Christopher. "D.C. Renewal Ready to Roll." *Evening Star,* December 27, 1970, B1.

Wright, Earl. "More Than Just a Haircut: Sociability within the Urban African American Barbershop." *Challenge: A Journal of Research on African American Men* 9, no. 1 (1998): 1–13.

Yates, Clinton. "'Columbusing Black Washington." *Washington Post,* October 8, 2012. Retrieved September 12, 2013. http://www.washingtonpost.com/blogs /therootdc/post/nouveau-columbusing-black-washington/2012/10/08 /62b43084-10db-11e2-a16b-2c110031514a_blog.html.

Young, Joseph. "D.C. Residents Call for Fewer Bars on H Street." *Washington Informer,* January 19, 2012a. Retrieved March 12, 2013. http:// washingtoninformer.com/news/2012/jan/19/dc-residents-call-for-fewer-bars -on-h-street/.

——. "H Street NE Corridor Struggles for Identity." *Washington Informer,* February 2, 2012b. Retrieved March 12, 2013. http://washingtoninformer.com /news/2012/feb/02/h-street-ne-corridor-struggles-for-identity/.

Zuk, Miriam, Ariel H. Bierbaum, Karen Chapple, et al. "Gentrification, Displacement and the Role of Public Investment: A Literature Review." Working paper, 2015. Retrieved April 7, 2017. https://www.frbsf.org /community-development/files/wp2015-05.pdf.

Zukin, Sharon. "Gentrification: Culture and Capital in the Urban Core." *Annual Review of Sociology* 13, no. 1 (1987): 129–47.

——. *The Culture of Cities.* Cambridge, MA: Blackwell, 1995.

——. "Consuming Authenticity: From Outposts of Difference to Means of Exclusion." *Cultural Studies* 22, no. 5 (2008): 724–28.

——. *Naked City: The Death and Life of Authentic Urban Places.* New York: Oxford University Press, 2010.

Zukin, Sharon, Scarlett Lindeman, and Laurie Hurson. "The Omnivore's Neighborhood? Online Restaurant Reviews, Race, and Gentrification." *Journal of Consumer Culture* 17, no. 3 (2017): 459–79.

Zukin, Sharon, Valerie Trujillo, Peter Frase, et al. "New Retail Capital and Neighborhood Change: Boutiques and Gentrification in New York City." *City & Community* 8, no. 1 (2009): 47–64.

Index

Illustrations and tables are indicated by page numbers in *italics*.

crack epidemic, xv, 72
Cramer, Lauren, 21, 147
creative class, 128
"Creative DC Action Agenda," 128
Creative Hands Massage, 195n79
"creative placemaking," 12
credit: purchasing of goods on, 32–33, 95
crime: 1980s/1990s rise in, 53, 125;
    blackness and, 127; at Eighth and
    H corner, 155–56, 156; and Prince
    George's County, 171; statistics, 155,
    156; surveillance and, 157
cuisine, 26, 124–25, 130–34
cultural appropriation, 115, 130
cultural homogenization, 88
cultural tourism, 89, 93, 101–6, 105, 109
Cultural Tourism DC, 88, 101–2, 191n50
culture: aestheticization of, 16; and
    American exceptionalism, 159; Black
    Americans as lacking, 29; commodifi-
    cation of, 65; food, 130–31; go-go,
    55–56; in Moynihan Report, 29–30;
    neoliberalism and, 11; of poverty,
    181n5; white, as American, 91

Dalmage, Heather, 91
Daniels, J. Yolande, 143
Dart Drug Store, 56, 143
Dávila, Arlene, 54–55
DC Coliseum. See Uline Arena
DC Cool (marketing campaign), 120–21
D.C. Economic Security Administration,
    146, 152
D.C. Historic Preservation Office, 88
D.C. Home Rule Act, xiv, 190n2
dcist.com, 159
Deckha, Nityanand, 191n53
defensive architecture, 127. See also riot
    architecture
Delhi, India, 180n53
Delta Towers, 198n37
Department of Small and Local
    Business Development (DSLBD), 98
De Place: Institute of Healing and
    Happiness (restaurant), 137

Deputy Mayor for Planning and
    Economic Development (DMPED),
    9–10, 65, 70–71, 73
desegregation: racial polarization and,
    104; white flight and, 28–29. See also
    integration
Desta, Yalemzwed, 137–38
Desta, Yenu, 137–38
Destination DC, 120–121
Detroit, Michigan, 39, 41, 44, 88, 151,
    182n14
devaluation, 8, 13, 17, 25, 52, 67–70, 160
diaspora: African, 137, 195n76; Black, 171
disciplinary architecture, 127. See also
    riot architecture
discrimination: diversity and, 115;
    employment, 32, 34, 41–42; housing,
    29, 32, 34, 41; persistence of, after
    desegregation, 29; by white-owned
    businesses, 43–45. See also Jim Crow;
    racism
Disneyification, 88, 138
displacement, xvi; Barry administration
    and, 63; belonging and, 119; of
    businesses, 11, 120–21, 122, 128;
    cultural, 12; diversity and, 23;
    gentrification and, 15–17; neoliberal-
    ism and, 4–6; and Prince George's
    County, 170; in Southwest D.C.,
    184n75; and transit-oriented develop-
    ment, 197n25; and uprisings, 40
diversity: aestheticization of, 22–23, 81,
    166; as aesthetic style, 77; authenticity
    and, 77; Benetton mode of, 77; Black,
    137–39; blackness and, 4; "Chocolate
    City" moniker and, xi; commodifica-
    tion and, 65, 92; commoditization
    and, 78; consumption of, 127–30;
    depoliticization of, 113; discursive
    work of, 62; displacement and, 23;
    food and, 131; gentrification and,
    65–67, 154; as lifestyle amenity, 89;
    linguistic power of, 112–13; marketing
    of, 18–19; in Near Northeast Historical
    Study, 94–96, 97; neoliberal exploita-

tion of, 5–6, 22; neoliberalism and, 85, 115; nostalgia and, 89; in official plans, 77; social justice and, 113; strategic value of planned, 76–81; and "the Plan," 84; universality and, 106; and Whole Foods Market, 111

diversity segregation, 198n63

DMPED. *See* Deputy Mayor for Planning and Economic Development (DMPED)

Dr. Granville Moore, 83, 101

Downtown Locker Room (DTLR) (clothing store), 159–160

drum circles, 196n8

DSLBD. *See* Department of Small and Local Business Development (DSLBD)

DTLR (clothing store), 159–60

Dusk of H Street (mural), 132, *133*

Dvorak, Petula, 15–16

Dwyer, Owen, 197n30

Eatonville (restaurant), 190n60

Economic Security Administration, 146, 152

Edwards, Prince, 8

"1814 ESB" (beer), 1

Eighth and H corner, 9; criminal activity at, 155–56, *156*; history of, 145–46; as relic, 144, 166; and surveillance, 154–57, *156*; as transportation hub, 149, 152–53

Eighth and H Crew, 56, 145

11th Property Group, 121, 193n28

Ellington, Duke, 165

Englert, Joe, 81–84, 102, 147, 189n60

entrepreneurship, 11, 61, 73–74, 79, 81, 100, 103, 128–29. *See also* business

equitable development, 127, 149, 194n44

Eritrean immigrants, 195nn76–77

ethical consumption, 113

Ethiopian immigrants, 137–38, 195nn76–77

Ethiopic (restaurant), 137–38

ethnic cuisine, 131

ethnic identity, 30, 181n3

Events DC, 102

exceptionalism, American, 82, 159

exclusionary zoning, 29

Fair Housing Act, 32

family: in Moynihan Report, 30

Family Services Administration, 146, 152

Fantles (drugstore), 57

fast food, 54, 124–125. *See also* cuisine

Father's Day celebration, at Sherwood Recreation Center, 146–47

Fauntroy, Walter E., 48–49

Feldman Group, 193n28

Fenty, Adrian, xii, 25, 70, 84, 128

festival, H Street, 57–58, 98–99, 139–42, *140*

Financial Responsibility and Management Assistance Authority, 63–64

fire insurance, 48

fish, *135*, 135–37

Florida, Richard, 128, 192n13

Fontana, David, 174

Fonvielle, Henry, 143, 147–48, 158–59

food, 26, 124–25, 130–34

Ford Foundation, 48

Foucault, Michel, 157, 178n9

Fourteenth-U Street corridor, 6, 35, 37, 84, 96, 143

Fredericksburg, Virginia, 107

"Free D.C." campaign, 35

Fuller, Catherine, 56, 143

Fuller, Greta, 24–25

futurity, 87, 176

Gaia (artist), 132, *133*

gates, security, 126–27. *See also* riot architecture

gentrification: aesthetics of, 17, 114; ambivalence of, 83–84; authenticity and, 16–18, 180n47; and Black mobility, 154; blackness in, xi; commodification and, 65; and decline of Black residents, xv–xvi; defined, 17; displacement and, 15–17; diversity and, 65–67, 154; equitable development vs., 194n44; hipsters and, 119; historic